THE
GRIZZLY
MAZE

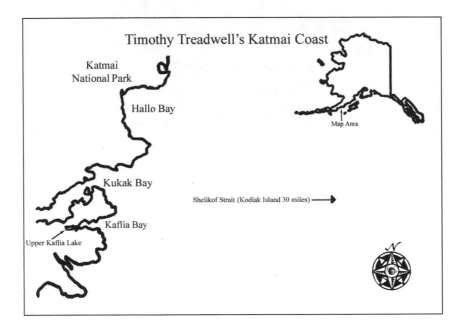

Timothy Treadwell's Katmai Coast

Katmai
National Park

Hallo Bay

Kukak Bay

Kaflia Bay

Upper Kaflia Lake

Shelikof Strait (Kodiak Island 30 miles)

Map Area

N

THE
GRIZZLY
MAZE

TIMOTHY TREADWELL'S FATAL OBSESSION
WITH ALASKAN BEARS

NICK JANS

DUTTON

DUTTON
Published by Penguin Group (USA) Inc.
375 Hudson Street, New York, New York 10014, U.S.A.
Penguin Group (Canada), 10 Alcorn Avenue, Toronto, Ontario, Canada M4V 3B2 (a division
of Pearson Penguin Canada Inc.); Penguin Books Ltd, 80 Strand, London WC2R 0RL,
England; Penguin Ireland, 25 St Stephen's Green, Dublin 2, Ireland (a division of Penguin
Books Ltd); Penguin Group (Australia), 250 Camberwell Road, Camberwell, Victoria 3124,
Australia (a division of Pearson Australia Group Pty Ltd); Penguin Books India Pvt Ltd, 11
Community Centre, Panchsheel Park, New Delhi - 110 017, India; Penguin Group (NZ), cnr
Airborne and Rosedale Roads, Albany, Auckland 1310, New Zealand (a division of Pearson
New Zealand Ltd); Penguin Books (South Africa) (Pty) Ltd, 24 Sturdee Avenue, Rosebank,
Johannesburg 2196, South Africa

Penguin Books Ltd, Registered Offices: 80 Strand, London WC2R 0RL, England

Published by Dutton, a member of Penguin Group (USA) Inc.

First printing, July 2005
1 3 5 7 9 10 8 6 4 2

Copyright © 2005 by Nick Jans
All rights reserved

Ⓩ REGISTERED TRADEMARK—MARCA REGISTRADA

Library of Congress Cataloging-in-Publication Data

Jans, Nick, 1955–
The grizzly maze : Timothy Treadwell's fatal obsession with Alaskan bears / by Nick Jans.
    p.   cm.
Include bibliographical references and index.
ISBN 0-525-94886-4 (alk. paper)
    1. Bear attacks—Alaska—Anecdotes. 2. Treadwell, Timothy, 1961– 3. Grizzly bear—
Behavior—Alaska. I. Title.
QL737.C37J36 2005
599.784'092—dc22   2004030920

Printed in the United States of America
Set in Sabon
Designed by Leonard Telesca

To Grandfather, in his woods

Contents

Acknowledgments

I'm indebted to an absurd number of people. From Anchorage to Juneau to the Katmai Coast and over to Kodiak, not to mention as far afield as Germany and California, I found myself humbled again and again as individuals offered up what they knew, and trusted me, a total stranger, to somehow get it right. Some went far out of their way to help me gather, clarify, or mentally sort the raw stuff from which this book is woven—hundreds of hours of interviews and discussions and musings; countless pages of reading; and thousands of miles of travel. If there are those I should have contacted but did not, forgive my oversight, lack of time, or outright shyness in some instances. In any case, I'll make an attempt to offer gratitude in a fashion that doesn't overly resemble a grocery list.

First, thanks to the two people who truly made this book happen: Elizabeth Kaplan, agent extraordinaire, and Gary Brozek, senior editor of Plume Books. Elizabeth has the distinction of being the first and only agent who ever returned my calls; her no-nonsense professionalism quickly won my enduring respect. I can say the same of Gary, who believed in the project from the start and offered a fine balance of freedom, guidance, and long-distance camaraderie as I struggled with issues of structure and flow, voice and balance, and finally threw out twenty-five thousand hard-won words.

A number of individuals were inordinately generous with their support or expertise. Andy Hall, senior editor at *Alaska* magazine, instantly recognized the size of the story and stuck out his neck to support both me and it. Joel Bennett gave freely in all respects; his integrity and generosity of spirit have served as both inspiration and example. Willy Fulton also has my special gratitude for the hours he invested in speaking with me and the insight he provided. Dr. Tom Smith of the USGS always found time to share what he knew; likewise, Chuck Bartlebaugh of the Center for Wildlife Information extended invaluable support. My deep thanks also extend to Jewel Palovak for her forthrightness at a difficult time. Larry Van Daele of the Alaska Department of Fish and Game also provided key information. Gary and Jeannie Porter of Bald Mountain Air provided logistical support, hospitality, and keen insight. Missy Epping of the National Park Service deserves special mention for the help she gave, not once but many times.

The following people supplied interviews or information that helped form the backbone of this book. In no particular order, Matthias Breiter, Perry and Angela Mollan, Chris Day, Sterling Miller, Tom Walters, Forrest Bowers, Allan Jones, Barbara Rudio, Phil Schofield, Larry Aumiller, Andreas Kieling, Dan Eubanks, John Bartolino, Dan Doorman, Joe Fowler, George Bryson, David Kaplan, Dick Ross, Leslie Kerr, Joe Allen, Kathleen Parker, Allen Gilliland, Lynne Grandvionnet, Lee Hagemeier, Dr. Franc Fallico, Lynn Rogers, Steve Stringham, John Quinley, Chuck Keim, Matt Robus, Bruce Bartley, Jane Tranel, Becky Brock, Don Pitcher, Greg Wilkinson, Joel Ellis, Deb Liggett, Sam Egli, and Larry Rogers. I'm sure I've forgotten someone; please forgive me.

A special thanks to my good friend Tom Walker for his sage input and vital guidance. Marty Owen, harbormaster of Kodiak, piloted me through rain and fog to a key interview. Michael O'Connor of Katmai Wilderness Lodge was most generous, and my time there was serendipitous on several counts. Lynn and Carol Norstadt proved their value once again as tireless and astute readers; better friends would be hard to find. Seth Kantner, another fine friend, was also generous with his judgment and time.

And as usual, my wife, Sherrie, provided unstinting support. I don't often claim that I'm blessed, but I don't know how else to explain her presence in my life. Last of all, a scratch behind the ears and a tennis ball to Chase, Gus, and Dakota, who provided daily lessons in unconditional love. Also, a sad farewell to Dakota, whom I loved dearly in return.

an outgrown Bear whc. is good meat
His skin to gett I have used all ye ways I can
He is mans food and he makes food of man. . . .

—Journal of Henry Kelsey,
Hudson's Bay Company,
September 1691

Into the Maze

"Ready?" pilot Gary Porter's voice crackled over the headset. From the copilot's seat I nodded. We dropped in a smooth arc, losing altitude until at last the floats settled in with a hissing thrum. As we taxied down Upper Kaflia Lake I reflected that, considering this was Alaska's Katmai National Park, where spectacular scenery is commonplace, this was a rather ordinary little valley: a narrow lake maybe a mile and a half long, cradled by a pair of upswept, undulating ridges. Dense clumps of alder and willow started at the water's edge and clung to the slopes, fading into stone and streaks of volcanic ash. Three weeks ago the land would have blazed with autumn colors; but this was early October, and the land was fading to brown, turning inward, waiting for snow.

"That's the place up ahead," said Gary, and I fumbled with the camera gear in my lap. As the DeHavilland Beaver coasted in toward shore, engine silent now, we could see an odd splash of white in the brush. Clad in hip boots, Gary and I swung open the doors and stepped down onto the floats. From there I could read the top lines of one notice:

DANGER

BEAR-CAUSED FATALITY

UNDER INVESTIGATION

The other sign was a map crosshatched with shaded areas. Strung from a thirty-foot section of white cord, the two notebook-sized, laminated sheets flickered in the breeze, as if somehow they could contain a sweep of country spanning four million acres.

This was the place where Timothy Treadwell and Amie Huguenard had died just five days before—attacked, mauled, and eaten outside of their tents during a violent rainstorm.

> *Come out here, I'm being killed out here!*
> *Play dead!*
> *. . . . Fight back!*

Their desperate struggle for life had been captured on a camcorder's audiotape, starting with cries for help and fading into high-pitched screams. A day later, would-be rescuers, hoping to find someone alive, had been menaced by bears at close range and shot and killed two, including a thousand-pound male whose stomach was filled with flesh, bone, and clothing. But today, except for those fluttering signs, this grass-crowned knoll, rimmed by a dense curtain of alder, seemed just like the valley: pretty but unremarkable, a tiny island adrift in an ocean of land. As sunlight filtered through high clouds, casting everything in a luminous golden light, I struggled to imagine the horror that had taken place here.

Then the soft breeze eddied, bearing the stench of death—a sickly-sweet, overpowering odor that cut through any illusion of serenity: the rotting carcasses of the bears the park rangers had shot. Shards of bear bone and clumps of hide lay scattered around the grassy swale before us, just a few yards away. Scavenging magpies and ravens called back and forth. The nightmare had been real. And this was where it had happened.

The questions I'd been wrestling with for the past five days swirled up again, sharp as the scent of carrion. The facts didn't add up. After twenty-five years living and traveling in bear country, first as a packer for a big game guide, then as a hunter, finally as a photographer and writer, I knew the danger posed by bears well enough. Attacks, while always a possibility, were isolated instances, and experience tended to tip the odds in your favor. If Timothy Treadwell wasn't experienced, who was? He'd spent thirteen summers among the big coastal brown bears here, and claimed to have an empathic connection to them—a gift, admirers said, that at times approached magic. He gave the bears names, claimed to understand their postures and vocalizations, moved among them as one of their own.

Yet, in the history of the Katmai Park and National Monument, stretching back over eighty-five years, not one person had ever been seriously mauled, let alone killed—until Timothy Treadwell. The apparent contradiction was cause enough for head scratching. This tragedy, however, went that ghastly step further. A bear, or bears, had turned predator—an occurrence so rare it came as a shock, even to people who knew these animals. This double killing wasn't just an anomaly for Katmai National Park; it was the first of its kind in the history of Alaska. What had gone wrong for Treadwell and Huguenard? What, exactly, had happened?

From those central questions, others spread in concentric ripples. Timothy Treadwell—who was he, beyond a face or a name, and what had brought him here? What were his hopes, fears, and dreams? And now that he was dead, why had he become such a controversial figure, galvanizing people from all walks of life, many of whom, just days before, hadn't even been aware of his existence? Was he a martyr, a fool, a lunatic, or, as some claimed, a cynical grifter, riding a self-created wave and playing it for all it was worth?

The Grizzly Maze, Timothy Treadwell had named this place where he died: a labyrinth of tunneled trails bears had worn through the dense brush over centuries of passing—dim, narrow passages where a person could only go by crawling on all fours, with no telling what lay around each bend, and no retreat possible. It's a place we've all been, if only in dreams. A fitting metaphor for the maze humans and bears have wandered together across time, and for the story of Timothy Treadwell, which already seemed to defy the sure paths of logic. The dark mouth of one of the many entrances to the maze was here at Kaflia, beckoning.

"Do what you have to." Gary shrugged. "I can't stop you, but I have to stay here." He, his wife Jeannie, and I stood on the Beaver's floats, looking toward the shore. Though the recent storm had stripped half the leaves from the alders, the curtain of brush, which started at the lake's edge, was still claustrophobic.

Other bears had been feeding on the carcasses, and had to be close by, though we'd spotted nothing on our flyover. The only real clearing was a marshy swale off to the right. I scrolled farther down the Park Service's notices:

—CLOSURE—
FROM CAPE CHINIAK (HALLO BAY) TO
CAPE ILKUTGITAK (AMALIK BAY):
ALL AREAS, EXTENDING INLAND 15 MILES,
ARE CLOSED THROUGH DEC. 1, 2003

ENTERING A CLOSED AREA OR REMOVAL OF THIS SIGN
IS PUNISHABLE BY FINE UP TO $500 OR
IMPRISONMENT FOR 8 MONTHS, OR BOTH

U.S. DEPARTMENT OF THE INTERIOR
KATMAI NATIONAL PARK AND PRESERVE

Going through channels, I'd been granted a special permit to land at Kaflia, with the stipulation that my feet wouldn't touch the shore. I could stay right on the plane and still do my job for *Alaska* magazine—take a few pictures of the notices, the brush, and some scenics, then do some flyover views of the bear trails that webbed across the knoll like spokes on a wheel. I'd even left my bear spray back in Homer.

Now that I was there, however, I knew where I was going. Though I hadn't known Treadwell at all, some of my friends, like Joel Bennett, had, and he lived for me in their stories told over the years. I saw in him that same love of wild things that had brought me to Alaska, mingled with the fear I'd always faced alone, and the death that could easily have been mine instead. All the bears I'd walked past without knowing, or sat and watched, taken pictures of, or hunted and killed—they were all waiting somewhere on that brushy hill, where all trails converged.

I started off with wide-angle images of the notices at the water's edge. Though my pulse thudded in my ears, I forced that energy into technical issues—bracketing, backlight, shutter speed, and depth of field. As I moved into the swale, taking a step at a time, pausing to listen, details seemed unnaturally heightened—the delicate patterns of frost at my feet, leaves steaming dry in the sun. Then the first scraps of tattered bear hide, and shards of bone. Watching the world through my camera, switching lenses occasionally, I kept firing away. The world became a series of fragmented images: a furrowed trail leading uphill toward the camp. Footprints, human and bear, cast in frozen mud. Bent and broken branches. And permeating everything, the insistent smell of death, which had no color or shape.

Twenty feet up the trail lay a bear's cache—a litter of brush, grass, and earth piled over a carcass to shield it from foxes, birds, and other bears. Two leg bones, obviously from the smaller of the two bears shot by the rangers, lay on top of the mound, polished clean. I heard the camera's motor drive whir, but over that came a soft, steady crunching noise—the sound of something heavy walking through frozen grass somewhere below on the swale, hidden from view by brush and the knoll's curve. Skirting to the right, I saw the bear about the same time he saw me.

It was a big, dark male, maybe eight hundred pounds—rippling with muscle and fat, gorgeously furred, and, at his predenning prime, immense by most standards. But along the Katmai Coast, he was just another bear—large, but a step down the social hierarchy from one of those truly huge, dominant males. Dangling from his jaws was a mass of bone and gristle from just such a bear—a pelvis, part of a spine, and a femur stripped of flesh—a fifty-pound scrap of what had once been Treadwell's presumed killer. The male stared uphill, locked on my shape.

About fifty yards separated us. The plane was roughly that distance away, below and behind me. From the lake, Gary and Jeannie had no way of seeing either me or the bear. I backpedaled slowly, rounding my shoulders and averting my gaze to appear—I hoped— nonthreatening. I suppose I should have been afraid, but I took cues from the bear, which didn't show the least sign of agitation. In fact, he went back to gnawing, glancing my way only now and then. Over the next ten minutes I shot half a roll until the animal shifted behind a small clump of willow. The air was so unnaturally silent that I could hear the scraping of teeth on bone.

I decided to leave the bear and circle away, back up the trail toward the campsite. A dozen yards farther, on a grassy, willow-rimmed bench, I found a second bear cache, obviously disturbed and seemingly empty, and just beyond, a circular, flattened area tucked back in the alders that seemed to have been Treadwell's campsite. When I bent low, the stench was almost nauseating, and I began to feel the growing distance between me and the plane. The stillness and the warm, filtering sunlight, the chitter of juncos and chickadees, only made things more eerie. Just a few more yards and I'd head back, I told myself.

The crackle in the brush, just a few paces away, might as well have been a grenade exploding. I was standing in the middle of the second cache, looking down and studying it through my view-finder, wondering how to create a telling image of dirt and sticks, when the noise erupted. Whipping upright, I caught a glimpse of brown fur in the alders, no more than twenty feet away.

How did he get so close, so quietly? I remember thinking. The world shifted into fast forward, time and space compressing, yet still strangely clear. I knew at once: It was that big male down the hill, and he'd stalked me. Running was seldom a good idea—I knew that. But standing right over a claimed kill, I had nothing to lose. At this distance, the rush would be instantaneous, the bear coming low and hard, slamming into my legs with the irresistible force of a breaking wave, a blur of teeth and claws and fur, an eruption of blood and tearing flesh. Without making a conscious decision, I was in motion, bounding down the steep-sided knoll through the brush in huge, weightless steps, the surge of adrena-line an uncoiling spring in my chest. The bright distance of the world, the narrowing cone of my own vision, the explosion of my own movement and my detached awareness—I was playing col-lege football again, complete with the noise of the crowd, distant shouts that I realized were Gary and Jeannie, shouting RUN, RUN!

I felt my ankle catch, twist, and buckle, and I went down hard, too fast for my arms to react. There was a tremendous blow, my teeth clashing together as ribs thudded into frozen ground. I scram-bled up, still aware of Gary and Jeannie's shouts, realizing that if they of all people were shouting for me to run, things were look-ing grim. Any second now—I was ready for the impact, envision-ing in a flash my next move: curled up, facedown, hands clamped behind my head, enduring the incredible, rag-doll-thrashing force of the bear. Three more leaps, the yellow of the plane's fuselage just thirty feet away, bright through the last screen of alders, and my ankle folded again. This time I went down even harder, a hummock slamming the wind out of my lungs, my face and shoulders smashing through a skim of ice into stinging cold water. I looked up to find the Beaver's floats almost close enough to touch, and saw my Nikon underwater, tightly gripped in my right hand. I'd landed face-first in the same little creek I'd stepped over on my way in. Still acting on reflex, I snatched the camera out and staggered up once more, then sagged down on a knee, coughing and tasting blood. For the first time I looked behind me. There was no bear—only the empty trail, and the bright stillness of that same October morning.

"Are you okay?" It was an inevitable question, I suppose. I nodded an affirmative, then ran a personal inventory. Lower lip bleeding and swollen. Bruised ribs. One wader half full of ice water. Right ankle spindled—an old, recurring injury. I knew from experience that I wouldn't be running anywhere for a month, but for now I'd be able to make a cast of duct tape and limp along. The only fatality was one waterlogged camera body.

Gary raised an eyebrow, his mouth tight beneath his mustache. "Didn't you hear us yelling for you not to run?" Of course I had—but only the last part, each time they'd yelled—don't RUN, don't RUN! I'm not sure I'd have listened anyway.

Replaying the whole sequence, I realized what had probably happened. The first bear, the big guy down in the swale, hadn't stalked me. Instead, I'd walked up on a second bear, bedded down in the grass. It was easy to generalize all the bad karma of this place, and create an imaginary army of slavering killer beasts; but in all probability, the bear had behaved in typical Katmai brownie fashion—rolled up for a look, scratched, and gone back to sleep as soon as the commotion faded. Again, the question came back:

What had been different, what had gone wrong with Tim and Amie five days before?

We all agreed it was time to move on. Daylight was burning, and we hoped to find Joel Ellis, the lead ranger involved in the attempted rescue and body recovery, at the National Park Service station at Brooks Falls. Though the trail seemed narrower this time and the alders thicker, I hobbled up and retrieved my gear. Both bears had evaporated into the brush.

The Beaver's radial engine rumbled to life. As we taxied down the lake, positioning for a takeoff into the wind, Gary spotted a bear in the water, along the far shore. Cutting the engine, we drifted to within fifty yards. It was a huge animal, twelve hundred pounds or more. Like most dominant males, he seemed uneasy around humans, eyeing us as he clambered heavily from the water. Rather than disturb him further, we moved off. Skimming low over the knoll after takeoff, I glimpsed a dark shape at the edge of the lake, close to the tiny white signs at water's edge. A different bear, maybe that first male, or the one in the brush, was standing, nose to the ground, right where I'd been flat on my face, as if to remind me I'd just used up my luck. Maybe the only real difference between me and Timothy Treadwell was that mine had been better.

The Birth of Treadwell

Timothy Treadwell was the sort of guy most Alaskans loved to hate. You don't go around on Kodiak Island or Katmai crawling on all fours, singing and reading to bears, giving them names like Thumper, Mr. Chocolate, and Squiggle. You don't say things to them like "Czar, I'm so worried! I can't find little Booble." Not unless you're from California, that is, and your name is Timothy Treadwell. He looked the part—boyish good looks and a shock of blond hair half-tamed by a backward ball cap. It was as if his surfboard had taken a wrong turn off Malibu and somehow he'd ended up on the Alaska Peninsula—home to the largest concentration of brown bears on the planet.

But he hadn't arrived by accident. Treadwell had been a fixture along the Katmai coast for thirteen years, camping out each spring and summer, alone, in the heart of bear country, deliberately seeking them out. He carried no gun (even if firearms had been legal in Katmai National Park, he still wouldn't have carried one) and eventually even swore off nonlethal means of protection, including pepper-based bear spray. Armed with little more than good intentions and a boundless, tail-wagging enthusiasm, he set out to become the bears' ambassador of goodwill, and their self-appointed guardian.

* * *

That's a sort of Timothy Treadwell 101. Those quick-sketched facts are by themselves remarkable—but even more so given the frame that surrounds the drawing. Perhaps the most remarkable thing about Timothy Treadwell is that one can argue he didn't exist. Or maybe it's more accurate to say he gave birth to himself— more than once.

The unraveling of his trail is made all the more complicated by the fact that in his one book, *Among Grizzlies* (cowritten by longtime friend Jewel Palovak), he gives no more than a join-the-foreign-legion, attenuated version of his early, pre-California and -Alaska life—about a page, all told. And what's there seems to be its own blended version of reality and revision. In literature, Timothy Treadwell is what you'd call an unreliable narrator; it's a common device in fiction, where the storyteller, created by the author, gives broad, early hints that he's not entirely to be believed as he relates his own tale. In nonfiction, however, as in court, telling a few stretchers or leaving yawning blank spots tends to leave the reader, or observer, wondering what finally *is* true.

By that brief account, he was born into a typical middle-class background on Long Island, New York. Not really a bad kid, but a handful. All along, he sensed a kinship with animals; he "donned imaginary wings, claws, and fangs" and daydreamed his way through school but somehow passed. A transforming event: He got into a fight with some older kids who were torturing frogs, and in his rescuing the animals, "an ecowarrior was born." Then came the tumult of adolescence—getting arrested, drinking, wrecking the family car, barely passing high school, and leaving shortly after, his home life in a shambles. He reflected, "In my chaotic state, abandoning my family was the best gift I could give them."

Cut to Long Beach, California, where Treadwell, in his own saga, emerges as "an overactive street punk without any skills, prospects, or hopes" and with "a voracious drinking problem."

He slides into hard-core drug use and the accompanying lifestyle, which includes being roughed up by gun-toting dealers who ram him headfirst through a Sheetrock wall. Finally, he overdoses on a heroin speedball and is plucked back from the edge of death by a Vietnam vet with a heart of gold, who slaps him into shape and points him toward Alaska and bears, where he discovers his true purpose in life: watching over those noble and imperiled creatures.

It all makes a swell story. But as with Jesus, there are some missing years, not to mention information. Let's say Treadwell graduated high school at the usual age; he first traveled to Alaska in 1989, which puts him then at thirty-two or thirty-three. That leaves the first eighteen years of his life summarized down to an asterisk, and fifteen more compressed just slightly less.

Let's backtrack a bit, straighten a few curves in the trail, and tie some flagging on the alders here and there. First, he was born Timothy Dexter. He later adopted Treadwell as a stage name (considering his ultimate career choice, good symbolic move, and better mouth feel). Then there was that struggling-through-high-school and leaving-home stuff. We have the vision of a waif departing with a backpack, thumb out—or something like that. What got omitted includes the small matter of two years at Bradley University in Illinois, a prestigious liberal arts school that doesn't exactly scrape the bottom of the academic barrel. Tim Dexter, it turns out, was an ace on the three-meter springboard in high school—good enough to land a scholarship and bright enough for Bradley, where he went on to set school diving records in his first two seasons. You don't do that sort of thing without plenty of talent, drive, and focus. And far from being cut off from home, he returned to Long Island each summer and worked as a beach lifeguard. Tim is remembered by those who knew him as a partier and a bit of a hothead, a pretty-boy type, a talker with lots of acquaintances but few close friends ... not to mention a damn good diver. But really, just another kid.

Tim Dexter's family life wasn't without turmoil; that litany of teen angst—the car wreck and all the rest—was apparently real enough. In his third year at Bradley he got hurt and couldn't dive, lost his scholarship, dropped out, and eventually headed west in 1981 to southern California—Long Beach, then Sunset Beach, and eventually Malibu. There he eventually found work as a waiter and bartender in increasingly respectable, even upscale, establishments and a social life in the attached party-and-surf subculture. For a time he lived with his sister, but he soon moved out. Overall, a rosier portrait than the minimum-wage, drug-addled-street-punk image he projected in his bio—a generic history that could be applied to tens of thousands of twenty-somethings, with little remarkable to recommend it.

That may have been just the problem. His entire life, childhood to death, suggests his deep yearning for the extraordinary, and twenty-five hundred miles still wasn't enough to blot out Tim Dexter's all-too-mundane past—especially from himself. No one out West besides that sister knew him or could possibly have cared where he came from; yet he developed a new identity and persona that would have made a method actor proud. Timothy Treadwell, English waif, was born—complete with a Union Jack emblazoned on his surfboard and a Cockney accent so studied it fooled everyone, including the occasional Limey tourist and the English owner of a bar where he once worked. He was an orphan, he explained, thrown out on the street with no place to go. And some people bought his line, at least for a while. Never short on charisma, he chatted his way into sympathetic situations. But forged identities have a way of unraveling sooner or later, with the inevitable hard feelings; as Karyn Kline, whose brothers and parents took him in back in the Long Beach days, recalled in an interview with Craig Medred of the *Anchorage Daily News*, "We all felt sorry for him at first, then the family caught on." No one likes to be conned, and out he went.

Treadwell apparently shrugged and reinvented himself once more. He was Australian now, or at least had grown up there. His new accent, which he could turn on and off at will, was once again nut-on. A 1997 review for *Among Grizzlies* in the well-regarded journal *Booklist* identified Treadwell as an "Australian-born bear lover"; after his death, a spokesman for Treadwell's parents had to rebuff a representative from the Australian media convinced of the Down Under connection.

While Treadwell's origins and last name were a fable, at least some of his claims of rough living ring true. In Long Beach he had a reputation as a fighter; he was arrested twice—once for brawling, and once, in Beverly Hills, for illegal discharge of a firearm. Kline remembered, "Tim was always in fights. He left when he heard several people were out to get him." And she surmised they were indeed drug dealers, which dovetails with his story. Considering his social circle, thrill-seeking profile, and the '80s time frame, it would have been remarkable if he *hadn't* dived on a few lines of coke and whatever else came along.

By the late '80s Tim Treadwell was living in a small, bare-bones apartment in Malibu, still gigging as a waiter and bartender. Working at Gulliver's, a seafood restaurant in Marina Del Ray, he met fellow worker Jewel Palovak—who, while absent from his book as a character, would eventually cowrite it. She also ended up sharing the rest of his life, first as lover, then as his most enduring friend. The fact that his partner isn't even mentioned in his book hints at the compartmentalized reality Timothy Treadwell presented both to the world and to himself.

"We had kind of a normal California life," Jewel told me. "You know, had a couple of cats, surfed, tended bar, went on little trips together. . . . He was always a good boyfriend and fun to be around." Regarding Treadwell's darker side, the violence and drugs, she claimed she never saw it; seems he'd cleaned himself up. But not completely. "Oh, he totally drank. Beer, mostly, and never out of control, but steady. . . . I lived with the man and it was never anything violent or abusive, but that stuff [alcohol] just leaks into the rest of your life." Eventually they'd call off the romantic thing, but their relationship remained close.

Meanwhile, the same restless impulses that had pushed him west and away from who he was were still at work. Timothy Treadwell had ambitions. Like so many who gravitate toward southern California, he saw his name up in lights—no surprise, given his theatrical instincts—but the chances of actually going Hollywood, he must have known, were slim at best. He was an astute fan of films and showbiz trivia, and knew his MTV videos. But his pull toward animals and nature, there since childhood, never lessened. Though he lacked credentials or experience, or even a firm notion of exactly what he might do, Jewel's encouragement propped him up.

He took shakedown trips to western national and state parks—and dreamed of Alaska and bears. And in 1989, he headed north astride a secondhand motorcycle, with a cheap point-and-shoot camera (a Canon Snappy, Jewel remembers), a few rolls of print film, an even cheaper sleeping bag, and big plans. Timothy Treadwell was about to be reborn yet again. And this time the self-written label would stick.

What to make of Timothy Treadwell at this point—bridge burner, dropout, serial fibber, self-admitted addictive personality, and ex-candidate for anger management? Pretty easy to brand a capital L on his forehead and write him off. But instead, think of a guy that much at war with himself that he ran from it, trying, hoping desperately, to be someone else. A kid who would risk getting the crap kicked out of him trying to save a bucket of frogs and, right or wrong, never backed down. Had the sack to do a reverse pike, head inches from the diving board. And later, at the age where most of us have sighed, settled in, and laid down our cards, demanded a reshuffle and headed out alone for Alaska. Maybe I'm getting fuzzy, but I find it hard not to like him—this guy I know but never met.

Alaska isn't exactly the sort of place you take in on a summer road trip. Think of the entire U.S. east of the Mississippi and you've just about got the size. The variety is another matter—everything from rain forests to desert, coastal swamps to glacier-clad ridges three miles high. Now sprinkle in just six hundred thousand people, most of whom live in a virtual thumbtack of space, surrounded by big, rough country going on to the horizon. I've made it my home for half my life, traveling thousands, sometimes tens of thousands, of miles a year within the state, and I still don't get it. I'm not sure anyone can.

So there's Timothy Treadwell bopping along on his motorcycle, greener than grass, soft from California living and searching for his own private Alaska. Tied to a ribbon of highway, where do you find the nearest herd of bears? Not as easy as you'd think. With the exception of mothers with cubs, they—either black (*Ursus americanus*) or brown/grizzly (*Ursus arctos*)—tend to be quiet loners, naturally shy of human contact. Even in prime habitat—which means most of the state—they're everywhere and nowhere, drifting, crepuscular shadows, elusive as dreams. You might glimpse one loping across the road, but chances are you won't. How do you bond with something you can't see? Of course, Timothy hopes, above all, for grizzlies—the embodiment of wilderness, once common in California, now extinct in all but two percent of their former lower-forty-eight range. And in Wrangell–St. Elias National Park, hiking along the Chitina River, he finally meets one face to face:

A grizzly! . . . Its nostrils flared, inhaling deep puffs of my scent through a black-tipped snout . . . the bear pivoted on its back paws and bolted in a violent retreat. . . . The message was clear to me. After decades of adversity caused by man, the bear was wary of people. For me, the encounter was like looking into a mirror. I gazed into the face of a kindred soul, a being that was potentially lethal, but in reality was just as frightened as I was. (*Among Grizzlies,* p. 10)

And a few weeks later, he flies into what he cryptically labels "a remote region of western Alaska." Here, more bears up close and an even stronger epiphany: He trips and falls, and a thousand-pounder gently sniffs him and steps over his body. And he sings to the bears for the first time—an unconscious, on-the-spot ditty—which seems to have a magical, calming effect, not only on himself, but on them. He's stumbled onto a peaceable kingdom where the bears seem neither ferocious nor afraid of man—a childhood dream made real.

So back to California he goes, determined to somehow save "the" bears—from greedy developers, evil sport hunters, and poachers that threaten their very existence—and, by projection, save the mirror image of himself that he glimpsed in that first grizzly. He's still drinking, but according to Jewel, he does stop for a month.

The next summer he returns to Alaska—still with shitty gear but plenty of determination. He flies in to a remote wilderness setting (unnamed, he says, to protect it from exploiters) and camps in the middle of a huge concentration of bears, grazing on a vast meadow. He soon discovers in himself a talent: He has a way with bears. Not only do they not attack, they seem to give a collective ursine shrug and include him—if not as one of their own, at least as a somewhat odd-smelling and harmless hanger-on. But it's far more for Treadwell. He's found love—so powerful it borders on obsession.

He encounters a young bear, names her Booble, and becomes her "adopted human companion." Soon there are others: Warren, Beacon, Mr. Chocolate, Hulk, Hefty, Holly, Mickey, Windy, Comet, and dozens more, each with their individual personalities, anthropomorphically interpreted by Timothy. And there's Timmy, a red fox he names after himself, that follows him around and pulls charming pranks, most of them involving scatological acts directed at Timothy's gear and food. The lush, Edenic area, untrammeled by humans, he dubs the Grizzly Sanctuary. And as its discoverer, he assumes the role of protector. On a beach, surrounded by clam-digging bears, Timothy Treadwell experiences a born-again moment that will shape his life:

> I begged forgiveness from a higher power, then made my pledge: "I will stop drinking for you and all bears, I will stop and devote my life to you." . . . my battle for preservation had begun. (*Among Grizzlies*, p. 33)

A beautiful and touching tale. And some of it—the bears all around, Timmy the fox, the essence of his own transformation—is even true. The pictures he took are proof. Later on, others, including my friend Joel Bennett, would shoot footage of Timothy and his bears in breathtaking proximity, cementing the actuality for millions of television viewers. But in the self-told drama of Timothy Treadwell, the interwoven pattern of myth and reality continues. As before, selective omission plays a major role.

Without doubt, too, Timothy discovered this place he called the Grizzly Sanctuary; however, his discovery, like Columbus's, was a highly subjective experience. The place already had a name—Hallo Bay—and it was firmly within the boundaries of Katmai National Park and Preserve, and had been under federal protection since before World War I. And if the bears needed Timothy Treadwell's protection, it came as news to the National Park Service, which considered that its job. As far as the rangers were concerned, he might just as well have plunked himself down in the middle of the Grand Canyon, vowing to safeguard it. The two thousand–plus brown/grizzlies that wandered the park weren't considered by officials—not the Park Service, the federal government, or private or state-of-Alaska biologists—to be endangered in any way, shape, or form. In places there were damn herds of them, thicker than anywhere else on earth, and their numbers seemed to be increasing.

Also, while the Katmai Coast of Alaska ranks among of the wildest and roughest stretches of real estate on the planet, hanging out with Katmai bears was hardly a new idea. The incredible concentration of coastal brown bears in certain areas had long made the area a mecca for tourists, bear biologists, and professional photographers; noted naturalist, bear hunter, and historian Harold McCracken first visited the coast in the early 1900s. By the time Timothy Treadwell arrived on the scene in 1989, bear viewing was a nascent industry pioneered by pilot Butch Tovsen, who first flew Timothy to Katmai from nearby Kodiak Island. By the mid-'90s a dozen or more private outfitters would keep busy ferrying people in. A busy June day might mean several flights of visitors, all anxious to watch the dozens of bears feeding on emerging sedges in the area Timothy called the Big Green. A smaller but steady stream of viewers, both solo and guided, would arrive by boat as well. While he did occasionally mention bear-viewing visitors in his narrative, Treadwell gave the impression that he was gloriously alone at Hallo Bay far more often than he was.

The next basic misrepresentation by Timothy Treadwell was at least partially unintentional, a product of his rich but geographically limited bear experience. Even more so later, after he'd spent a dozen seasons at Katmai, he'd have had a tough time internalizing this essential fact: All bears of the same species are far from behaviorally equal. Though he chose to call the bears he met at Hallo Bay "grizzlies," they were and are considered by Alaska biologists to be brown bears—the coastal version of the species *Ursus arctos*, which also includes an inland variation, commonly known in North America as "grizzly" (*Ursus arctos horribilus*).* But what's more sexy? Timothy chose *grizzly* for reasons any publicist could tell you, and justified it in print by rightly claiming they were the same species.

The distinction between grizzlies and brown bears is, most Alaskans would argue, the difference between pit bulls and Labrador retrievers. For a number of reasons—first and foremost being abundant food in concentrated areas—brown bears, while generally far larger than their interior brethren, are less aggressive, not only toward each other, but toward just about anything else. They're used to crowds, and have developed manners that allow them to bunch up with minimal conflict. Grizzlies, on the other hand, are hard-core loners (mothers with cubs an obvious exception), usually spread thin over thin country. They tend to run—either straight away from or, far less commonly, straight over, an interloper. None of this mellow stuff. If Timothy Treadwell had continued to poke around in Alaska's interior, places like Wrangell–St. Elias or farther north in the Brooks Range, he wouldn't have written the same book—instead, a story of rapidly vanishing, furry butts, long patches of nothing, and occasional bursts of adrenaline-soaked fear. Because Timothy never spent time with those inland grizzlies, he never fully appreciated the difference. As far as he

---

*While most bear biologists, along with many Alaskans, call all members of the species *Ursus arctos* "brown bears," other scientists make the following distinction: Any bear living farther than twenty-five miles from the coast is a grizzly, while one nearer to the ocean is a brown bear. But a grizzly may visit the coast in his travels, thereby swapping nomenclature. To further confuse matters, some black bears (*Ursus americanus,* an entirely different species) are in fact brown in color, and some brown bears (*Ursus arctos*) are so dark they're sometimes mistaken for their smaller cousins. To lessen confusion, I use the term *brown/grizzly* in this book, except where context makes the matter clear.

was concerned, the bears before him were real enough to render such distinctions moot.

And whether they were brownies or grizzlies, they were still bears—and their world, even in Katmai National Park, is brutal. Only one in ten cubs lives to adulthood; starvation, accidents, and cannibal predation by large male bears take the rest. Even females, worked into a rage, have killed both their own and other bears' cubs. Fights are common enough that many bears, especially larger males that battle for dominance in mating, personal space, and feeding areas, carry horrific scars. "If bears treated people the way they treat each other," says bear-viewing guide John Bartolino, "there wouldn't be anyone on the Katmai Coast." Though Timothy repeatedly writes of the personal danger he faces, he also dismisses it. The bears are misunderstood, he says, and one of his missions is to prove that brown/grizzlies are peaceful creatures that pose little threat to humans. And he intends to prove it by putting his own body on the line.

Timothy Treadwell, alone and alive as never before, sets to work among the bears of Hallo Bay, watching and following them as they feed, sleep, play, brawl, and mate. He's both observant and patient, and soon learns to identify dozens of individuals—a complex skill, even for a trained field biologist with years of experience. And though his outdoors skills are about what you'd expect of a Malibu cocktail waiter, he somehow manages to get by. The notorious Katmai coastal storms shred his Kmart-quality, ill-pitched tent; he subsists on peanut butter, PowerBars, and Tang, plus an assortment of sugary junk food that includes candy corn and Coke. He lives days at a time in soaking-wet gear and, when the relentless wind and rain abate, gets eaten alive by mosquitoes and no-see-ums. He grows tougher and leaner, beyond the athletic litheness of his diving days. His street-survivor instincts get honed toward a primal edge. He learns to sleep with bears brushing by his tent in the night, and to defuse confrontations with the animals. As Jewel would later say, "We had no idea he'd be able to do what he did."

Exactly what he *is* doing will become a topic of considerable debate. But at this point, the only agenda actually supported by his actions seems to be (in the words of biologist Sterling Miller) "to become friends with the bears." He creeps close among them, parks himself near trails and waits until they walk by, murmurs and sings to them, sleeps in their nest-shaped daybeds in the rye grass. He says things like "Hulk, how can I help you if you want to hurt me? You are the champion, but I'll be yours if you let me live." (*Among Grizzlies*, p. 75) The bears respond on cue in Dolittlesque fashion: "[Hulk's] face became animated, and I felt a warm feeling flow toward me. He was sad now, but one day he would love again." (*Among Grizzlies*, p. 105)

While out at Hallo Bay, Timothy becomes increasingly feral—both a conscious and an unavoidable process. It doesn't take too many days camping alone before the sight of people, with their bright nylon and nattering voices and raucous airplanes, even far down the bay, becomes strange, a barrage on senses lulled by the rush of wind, the silent passage of bears. More and more, Timothy imitates his ursine companions—their body movements, postures, and habits, their vocalizations. Even as he casts the bears in human form, he strives to become one of them. He tells himself, "I am grizzly." He plunges across ice-water glacial torrents, walks on all fours, and thinks in grunts or growls. He was never one to back away from the dramatic possibilities of the moment, and here he's on the stage of his life. In his own words, "my transformation was complete. . . . I felt wild and free." Timothy also moves his campsite from a relatively out-of-the-way spot to a central spot on the Big Green, where his position assures he will be surrounded by bears, 24/7. Again, the bears shrug and go about their business.

At the end of each of those first few summers, Timothy Treadwell returns to Malibu—no doubt a jarring experience to find it all still there, same guys on the same barstools and all the rest—and picks up that end of his life. Back to bartending. Meanwhile, he has pictures to show and stories to tell, and people are suitably impressed. He and Jewel put in serious time sitting around the table in her dad's kitchen, discussing how he—more accurately, they—might shape this burgeoning passion and turn it into something more. "I can't remember what we were trying to do at the start," Jewel recalled. "Maybe something to do with science or photography." Timothy enjoys modest success selling photos at craft fairs, and eventually he ends up doing free presentations for elementary students, and loves the children as much as they love him. With his own kidlike enthusiasm, jumping up and down and having the kids repeat bear facts after him, he's a natural. What's more, the youngsters are learning and caring about bears. Somewhere in those first years—Jewel can't remember exactly when—the idea of Grizzly People is born: a grass-roots, nonprofit organization dedicated to protecting the bears, studying them, and educating people, with a special emphasis on his most willing and accessible audience. Timothy has become, in more than one sense of the word, the Pied Piper in a children's crusade.

Lifeguard to the Bears

Through the early and mid-'90s, Grizzly People, this army of two, marches onward and uphill. Each year Timothy heads north to spend the summer among the bears, and Jewel, back in Malibu, takes care of the practical end of things—courting sponsors and lining up speaking engagements for the off season, taking care of administrative details, all the while juggling her waitress job. She's a natural. "It was fun and personally rewarding," she says. "I like to get things organized and done." Private donors chip in; greenie housewives, students, showbiz types from the restaurants, and friends—not much at first, but enough for Tim and Jewel to push their dream forward. "I never thought," Jewel says, "that my life would take a turn like that." She and Timothy have become full-fledged, committed animal activists.

The bustling fishing port of Kodiak, on the mountainous western Alaska island of the same name, becomes Timothy's base of operations. Though the greater Kodiak metropolitan area—if one can call it that—is home to just twelve thousand residents, due to the fishing industry the city is a commercial hub with daily jet service from Anchorage, and from there direct to L.A. A handful of bush flying services provide access to the sprawling wildernesses of both Kodiak National Wildlife Preserve and Katmai

National Park. Pilot and guide Butch Tovsen, who first showed Timothy Hallo Bay, ferries him back and forth, and he strikes up a friendship with hunting guide turned bear-viewing entrepreneur Bill Sims. Tom Walters, who in 1994 builds a bear lodge out at Kukak Bay, adjacent to Hallo, takes Timothy under his wing too. Kodiak resident Kathleen Parker, an ex–L.A. street cop twelve years his senior, a woman who hunts her own meat, gives him a base to launch what he now calls his Expeditions (Expedition '94, '95, and so on) and a place to keep his gear over the winter—not to mention some Alaska-flavored guidance and mothering. Though an unlikely match on the face of things, she becomes his closest ally and friend on the island. Later on, after he has a falling out with Walters, Dean Andrew of Andrew Airways and pilot Willy Fulton will step up. While some of these relationships are commercial, everyone seems to cut Timothy slack in one way or another, and much of the time he or his supplies ride for free. In the case of Sims, they work out a symbiotic relationship where he trades rides for guiding the pilot's bear-viewing customers. Timothy, as always, has an uncanny way of bringing out the caregiver in people. Says Walters, "Everybody helped him out. We all assumed he was broke."

Meanwhile, Timothy expands his range each season to include not only Hallo, but Kukak Bay, just to the west (which he dubs the Forbidden Zone) and Kaflia, one bay above Kukak—his Grizzly Maze, which he first glimpses in '94. He redirects the karmic flow he's received from his benefactors, continuing in his self-appointed role as guardian of the bears; he even introduces himself as such to some of the bear-viewing tourists and begins giving impromptu lectures on bear natural history and guided tours.

Besides Katmai National Park, Treadwell also spends chunks of time on Kodiak Island through the mid-'90s. Kodiak, besides being his staging point for Katmai, has a huge population of bears itself—huge not only in numbers, but in their legendary size. The world record was shot here, an animal with a head the size of a human torso.

This verdant, rain-washed island, the second largest in the United States (after Hawaii), is a totally different ball game from Katmai National Park, which lies on the Alaska mainland, thirty miles due east. While nearly all of Kodiak is a national wildlife refuge, it's entirely lawful, during two tightly regulated spring and fall seasons, to hunt bears (a contrast to Katmai National Park, where it's patently illegal). And unlike Katmai, which is without permanent settlements, Kodiak has those thousands of people, most of them living in or near the city of the same name. Many of them make part of their living, directly or indirectly, from the hundreds of well-heeled hunters from around the world who come every season, hoping to bag the trophy of a lifetime. By the time air charters, guide fees, hotels, meals, licenses, souvenirs, and all the rest are factored in, the local bear hunts on Kodiak bring in $4.5 million a year. Enormous stuffed bears, skulls, and hides garnish both local businesses and the Alaska Department of Fish and Game office, along with dozens of photos of hunters posed behind dead behemoths. Strange as it seems to an outsider, folks are proud of their bears, and not just as a renewable resource. They're a source of identity, part of what Kodiak people are.

By all accounts, the Kodiak brown bear population is stable and well managed; according to regional bear biologist Larry Van Daele, the two hundred–odd bears taken each year in the refuge (the total number of permits is around three hundred) are of at least equal size to those killed fifty years earlier—a sure sign of the population's health. In '93, Van Daele tells me, he measured a sedated bear that would have been an all-time world record—and as far as he knows, the bear was never shot and eventually died of old age. So it's not that the good old days of big bears are gone with the buffalo. In short, Kodiak is a tough place to sell the ul-tragreen brand of bear preservation that Timothy Treadwell es-pouses freely, to anyone within hearing range. He eavesdrops on bear-hunting conversations and cuts in, frequently goading locals with antihunting rhetoric.

He also regularly plunks himself down at popular bear-viewing areas such as O'Malley, Karluk Lake, and the Frazier Lake fish weir, where the animals congregate in summer to feast on spawn-ing salmon.

"He was camping right on a gravel bar that was a bear runway," recalls Don Pitcher, who worked for the Alaska Department of Fish and Game in the mid-'90s at Frazier Lake. "One time we saw him below us, and he was sneaking up on some cubs, getting be-tween them and the sow, closer and closer, and that mother bear was getting really upset. We were shouting for him to back off and he just sort of waved us away. We kept yelling, and finally he stopped. She collected her cubs and ran off. We thought we were going to see him get ripped up." Asked to summarize his impres-sion of Timothy Treadwell, Pitcher says, "Nice guy, but zero woods sense—and he never seemed to get any better. We saw him a num-ber of times crowding bears and forcing them to move away. . . . He kept food in his tent, for God sakes. He fell into a campfire and burned the hell out of his leg, really ugly and serious, and he just blew it off. We used to invite him up to dinner at our camp so he wouldn't get killed down there."

Says ex–Alaska Fish and Game biologist Dave Kaplan of Ko-diak, "He told me he was the bears' lifeguard and seemed to have some sort of grandiose version of things that just didn't fit the reality I knew."

Timothy would no doubt have had an alternate version of events, but local sentiments seem rather united—not just among the bear-hunting and bear science crowd, but conservationists as well. When he meets with the Kodiak chapter of the Audubon Society, hoping to gain their support or endorsement, they listen politely but straight out refuse their seal of approval. Says Barbara Rudio, the organization's president at the time, "People from Kodiak are awed by the bears and consider being around them an honor, and want to make ourselves as unobtrusive as possible. . . . There are proper ways to act around bears and he [Timothy] certainly wasn't demonstrating it." Forrest Bowers, a state biologist who was raised on Kodiak, is somewhat less kind in his evaluation of Timothy Treadwell. "There was nothing wrong with his concept, but the way he went about executing it and his spin on things turned a lot of people off. . . . Frankly, he seemed like he'd done too much acid." As an arms-akimbo whole, Kodiak seems to resent this wet-behind-the-ears surfer boy with wraparound shades telling them what to do with their bears. They got along just fine before he was here. Endangered? Not even most greenie locals, who would like to see some areas of the island protected from bear hunting, will go along with that. At least one flying service refuses to carry him.

Not surprisingly, Timothy Treadwell finds the comparatively un-trammeled Katmai Coast much more to his liking—a four-hundred-mile sprawl of jagged, windswept, near-vertical real estate just across Shelikof Strait from Kodiak. It's a hodgepodge of glacier-draped crags and postvolcanic angst framing tidal flats, surf-battered cliffs, and relatively narrow, brushy valleys drained by salmon spawn-ing streams. With its luxuriant rye grass fields, clam-rich flats, and salmon, the coast attracts an astounding assemblage of bears. And besides being mostly within the hunter-protected confines of Kat-mai National Park, there's not one permanent settlement in hun-dreds of miles. Out here, there aren't so many eyes and opinions. From the mid-'90s on, Timothy spends more and more time there. Ironically, his mission to protect bears from people seems to re-quire a certain distance from the latter.

For weeks, even months, at a time, Timothy lives among the bears of Katmai, learning the subtleties of their interactions and behavior. He's a quick study, which is a good thing. Filmmaker Joel Bennett attributes at least part of his intuitive grasp of bear body language to his rough-and-tumble experiences on the streets of southern California. No doubt Timothy's athletic past has also helped prepare him to make fearless, on-the-fly decisions. One could say he has a gift, or that he's just plain stubborn. Either one works. But Timothy doesn't think much about such matters of why and wherefore. He's too busy focusing energy on the bears.

Easy to see what Timothy finds so enthralling. Brown bears are complex creatures, so intelligent, so emotive, that at times they seem eerily human. Like ourselves, they have the capacity to play, to contemplate, become frustrated, and throw fits of temper. And expressions we recognize (or imagine we do) play across their broad faces: scowls; grins; looks of puzzlement or contentment. They clearly display the ability to solve complex problems. Naturalist Enos Mills declared, around the turn of the century, "I am convinced that the grizzly is an animal who reasons." He wasn't alone in that assessment. Across the past century, stories abound of individual bears, some of them notorious "outlaw" grizzlies, evading poison, set guns, and all manner of contrivances while continuing to wreak havoc on livestock. In a parallel, well-documented, and more recent example, Montana biologists in the 1980s had a prolonged and losing run-in with a crafty male they called the Mud Lake Bear. The scientists claimed he learned to drop rocks or sticks on the triggers of live traps and snares, demonstrating he knew exactly how the gadgets worked. He found and dismantled remote cameras, even tore surveyors' tape from trees—in short, made a three-year career of deliberately seeking out and wrecking increasingly elaborate trap sets over a wide area, apparently in retribution for having been trapped, measured, and tagged himself.

He was apparently thinking not only in terms of *how* to do things, but *why*. As further support for the formidable intelligence of bears, Doug Seuss, trainer of the famed ursine movie star Bart, claims his charge often mastered a scene in one or two takes— better than some human actors can claim.

No surprise, then, that individual bears exhibit distinct tendencies that are tough not to label as personality. Some bears are generally even tempered and laid back; some are nervous and retiring; then there are nose-to-the-grindstone serious types, as well as short-fused bullies. There are homebody bears and adventurous ramblers; carefree goofballs and chronic worriers. And ursine individuality goes beyond mere disposition. These animals have distinct styles and preferences in matters from clam digging to choosing den sites to wooing mates—some probably learned from observing mother or fellow bears, others seemingly original, the product of spontaneous invention and adaptation.

Take fishing methods, for example. There are bears who "snorkel"—stick their entire heads under the water, eyes open, in search of salmon. Others specialize in diving up to twenty feet to retrieve fish carcasses. Some are adept at chasing and pouncing on shallow-swimming salmon, or deftly grabbing them in midair at waterfalls. And like some people, there are bears that never seem to get the hang of fishing by any means. These all-thumbs types rely on scavenging remains left by more skilled bears—becoming the welfare bums of their kind—or they turn to crime, relying on strong-arm robbery of subordinate animals. While of course local conditions dictate techniques, methodology seems a direct extension of the animal's individuality. That sort of diversity runs through the whole gamut of bear behavior. Even seasoned biologists and bear-viewing guides struggle to avoid making anthropomorphic projections and developing personal ties and favorites, as some freely admit. But Timothy, in this regard, shoves the throttle forward.

Crawling on all fours, singing and talking in that sort of odd, high voice normally reserved for babies and cockapoos—*Hey, little bear, love you, aren't you beautiful, that's right, love you*—Timothy sidles up to wild bears time and again, intent on building personal relationships based on mutual trust and goodwill. As his confidence and knowledge grow, he feels he's knocking on the door of interspecies kinship, especially with animals like Booble, who seem to move, he says, beyond mere tolerance to actually enjoying his company. A wounded bear he names Mickey sleeps near his tent for weeks and recovers; mothers often leave their cubs nearby when they go off to forage, as if asking him to baby-sit. By his own admission, he even goes so far as to plant a kiss on one bear's nose after it licks his fingers.

The camera and video recorder keep whirring, and he fills note-books with observations, scrawled in wavering schoolboy print. He's found himself. This is where he was meant to be all along. A sense of wild power and clarity must flow through him, and a sense of his own smallness. That's what spending large chunks of time alone in the country does; the walls of paradox flicker, fade, and occasionally dissolve. When he tells Kathleen Parker and others, and writes again and again in his book, that he may not return this time, it's more than melodramatic rhetoric. He knows damn well the danger. On the other hand, part of him, the same reckless kid that dared the diving board to hit him and waded into fights, booze, and cocaine without blinking, believes he will never die. Which voice he believes most depends on the moment.

The bears are by and large incredibly tolerant and peaceful, typified by the animal he calls Ms. Goodbear, after a stuffed Teddy he once owned. But from time to time, just often enough that he never quite forgets they're out there, he faces bears—certain ones, especially smaller but powerful, three- to five-year-old adolescents (known to biologists as subadults), and the occasional large male—that are different. They menace, bully, and huff at Timothy, approach head low and don't back down. But with no place to run and nothing to fight with, he learns to play his remaining cards well. Sometimes he finds that the best thing is to ignore a bear; others, like a troublesome subadult incongruously named Cupcake, he bluffs into leaving by standing his ground, making himself look as large as possible, and even by charging, as a dominant bear might. Only once, sometime in his first several years on the coast, does he use pepper-based bear spray, the ursine-sized equivalent of Mace: He hoses down Cupcake at point-blank range when he feels he has no other choice. However, he's so distressed by the bear's apparent agony that he decides he'll never use it again. And he doesn't—in fact, entirely stops packing it along. Fear, he decides, isn't the message he wants to send—ignoring the advice of other experienced bear hands who maintain that the animals hold no more grudge than they would with, say, a skunk. The spray is a harmless negative stimulus, these guys claim. But Timothy feels that good intentions are the only shield he needs.

At least twice, though, Timothy himself is on the receiving end of that fear communiqué, reduced to a quaking ball of nerves. In one case at Hallo Bay, witnessed from a distance by a bear-viewing guide in the mid-nineties, an older male who is courting a female loses his temper at Timothy's persistent, point-blank presence and stops just short of knocking his head off. Timothy, obviously shaken, retreats to his camp. Another time, threatened by a bear trashing his tent, he makes a radio call in a total panic to Euyak Air, asking for an immediate dust-off. And yet he refuses to lean on bear spray or newly developed (and highly effective) portable electric fences to ensure his own safety. You could call Timothy Treadwell stupid or foolhardy, I suppose, as many did before his death and many more have done since. But even if you believe he was a dunderhead, a suicidal maniac, or just a guy who wasn't thinking things through, it's hard not to nod at his raw courage and steadfastness of conviction.

Even the Sanctuary offers only limited escape from humanity's pressure. Poachers, Timothy says, remain a constant threat, both to himself and the bears. He relates threats, both veiled and direct, and tells friends and backers that if he disappears or turns up dead out there, it's more likely one of these illegal hunters than a bear. Timothy claims they're after trophies, or gall bladders and other body parts destined for Asian markets, where such items bring tidy sums to small fortunes. Along the desolate outer Katmai Coast, these men come and go in unmarked small planes and boats, and often turn tail when they spot him. To hear Timothy tell it, he's become a human shield, operating alone and unarmed in the front lines against a looming menace. He writes of confronting his first poachers sometime in the early '90s (exact dates regarding Timothy are often vague)—sinister men with scoped rifles who come ashore from a yacht and stalk Beacon, the most beautiful of the Sanctuary bears. Only his charging the men, screaming obscenities, forces the poachers to flee—but not before one man levels a rifle at his chest. The incident's a dramatic high point, one that justifies his presence here, not just to himself but to supporters back in California.

But few people who know the area—park officials, state biologists, pilots, local fishermen and outdoors people, bear-viewing and hunting guides, even Alaskan friends like Parker, Fulton, or filmmaker Joel Bennett—are convinced of Timothy's claims of persistent poaching.

"He never saw one poacher," scoffs Chuck Keim, a commercial fisherman turned Katmai bear-viewing guide whose experience along the coast goes back to 1974. "I don't think he even knew what a poacher looked like. And if he had run into someone that desperate to hunt illegally in the park, they would have shot him, stuffed him in a crab pot, and he would have just disappeared. That business of his was a total fabrication."

"In my sixteen years of law enforcement in western Alaska, I've never heard of a bear poaching case on the Katmai Coast," says police officer turned National Park Service pilot Allen Gilliland, a member of the rescue team, the man who would find Timothy's remains. "I think there would have been at least one investigation in that time if anything much were going on, and I would have heard of it."

Probably the most scientific support of minimal poaching is the post–*Exxon Valdez* oil spill study conducted by Alaska Department of Fish and Game bear biologists Richard Sellers and Sterling Miller in 1989 and 1990—Treadwell's first years, when he insisted that poaching was rampant. Using a helicopter and sedative dart guns, Miller and Sellers's crew immobilized, studied, tattooed, and radio-collared dozens of bears along the Katmai Coast, many in the same areas Treadwell would later frequent. The collars allowed the biologists to track the animals by radio beacon; should a collar become inactive, due to being shed or the bear dying, it would send out a distinctive signal. And, says Miller, "there was never one incident of the study bears being poached, or dying in a suspicious manner."

In fact, in the history of the Park and Preserve, going back eight decades, there is not a single documented case, solved or not, of a bear being illegally killed inside park boundaries.* On the other hand, the Park Service concedes that poaching once *was* an issue—in the 1960s and '70s, before regular patrols of the Katmai Coast began. Kathleen Parker says she knew there were ille-

---

*This would change in 2004 with the shooting of three bears at Funnel Creek, outside the park boundaries but inside the preserve.

gal killings in the '70s, mostly young men off the commercial fishing boats, looking for a thrill after work. Timothy also pointed to the testimonial of an unnamed rogue guide (apparently Ron Hayes, who was indeed convicted of numerous poaching violations, albeit elsewhere in the state) who claimed his clients shot over a thousand bears in the 1960s and '70s, some legally and some not, many of them along the Katmai Coast, inside park boundaries.

But by the mid-'90s just about everyone who knows the coast agrees there were simply too many planes and boats, and too many people coming and going at places like Hallo Bay and Kukak Bay (including bear-viewing camps or lodges at each of the above), for poaching on any scale to take place. And the potential penalties—forfeiture of all equipment, fines, jail time, and loss of guiding license—are too steep a price for most guides to risk. Gary Porter, who during bear season drops off legal, resident sport hunters outside park boundaries, claims eighty-plus percent success rate for his clients and says, "No one in their right mind would poach a bear out of Katmai National Park. There are too many bears everywhere else."

For hunters of world-class trophies, though, the lure of Katmai is clear: those enormous, once-in-a-lifetime male bears twenty years old and more, up to fifteen hundred pounds—the closest thing to a cave bear or saber-toothed cat, and worldwide, almost as scarce. A top-ten bear might be worth twenty grand under the table. But if some pirate guide were to poach, he'd most likely do so in April or mid- to late October, when bear hides (the whole point of a sport hunt) are prime, and no one, including Timothy, was around—he habitually arrived around June 1 and left by early October.

At least some circumstantial evidence supports Timothy's claims of illegal bear-killing. An early-'90s issue of the German-language magazine *Geo* featured a first-person account of an indignant sport hunter who was unknowingly drawn into an illegal bear hunt inside Katmai National Park. His exposé included images of skinned-out paws and gangs of trophy-clutching hunters, making the point clear that his wasn't an isolated case. The contentions of the *Geo* piece, though, have never been confirmed or denied, and they never led to a conviction.

"I don't think Timothy was entirely out to lunch on this thing," says independent Alaska biologist and bear researcher Steve Stringham, who counted Timothy as a friend, and shared at least some of his beliefs concerning bears. "I've heard rumors of certain guys who guide bear viewing in summer and hunting in fall. Some of their hunting activity is inside the park, but not all of it. Pretty easy to slip across the boundaries and claim you shot something somewhere else."

But despite the fact that Timothy Treadwell carried camera and video gear with him just about everywhere, in thirteen seasons and numerous claimed encounters, he never produced so much as a single out-of-focus snapshot or video of the lurking killers or their handiwork—though, in summer of 2003, just months before his death, he did find and film a disused campsite hidden in the timber at Hallo Bay with a log structure he called a "skinning post." However, park superintendent Joe Fowler said, "Investigating rangers found no evidence of poaching activity in the area." He characterized Treadwell's "skinning post" as merely a log lashed between two trees just five feet off the ground, the sort of rig someone might make to support a tarp shelter or hang some gear. And any hunter—which Timothy never was—would know that a bear, too heavy to drag, is invariably skinned where it lies.

Timothy finally did present one image of a poacher: a man fording a stream with a shotgun on his shoulder, apparently ignoring a bear maybe thirty yards away. The picture was used on a

Grizzly People brochure published in 1998, top left on the first inner fold—by placement, the most prominent and important shot in the spread. The caption reads, "A poacher stalks Tabitha." The "poacher" turned out to be Joe Allen, one of Tom Walters's bear-viewing guides from Katmai Wilderness Lodge.* Walters, who'd helped Timothy out numerous times, offered to sue Patagonia, the designer and printer of the brochure, for defamation of character. The offending pamphlets were pulled at once, and for a while, so was Patagonia's support of Timothy.

He had just needed an image to dramatize the poaching issue, Timothy told Walters, and thought no one would notice. But he stopped short of apologizing to a man who flew him for free, fed him, and let him stay at his house on and off over a course of years. Instead, he told Walters that Allen really wasn't such a nice guy, and that Allen occasionally threw rocks at bears. (This is, in fact, a common and surprisingly effective practice among some bear-viewing guides, seen as a kinder alternative to pepper spray, used to discourage overinquisitive animals at point-blank range. Says one experienced guide, "A person would get mad if you chunked a rock at them; the bear seems to think it's magic, and it always has worked for me. It's not a pelting, just something that jars them and changes their mindset.")

"Tim believed that the end justifies the means," says Walters later. "Quite frankly, he wasn't keeping poachers away. He admitted that much when I confronted him. I saw him every year, coming and going, and he never once mentioned a poacher to me—and he would have, caring as much as he did about the bears. That was nonsense he saved for his California crowd. Meanwhile, Joe was his friend and he stabbed him in the back,

*Firearms are technically illegal above the high-tide mark in Katmai National Park, but Walters points out that Allen was below that tide line. Regardless, in bear country, shotguns are strictly defensive weapons, not the tools of a poacher.

and never really apologized. I never really got angry with Tim, but I sure did get disappointed." Tom Walters is done with Timothy Treadwell. So is Joe Allen.

But publicly, Timothy sticks to his story—give or take. When interviewed by talk-show host Tom Snyder later that same year, 1998, Timothy will play the Tabitha card once more. The fact that it's the same bear out of all the scores that he knows seems to indicate he's referring to the same incident. In front of the kleig lights, though, the details flex a bit. "There was a time," Timothy tells Snyder, "a boat pulled up on [Tabitha]. These guys were like poster men from the NRA—they had machine guns, they had shotguns, high-powered rifles, they were gonna take her out. But I stepped out and—I would take a bullet for Tabitha." Timothy, in his ignorance of firearms, once more commits a faux pas any hunter would spot. Shotguns? Machine guns? Bolt-action magnum rifles with scopes would be more like it—and careful aim of a single killing shot. One is left to wonder if poor old Joe Allen, who wanted only to cross the creek and get on with his bear view, has morphed into an entire SWAT team, or if a gang of Mafia hit men had suddenly materialized on the Katmai Coast, determined to settle a score with the bear that did them wrong.

In any case, Timothy is never able to document the loss to poaching of any of the dozens of bears he knows by sight; a curious inconsistency, you could say; or one might argue, as he does, that his own presence is what saves the bears. Despite lack of any hard evidence, Timothy continues to adamantly proclaim the presence of poachers in Katmai, as will Jewel after his death.

Why insist on poaching at all? Camping in a national park doesn't require a mission statement or any justification. However, effective fund raising does. Even with all the handouts that Timothy garnered, the costs of operating in bush Alaska—plane tickets, equipment, supplies—added up. Then there was the cost of travel for Timothy's dozens of lower-forty-eight school presentations. A frugal guy, which Timothy certainly was, might have made it on the cheap for ten grand a year, and doing things right, all included, would have taken double or triple that. Not on a part-time waiter's salary. Grizzly People could only operate with outside support; and without some compelling reason, they'd have been asking folks to donate to Timothy Treadwell's annual summer vacation. But as long as the bears were endangered, beset by an evil menace, doomed if not for this brave man, they had a pitch. In the blunt words of Tom Walters, "He was a con artist, no doubt about it—nice guy, but I knew what he was too. Timothy just had himself a good gig, and he wanted to keep it going." The poaching angle was clearly the selling point, Timothy's *cause célèbre* that helped push financial support to another level.

Money trickles, and sometimes rolls, in. Timothy Treadwell may be broke, but there are plenty of people in Malibu and beyond who aren't. Save the bears? Honey, write this guy a check, willya? With this sort of hook, Jewel and Timothy attract an impressive array of sponsors—among them the outdoor clothing company Patagonia (printer of the poacher brochure), The North Face, Tamrac, and Konica Minolta, which loans Timothy thirteen thousand dollars' worth of professional-grade camera gear. There's now enough money for Grizzly People to expand and upgrade their operations. More trips and better equipment and, in the off season, more free school presentations. Meanwhile, Grizzly People, a supposed nonprofit organization, somehow isn't ever properly registered with the federal government with the official 501(c)(3) designation. Just an oversight, a technicality, one might argue— one that won't be noticed until caught in the glaring spotlight following Timothy Treadwell's death.

*   *   *

Local Park Service officials become increasingly restive, even downright irritated, over Timothy Treadwell's presence. Not only is he insinuating their failure to protect the bears, as far as they're concerned, he's putting both himself and the animals at risk by his up-close-and-personal style. In one instance, a bemused bear-viewing visitor reports in writing to the Park Service that Timothy was straddling a sleeping bear—standing over the animal, one leg on each side—while filming it. Another eyewitness account has him videotaping a young bear poking at his tent while someone else, apparently a woman, is inside. Encouraging such close contact with animals as powerful and space sensitive as bears is over the line, no matter how you slice it. Sooner or later, Park Service officials figure, even one of these copasetic, well-fed bruins is liable to go off, and it only takes a moment before the damage is done—not only to bears and people in the field, but to the park's reputation. "We were fairly alarmed by his behavior," says park superintendent Deb Liggett.

Also, Hallo Bay and the park as a whole are remote, but hardly an empty wilderness, with a steady and growing stream of bear-viewing visitors passing through, many straight out of Hoboken or Cedar Rapids. By hanging out with an entire population of bears, Timothy is habituating them to not only his presence, but to people in general. What are Ma and Pa Murphy with their point-and-shoot going to do when one of Timothy's bears, used to cheek-to-jowl contact, or at least comfortable point-blank proximity, ambles up? If they panic and run, as they very well might, or just get un-lucky, someone gets chewed. In the lower forty-eight, habituated brown/grizzlies (albeit in most cases with food involved) are im-plicated in the most human deaths—every single one of the eighteen recorded in Yellowstone and Glacier National Parks. Too, maul-ings set up inevitable chain reactions that generally result in dead bears—if not the bear involved, other bears, sometimes hundreds of miles away and weeks later, gunned down by nervous people who suddenly have an elevated awareness that they could be next. Biologists label this phenomenon bearanoia, and it generally spikes following a bear-caused death.

Over the years, Timothy is advised, warned, and urged to show restraint and take basic precautions, both for the bears' sake and his own—not just by the feds, but by biologists, photographers, pilots, and even similar-minded bear activists like Charlie Russell and Dr. Stephen Stringham. The latter two, despite a shared belief in intraspecies spirituality, can't convince him to use a bear fence or carry spray, and to be a bit more careful. Stringham, notorious in some circles for his own close-range work with bears, says, "Tim and I were friends, you know, and we had a good laugh over it. He just kind of chuckled and said, 'What do you think, some bear is going to come into camp at night and eat you?' I said, a normal bear, no, but some bear, yes. He just laughed it off."

German adventurer and filmmaker Andreas Kieling, whom Park Service officials and bear guides often mention in the same breath with Timothy Treadwell, also tried to caution Timothy. Kieling, known for his fearless, up-close bear-filming tactics (apparent in his Animal Planet special *Grizzly Encounters*), seldom carries any form of protection. Still, he makes it plain that he considers no bear to be safe. He points out that after a few weeks out on the coast, he's caught himself making potentially dangerous assumptions about bears. "You feel like you build up a relationship with this bear or that one—but it's a big error," Kieling says. "I think Tim was too positive about bears . . . he didn't like to know the truth."

On the other side of the ideological fence, longtime state bear biologist Sterling Miller (now retired, but still professionally active as president of the International Bear Association and as a bear specialist for the National Wildlife Federation) recalls admonishing Timothy to be more cautious. He received a letter in reply that stated, among other things, that Timothy would personally "be honored to end up as grizzly shit." Ruminates Miller, "Given his attitude, I believed it wouldn't be long before he would be so honored."

Tom Walters, never one to mince words, says, "I told him straight out, years ago, he was going to get himself killed."

As for the other side of the equation—the danger he might pose to bears—Timothy makes vague deflections, never quite admitting that the possibility even exists. He loves these bears. How could he ever possibly hurt them? Later on, he'll write in his book that in the event of his being killed by a bear, he's instructed the pilots who fly him to dispose of his remains so that he simply disappears. That's his safeguard to the bears. Of course, it's a pipe dream, asking people to commit a class A felony for his sake, and to risk their careers, even lives, on his account. He also repeatedly makes the claim that he has an understanding with the Park Service that no bears will be killed over him. In all probability, it's a fiction he spins for himself as much as anyone else.

One thing everyone seems to agree on: Timothy Treadwell, from start to finish, holds his own opinions and beliefs about bears, and keeps counsel largely with himself on the matter. And right or wrong, he has major cojones.

Besides the safety issue, Timothy is, as far as the Park Service is concerned, a squatter situated in the center of one of the most popular areas of the park, camping for weeks on end. But there's really nothing the Park Service can do. According to regulations, staying in one place all season—year round, for that matter—isn't illegal, simply because no one ever considered trying it at Katmai. An occasional pro photographer might stay for a few days, but he or she wouldn't set up a tent smack in the middle of the bears' feeding grounds and snoozing areas, or near main trails. Biologists, operating under research permits, camp in small groups and keep their distance from their study subjects. And there's Timothy Treadwell, alone, plunked down at the epicenter of bear town, like he's at home on the Barcalounger. No one, least of all the park rangers (who camp behind electric bear fences at the beach fringe of Hallo for a few weeks during the heart of bear-viewing season) know what to do or say.

However, crowding wildlife *is* explicitly verboten (fifty yards for single bears, and a hundred-yard buffer for females with cubs), as is improper food storage (specially made plastic BRFCs—bear-resistant food containers—are required). Rangers on patrol visit his camp regularly, no doubt snooping for violations, but generally they seem to take a laissez-faire attitude. Timothy is never charged with crowding bears. (Who approached whom? What are you supposed to do if a bear walks up and lies down ten feet from your tent?)

Finally, in 1997 the Park Service clamps down in a move calculated to wear Timothy down, or at least restrict his access to Hallo Bay. Park regulations are amended to include a prohibition against camping in one area for more than seven days—dubbed by insiders as the Treadwell Rule. He's forced to move his camp a minimum of one mile each time, a Herculean task given the roughness of the terrain and the amount of gear involved. But the authorities have underestimated his determination. He responds by showing up the next season with an outboard-powered Lund skiff to move his camps. After a series of near disasters with the coast's notorious tides and rough surf, Timothy abandons the skiff idea after only a season; donors provide him with the wherewithal to charter floatplanes from Kodiak—eight hundred dollars a pop—and the game of chess continues. Ranger patrols are often so infrequent that he's able to stretch the legal one week before moving into two, or three.

Still, while Timothy is warned of various infractions, he's ticketed only once in his thirteen seasons. In 1998, the Park Service dings him $150 for improper food storage and warns him for having a gas-powered electrical generator (to charge his video camera batteries) in a wilderness area. He is "outraged," he writes in a letter of protest, that rangers would search his camp in his absence. In a return letter, the Park Service points out Timothy repeatedly fibbed to them about nonexistent bear-proof, out-of-camp food containers and an adjacent cooking area. A picnic-grade Igloo cooler duct-taped shut and a cardboard box stuffed in a tent hardly qualify as BRFCs. Timothy mutters but pays his ticket, accepts a loan of the rangers' containers, and retools with his own BRFCs the next season.

At least some of the Park Service people, like Ranger Stephen Harper and chief back-country ranger Missy Epping, like Timothy, and consider him a help along the outer coast, where there are no permanent NPS stations. They hang around and eat together when passing through. He's charming. He's fun. He's a friend even if he doesn't exactly toe the line.

Filmmaker Andreas Kieling and other regulars along the coast claim Timothy received special treatment, especially from a ranger Kieling knew only as "Big John." "Timothy was untouchable," Kieling says. "He got away with things no one else could have."

Whether or not Keiling's assertion is true, Timothy feels the pressure. Even while his correspondence with the Park Service brims with goodwill, he responds to their scrutiny by becoming increasingly secretive and evasive, assigning code words to his locations when using a two-way radio or (later on) a satellite phone. And he spends more time at Kukak Bay and at Kaflia, his Grizzly Maze, hunkered back in the brush, with camouflage netting over his tents. Like Conrad's Kurtz in *Heart of Darkness*, he seems to be slipping farther and farther away from society's boundaries, into a wild landscape that will eventually envelop him.

Fifteen Minutes and Change

The maze of Timothy Treadwell's life is a study in ever-sharpening extremes. On one side, there's his California gig, redolent of palm trees, sushi, and sun; on the other, the stark Katmai Coast, pounded by weather and patrolled by foraging bears. Those were the starting values, jarring enough in 1989, when Timothy's Alaska sojourn began. But in a sense, in those early days, the same Timothy Treadwell moved through both worlds—an unknown, a marginal player at best, a gutsy, lonely adventurer with little to claim in the way of accomplishment and nothing much to lose. Watching him at the beginning, you'd have guessed long odds, betting on a dramatic uplift of his fortunes.

Some people, though, seem to possess either the power or will to shape their lives in a way that most of us can't—or won't. By coming to Alaska and finding this one place (arguably the only one) where he could coexist among seemingly peaceful, friendly bears, and muster the necessary support, Timothy fulfilled the first part of his dream. The second part—recognition, even fame—seemed, at first glance, more daunting. He was, after all, a high school graduate with zero training in animal behavior, professional photography, acting, or public relations, at least one of which seemed a prerequisite for that ultimate dive into stardom.

Nonetheless, as Alaska turned a collective cold shoulder to him, California opened its arms—maybe one of those quick, peck-on-the-cheek Hollywood *abrazos*, but a gesture nonetheless. Even as Timothy moved and breathed among the bears, moving secretly from place to place, the show business side of his life continued on a separate, but inevitably overlapping, trail.

To someone from southern California, someone who doesn't know squat about bears, let alone the coastal brownies of Katmai, Timothy's exploits are jaw dropping, and his videos and photos prove it's more than just hype. Add the urgent save-the-bears message, the educate-the-kids-for-free deal, to Timothy's natural charisma, and you have an attention-grabbing, tailor-made-for-TV story. Turner Broadcasting is the first to invest in a project, an hour-long Audubon special aired in 1992, "In the Land of the Grizzlies." It features on-location footage of Timothy doing what he does best—schmoozing with bears in point-blank proximity and being his flaky, passionate self. A national audience sits up and takes notice. *Who is this guy, anyway?*

At the same time, the project is, for Timothy, a bittersweet success. Originally the show was to be all him, but apparently the field producer, Liam O'Brien, finds Timothy difficult to work with. He doesn't always take direction well and seems both moody and self-absorbed. At one point he tells O'Brien, who wants another take of a sequence, that he "will not prostitute his bears." At the same time, O'Brien becomes interested in Alaska cameraman and filmmaker Joel Bennett, himself a longtime bear and wildlife advocate, and the story widens to include him—as well as a broader message on the imperiled state of bears worldwide. Timothy is relegated from top billing to a costarring role, and the buzz is out that he doesn't quite have what it takes to become, say, the next Steve Irwin (the Crocodile Hunter, at this point a growing Aussie celeb under the radar in America, but about to break big). Close, but no cigar. Still, Timothy Treadwell's name is up in lights for the first time, and the exposure gains him recognition and credibility—as well as a whetted hunger for more. The door of opportunity cracks open, and Timothy slides his foot in.

His big break, in terms of national exposure, is a *People* magazine feature two years later, in 1994. This time Timothy, a bit better prepped and focused, knows what to do. Phil Schofield, the photographer for the story, has recollections of his three days with Timothy at Hallo Bay, which reflect a sharp ambivalence:

> If there's one thing this guy knew how to do, it was how to go after publicity. He had a package and he had a plan. He knew why we were there, and knew we needed good pictures and anecdotes to make the story publishable—him becoming one with the bears. . . . I think his intentions were probably good, but it still was kind of a scam. I've known guys like him; the place he'd come from wasn't one he wanted to go back to. . . . He knew this was a huge opportunity for him and his project. And, sure, he was a very likable, personable guy. He had enough Hollywood in him to be able to turn on the charm. On the other hand, after watching Tim for three days, I could see how one would get sick of him.

Asked to fill in scattered impressions, Schofield adds,

> Tim seemed very ill prepared. He had all-cotton clothes, a tent that blew down while we were there, and the second day, he tipped a pot of boiling water on his leg and needed to be flown to Kodiak for medical attention.* But he was somehow comfortable out there, and very energetic. I sure didn't sleep a wink the whole time. There were forty or fifty bears every day, and Tim was right in the middle of them. We got our story.

---

*This is a different burn from the one Don Pitcher reported on Kodiak—apparently a recurring theme in Timothy's camping life.

People magazine has thirty million readers, and this brief story, photographed by Schofield and written by Lyndon Stambler, stands out among the usual celeb chatter and human interest blurbs. Timothy Treadwell has copped some major face time, and the coup results in a life-altering chain reaction. Within a year of the *People* story, the French company Marathon films their own feature, *Timothy and the Bears*. As the title suggests, this time Timothy Treadwell gets marquee attention, and it plays well in Paris. Publishing giant HarperCollins offers him a book contract. Again, Timothy's education hasn't exactly prepared him for authorship. But Jewel, a graduate of Southern Cal, steps in to cowrite the two-hundred-page ecomemoir, *Among Grizzlies*, released in 1997. While hardly a smashing commercial or critical success, a book is a book, and HarperCollins isn't small potatoes. Ballantine picks up the softcover rights, and the Treadwell ball continues to roll. Paramount Television follows in 1997 with a short feature on Timothy for their popular Fox-channel series *Wild Things*. Then comes the tour de force, the 1999 Discovery Channel special, "The Grizzly Diaries": Timothy front and center with the bears before a national audience, impeccably filmed and produced. A year later, NBC *Dateline* does a high-profile journalistic take as well, which has its own ramifications, not all positive.

Meanwhile, Timothy becomes a near regular on the talk show circuit, chatting up the likes of Tom Snyder, Rosie O'Donnell, and up the food chain to David Letterman. He takes a few lessons and hires a stiletto-heeled PR specialist—in the vernacular, a handler—to help him hone his theatrical persona, and apparently it pays off. Though he seems a bit self-conscious at times (Juneau filmmaker Joel Bennett, who did all of the on-location camera work for just about all the above features, and knows Timothy as few do, calls the first Letterman appearance in 2001 stiff and nervous), Timothy still comes across as genuine and charismatic in his usual surfer-dude way—backward ball cap, shaggy blond mane, and all. Video clips of him and the bears at handshake range bring oohs and ahhs from hosts and audiences alike. He tells the audience that bears are "just big party animals," and is enough of a hit that Letterman invites him back the following year. "I take my orders from the animals," he earnestly tells Tom Snyder.

Whether they like him or not, everyone agrees: Timothy Treadwell has a shtick. He knows it and it works. If there's a downside, it's that it encourages, even demands him to produce more of the same and, if possible, to upstage himself. One video clip that pops up on *Dateline* in 2000 shows him reaching out and inviting a bear to touch his hand with its nose. Apparently the bear does, or stops just an inch or two short. How do you top that? With what seems in retrospect chilling prescience, Letterman asks him, "Is it going to happen that one day we read a news article about you being eaten by one of these bears?" Of course, Dave's line is a big yuk for the crowd.

In the show biz world of southern California, even more so than everywhere else, getting on a screen of any size more than once makes you somebody. Among the more ecoconscious glitterati, Timothy Treadwell and his cause are accorded the sort of legitimacy that translates into major support—of both the moral and the folding variety. Leonardo DiCaprio and Pierce Brosnan are among the high-profile donors who now grace the Treadwell prospectus. DiCaprio beatifies Timothy on his own Web site, ponies up sizable bucks—in the twenty-five-grand-plus range (funding, among other things, Timothy's short-lived skiff experiment). Reclusive Colorado millionaire Roland Dixon, a sympathetic player in bear preservation, is rumored to double that. Add on the corporate sponsors, the blessing of the Sierra Club and the Great Bear Foundation (among others). One might surmise a swelling army of activists. Nonetheless, Grizzly People is still as grass-roots an organization as ever, made of exactly two people: Timothy and Jewel. Despite those irregularities in his organization's nonprofit status, and the ever-increasing monetary influx, Timothy remains true to his tightfisted roots. Maybe he doesn't serve drinks anymore, but no one offers evidence that he is anything but dedicated to the work of Grizzly People. His passion has become a full-time job.

While the bears sleep through the long Alaska winter, Timothy Treadwell basks in his celebrity and hits the lecture circuit. Traveling widely, with an emphasis in the West, he preaches his gospel of grizzly love anywhere he can fill a hall or room halfway full of people—sometimes accepting a speaker's fee, but often free of charge. He shows slides and videos, passes the hat to do battle against the poachers, and hands out autographed pictures of his favorite bears. He wades through classroom after classroom of elementary kids, bouncing with energy, stressing bear safety and awareness. The professionally designed Grizzly People Web site claims he reaches fifteen thousand children a year. That figure is almost certainly padded, but even half that is a staggering number, as anyone who's spent much time in a classroom will tell you. The letters from excited kids and grateful, impressed teachers pour in. And in between, he meets with supporters and presides over private viewings of his latest bear videos.

It would be tough—impossible, really—to be a blond, outdoorsy, semihandsome, and semifamous lover of bears and children and not be some sort of chick magnet. Women of all ages and sorts find Timothy attractive, as they'll freely tell you. He had a pronounced taste, longtime friend Kathleen Parker says, for "younger, sexy California-girl types"—understandable enough, but not exactly the sort suited to the Katmai Coast. But every two seasons or so a different woman shows up in Kodiak and spends a week or two out with Timothy and his bears. They are, by all accounts, interchangeable parts, and he likes it that way—even if some of them don't. Despite the spontaneous warmth that friends comment on, Timothy imposes a paradoxical distance—physical, emotional, or both—between himself and the world. His ability to strike up a conversation with almost anyone belies a complex and guarded inner persona. His self-imposed severance from his family, his repeated reinvention of himself, and his apparent aversion to commitment—all become concrete in Timothy's solitary refuge on the wild Katmai Coast. No surprise at his instinctive rapport with bears and children; they don't ask for much beyond the moment.

At the same time, Timothy adores women, and he's loath to do without. Semidisposable dates, then, are the perfect solution—companionship without long-term complication. But as he tells Kathleen Parker, having women with him out on the coast makes him nervous. He doesn't worry much about himself, but their presence reminds him of what can go wrong.

Apparently he's not always totally consumed by such concern. In the '98 Tom Snyder interview, he admits to engaging in a bit of intense interpersonal research with one of his girlfriends, surrounded by bears doing more or less the same thing. When Snyder orders the clip to roll, Timothy reddens while the audience howls. Whether a setup or not, it makes for great theater, and no doubt piques the interest of a few would-be recruits who imagine themselves in the picture.

To illustrate Timothy's almost uncanny ability to attract women without seeming to try, Joel Bennett tells me about an incident he witnessed in the summer of 2003, just a few weeks before Timothy died. They were out at Frazier Lake, working on Treadwell's film intro for the Disney cartoon feature *Brother Bear*. A beautiful young summer worker for the Alaska Department of Fish and Game, apparently quite irritated with all Timothy stood for, confronted him and started hazing him with sharp questions. "She wasn't just cute," Joel emphasizes, "but flat-out gorgeous, and close to half his age (then forty-six)." As Joel watched, Timothy somehow not only deflected her ire; within minutes she was batting eyelashes at him, obviously smitten. Joel snapped a photo of them standing together, and drags it out to show me. He's right about one thing—she's a looker, you'd think a bit out of his league. Nonetheless, there's the picture, and the body language says it all.

So—where does Amie Huguenard, the woman who will die with Timothy Treadwell, fit into this story? Good question. In the wake of the tragedy, reporters will trot out terms like "girlfriend," "partner," and "companion," fishing for the correct term. The truth is, no one, including Timothy's closest Alaska friends, seem to know what Amie was.

"I never heard him mention her once," says Joel, "and I was working with him just before she came up that last time."

"Timothy always told me about his girlfriends," says Kathleen Parker. "Always. And he never brought up Amie." Andrew Air pilot Willy Fulton, who flew Timothy (including a female companion now and then) over six seasons, tells the same story. "Sure, Tim and I shot the breeze about women," he says. "But not her. Tell the truth, I never knew much about her. She was pretty quiet the few times we met."

Amie Huguenard first sees Timothy Treadwell in Boulder, Colorado, in 1996 at a slide show and lecture he's giving at the University of Colorado campus, and is smitten by his passion and commitment. Five years later, in a letter of support for Timothy to the National Park Service, she will write, "As an advocate for the rights of wildlife, I attend many presentations . . . but none captured my attention like Timothy's. Finally someone willing to espouse wildlife ethics where it matters most—in the hearts and minds of young children." They meet, and one thing eventually leads to another—though it's hardly a fast-track romance. Amie doesn't fit Timothy's usual STR profile—some bouncy California waitress thing. At the time of their first face-to-face she's in her early thirties, a surgical physician's assistant who, while attractive in a wholesome, fit way, could hardly be described as sexy. She doesn't try to be. Just over five feet tall and a hundred pounds, she's a devotee of outdoor aerobics, including running, hiking, and biking. Makeup—let alone low-rise jeans and bare midriff tops—isn't her style. Her credentials have a bit more substance, including a master's degree in molecular biology. She's someone who approaches animal rights issues not just with her heart, but from an informed point of view. And when she sees Timothy Treadwell up on that stage, what attracts her is his passion for the bears, his commitment.

In spite of the moving target Timothy presents, Amie Huguenard doesn't give up. She sees in him, too, something that transcends mere interest or physical attraction. "I think she was in love with Timothy," says Parker. "In fact, I'm sure of it, just from the way she looked at him." In any case, it seems clear that making things happen is up to Amie, and she keeps tapping him on the shoulder, by phone or letter, e-mail, in person, any way she can. In 2001 she makes her first visit to the Katmai Coast; whose idea it was isn't clear.

In any case, a week at Hallo Bay, a good place to break into the world of bears. She hangs around Timothy as he hangs around the copasetic, grazing bruins there, and learns to almost sleep at night with them rustling around in the long, twilit summer evenings. Then on to Kaflia for a week—more intense, but still, it's summer and food is plentiful. The bears are relaxed. She watches as Timothy works his magic; after eleven seasons here, just about all the bears know him and have developed an exceptional level of tolerance for his presence, even by Katmai standards. Bears have long memories, and many of them he's known since they were spring cubs—thirty-pound fluff-balls—when he sidled up to their mothers and watched them nurse. This odd singing, cooing creature with his tripod and cameras has been around them every summer of their lives. Now some of these bears have cubs of their own and pass that tolerance along to them. Timothy jots down long notes on sightings, matings, and bloodlines—in essence, involved family trees—which are, due to his long presence, sharp-eyed ability to identify individuals, and tireless devotion, his most notable (perhaps only) contribution to bear science.

While this idyllic coexistence with her bear crusader may enthrall Amie Huguenard, state and federal biologists have all along been huffing and jaw-popping over Timothy Treadwell's presence. Whether state employees, with little official authority over national park areas, or federal workers defending their backyard, all of them consider bears to be their life's work and, by dint of years of schooling and many more of study, their rightful and exclusive province. So here's this California waiter plunked down in the middle of their study areas, acting like he's the Christopher Columbus of bears. What's more, he ignores all advice and standard protocols—the rules, both written and implied, which members of the scientific bear community hold as the Bible. You don't crowd or habituate bears and contaminate your study area by interacting with them. You don't treat them like people in furry suits. You sure as hell don't sing or talk to them.

Timothy's rising media star rankles the bear establishment further, goading them toward an all-out charge. It's one thing for this upstart to pull his goofball, New Age, commune-with-the-bears routine in anonymity; but to have it broadcast to tens of millions is another. No matter that Timothy continually promotes bear safety; the footage of him practically nuzzling and petting wild bears sends an opposing, hypocritical, and far more powerful visual—the equivalent of a father, Marlboro dangling from the corner of his mouth, exhorting his son not to smoke. And Timothy's real message isn't about bears, they argue, but himself, a cult of personality. Without that in-your-face bear-hugging act, which they see as self-absorbed and self-serving shenanigans bereft of the least shred of science, no one would pay any attention. In other words, if Timothy were actually practicing what he preaches, maintaining the legal Katmai distance of fifty yards to single bears and a hundred to females with cubs, there would be no talk show spots, no TV features, no book, no nothing. And none of his stated missions—guarding bears from poachers, studying them, or educating others—require the sort of proximity he practices; in fact, the argument is made that if there were poachers, Timothy's conditioning bears to not fear humans actually would put them at risk, making them easier targets. One scientist who witnesses Timothy interacting with bears in the field labels it "his own private *Jackass* show, minus the shopping cart"—a reference to the sophomoric MTV show that features a procession of mindless, death-defying stunts, the trademark of which is a downhill plunge in the aforementioned cart, all in the name of entertainment.

And the hell of it is, Timothy longs for the bear establishment's approval above all, even beyond that of the Park Service. He doesn't understand why it's not only withheld, but withheld so vehemently. In his mind, he's walked the walk and then some. He has endless pages of field notes documenting behavior and breeding; he's mastered bear body language and vocalizations; he's devoted his life to the bears' protection, laid it all out there. In 2000, he even attends the annual IBA (International Bear Association) conference, where cutting-edge papers are read, alliances forged, and tales from the field passed around. He finds himself sitting there, practically speechless for once in his life, no doubt intimidated by all these shingle-wielding Ph.D.s with their multisyllabic, statistic-driven palaver. It might as well be Swahili. There's no place for emotions, bears named Booble and Downy, and eye-dabbing interspecies bonding moments. He doesn't understand the whole process of peer review, whereby papers are circulated for examination and critique. When these guys, either here or in the field, ask to see his work, he taps his head and tells them it's in there— or he points to his book. He won't debate. He knows what he knows.

Whatever else *Among Grizzlies* may be, it hardly qualifies as a formal treatise. Though Timothy may understand a great deal about bears, it's strained and filtered through a decidedly unscientific perspective. Riddled with anthropomorphic interpretations and informed by emotion rather than logic, completely lacking any systematic approach or data, Timothy's book is worse than insubstantial to these men; it's downright offensive, a blueprint of how *not* to study animals of any sort.

"To me, what he was doing was disrespecting the bears," says Larry Van Daele, the biologist who would later conduct the necropsy and investigation following the tragedy. "There's so much more to a bear than Treadwell ever understood, so much more than this I-love-you, you're-my-friend, I'll-protect-you stuff. They're in a higher realm."

Among Grizzlies bubbles with gee-whiz statements such as "I had stumbled upon an amazing grizzly gathering, the likes of which may never have been seen before by humans" (p.120), and periodic references to "the secret ways of bears" that hint Timothy is somehow the gatekeeper to undiscovered behavior and insight. Yet, as USGS ecologist Dr. Tom Smith notes, "There's not one thing—not one single thing—in that book I didn't already know or couldn't look up in five minutes." The unwritten subtext to Timothy's gushing fountain of bear knowledge is that all the work that's come before amounts to chopped liver. And just about all his factual content is merely parroted from books he's read or the scientists he's talked with. The actual text, too, is riddled with biological bumbles, such as his repeatedly identifying razor clams as "razorback clams" and referring to "pine trees" that are in fact spruce. To people who trade in facts and respect them above all else, such inattention is a crowning insult to the craft and, when it comes to reputation, a kiss of death.

Timothy's posse, though, sticks by their man. Jewel Palovak asserts, "Timothy had plenty of good data to contribute. He wasn't a scientist, but someone could have worked with him. Hardly anyone in the scientific community even gave him a chance." Roland Dixon, Grizzly People's prime benefactor, dismisses the attackers as "just jealous."

Dixon may have a point. Timothy has clearly upstaged the entire bear-science establishment, garnering more media attention for himself and his cause in a decade than they've managed as a group over the last three. Considering that some of these folks have dedicated twenty, even thirty years to bear science, and that recognition is the name of the game, tough to imagine that some of them aren't just a bit green. As Stephen Stringham (himself an independent biologist on the fringe of the fraternity, who did offer to work with Timothy in constructing a study from his field notes—a project derailed by Timothy's death) observes, "Make no mistake about it. Bear biologists are as proprietary as any grizzly on a moose carcass."

But any way you play it, legit in Hollywood is a long way from legit in the world of bear science. If Timothy ever had a chance of gaining any sort of respect in that arena, by the turn of the millennium, it's slipped away.

The Grizzly Maze

A decade and counting into his new life, Timothy Treadwell rides the twin horses of fame and notoriety, balanced like a circus performer with one foot on the back of each. In California and the world beyond, he's made it. But as always, Alaska is another story. Supported by a few loyal friends but cold-shouldered by seemingly everyone else, Timothy continues to spend more and more time farther out, alone with the bears. He still starts off each season at Hallo Bay, where the animals congregate in mid-May through June to graze on the bounty of new-sprouted sedges and to forage on the clam flats.

But due to the boom in fly-in bear viewing, Timothy's Sanctuary has become an increasingly busy place. The next bay up the coast, Kukak, with its problematic tides and fewer landing places, is far less visited; Kaflia, the bay beyond that, is wilder still—more brushy, primal, and difficult, populated by bears scarcely or not at all habituated to human presence. Kaflia is the place Timothy ends up more and more often, the place he loves best. His code name is the Grizzly Maze.

Think of Kaflia as a set of three stairs leading into increasingly remote country. The lowest is Kaflia Bay itself, an almost V-shaped notch in the coast two miles deep, accessible from Shelikof Strait by boat. At its upper reaches it narrows into a saltwater lagoon, ringed by tidal flats. At the end of that lagoon lies a small, creek-fed lake where salmon spawn. Access here is strictly by float plane, or by kayak portage from the bay below. The valley above Lower Kaflia Lake is dammed by a rock outcropping that forms the highest stair, Upper Kaflia—a narrow, deep body of fresh water roughly two miles long and a half mile wide, framed by ragged, precipitous ridges streaked with volcanic dust. Draining the upper lake into the lower is a short, steep creek, more of a cascade than anything else, where salmon hearkening to the natal scent of their birthplace practically have to don track shoes for a quarter mile to shimmy uphill over a boulder-strewn streambed. When the reds are running, it's the easiest pickings on the whole Katmai Coast— and every bear within twenty miles knows it. They stack up almost as thick as the fish, sometimes several dozen along that ankle-deep, four-hundred-yard rivulet draining between Upper and Lower Kaflia Lakes. Their tunnel-like trails wind through the otherwise impenetrable alders and head-high grass, forming an unmapped maze—thus Timothy's name for the place. For a human, exploring these trails seems a poor idea of the first magnitude; *suicidal* is the word that comes to mind. Considering that *the* leading factors in brown/grizzly attacks are lone humans surprising bears in thick brush, and that such conditions define the Maze, we might cross off *suicidal* and substitute *insane*. Don't forget the individual in question will be completely without defense or weapons. But let's also not forget that Timothy is Timothy.

During his first visit to the Maze 1994, he camped out along the shores of the lower lake, wrapped in the silence of the rugged, junglelike landscape and the spectacle of the bears coming and going as they fished at the creek outlet. Clearly, these weren't the bears of Hallo Bay. Even Timothy sensed the danger of this place. He found what he called "killer bears" there—big, aggressive males intolerant of human presence—and he squeaked through some close calls early on. But inevitably he was drawn into the shadowy world of the Maze. Crawling on all fours, scrambling through tangles of alder and snaking through tunnels in head-high grass, Timothy ventured into a terra incognita where the monsters were more than figments drawn on a map. Salmonberry thorns and willows gouged at his face and hands; his knees became bruised and swollen, his clothes crusted with bear scat, mud, and sweat. Any of a hundred blind turns could have been his last.

Sure enough, he found himself surrounded by feeding bears along the alder-choked creek, sometimes so close they literally shouldered him out of the way and brushed against his body. But, intent on the urgency of packing on weight while the salmon were running thick, and shoulder to shoulder themselves with no short-age of food, they largely ignored his presence. Of course, they would have done the same with almost any other living creature, seagull on up. Timothy, though, felt not just tolerated, but included. The sense that he was one of the bears further intensified.

And in his repeated explorations over the next three seasons, deeper and deeper into the Maze, he found his heart of home. Kathleen Parker (along with Willy Fulton, one of the few people to ever accompany Timothy into the Maze) was with him in 1998 when they discovered the secluded knoll above the shores of the upper lake. There was enough level, dry ground for a campsite, easy access to a little bay where a floatplane could land. And no one except the bears went there; the shoreline of Upper Kaflia is too brushy, too hazardous, for commercial bear viewing or photography—or, for that matter, plain old walking around. Any visitors would choose the lower lake, just a quarter mile away on the near side of the Maze. Though there was a major bear trail within fifteen feet of this new campsite, Timothy was confident the bears would walk on by, as they always had. He'd found his island of solitude—and the place where he and Amie Huguenard would die five years later.

Kaflia pushed Timothy's relationship with both the bears and the land to another level. As Willy Fulton recalls, "He was a different guy at Hallo Bay; over there you could lay in the grass and just relax. Kaflia's a totally different place. You have to pay close attention. When the bears are ripping, it's wild. Bears popping in and out of the brush, fighting over fishing spots, some pretty crazy stuff." Timothy admitted as much to him. "Oh, yeah," Fulton continues, "he was always amped up when he came out of there. He knew exactly how dangerous it was, especially in the fall. That's one of the reasons I don't have any problem with what he did—he knew the risk and took it on."

In the confines of the Maze, Timothy continued to have near brushes with his "killer bears"—one of which he named Demon. In a passage as melodramatic as the bear's name, Timothy described a near-fatal scrape:

> Just as the dark male closed to within ten feet, his ears went back, and the most menacing, wicked eyes I'd ever seen turned to ice. The dark male was coming for me. In a last desperate moment, I lunged toward him, kicking and screaming . . . he slowly backed off, those wicked eyes blinking . . . at that point, he hadn't felt like working up a sweat killing me. (*Among Grizzlies*, p. 124)

Demon and the others let him breathe; and with time, Timothy sensed that even Demon and he had reached some level of truce, even tolerance. Given the number of seasons he navigated the Maze unscathed, it's hard to say he wasn't at least partly right to believe so. However, the bounty of the Maze, coupled with the modest size of its prime feeding areas and its close confines, make for a volatile environment—a place where bears are often on edge. As anywhere, they don't like surprises, which are guaranteed by the sheer density of vegetation, the lack of open space. Yet they're drawn to the food, a veritable salmon buffet.

Why Timothy's attraction to Kaflia and its maze? It's tough to pick the point at which acceptance of extreme danger slides into a submerged death wish. Timothy's self-described flirtation with hard-core drugs and violence seems an earlier manifestation of the same syndrome. A little of it resides in all of us; bungee jumping, three-hundred-horsepower sport sedans, and roller coasters wouldn't exist if we weren't a bit in love with the dark lady—all a matter of degree. If Timothy Treadwell had an addictive personality, his drug of choice was never booze or cocaine. Like an extreme rock climber or big-wave surfer, he intensely loved what he was doing, where he was, and who he was with, but what hooked him was the danger. Otherwise he'd have been satisfied with Hallo Bay, where there were plenty of bears to hang out with. Sure, there were people, there, too, but they got on the planes and flew away every afternoon. The bears remained. Still, he was skilled and/or lucky enough (depending on whom you ask) to survive in the heart of the Maze for major portions of ten seasons—longer than naysayers, and even some supporters, expected.

Even in his secret camp at Upper Kaflia—camouflage netting and all—there was no hiding from the world. The bear science establishment wasn't alone in its discomfiture over Timothy's presence; the ever-increasing popularity of fly-in bear viewing along the coast forced conflicts and issues that the Park Service could no longer ignore.

Since day one, Timothy had considered himself the guardian of the bears; and as his knowledge of them grew, along with his attachment to the landscape and a sense of personal history, so did an almost unavoidable sense of ownership. Giving them his own private names cemented the bond. They were *his* bears (he often referred to them as such), and he'd sworn a personal oath to protect them, to lay down his life if necessary. Whether the presence of poachers was to him a convenient fiction or a looming threat, the commitment was real enough. No one who knew him—friend or critic—doubts that. And if poachers didn't show up, bear-viewing guides and their clients certainly did; and they became, by default if nothing else, the target of his obsessive energy.

Throughout the 1990s bear-viewing visitor numbers grew exponentially in Katmai National Park. Over this time, the National Park Service didn't even recognize bear viewing as a category of service in its database of licensed concessionaires, though the number of registered air taxi operators (most of them featuring bear trips) doubled from twenty to forty. Ads for Katmai bear tours burgeoned in magazines and on the Internet, in proportion to the skyrocketing popularity of the trips themselves. In 2002, bear viewing would finally become a recognized, licensable activity, with fifty-five registered concessionaires. Twelve months later, the year of Timothy's death, the number would rise to sixty-nine.

Imagine the view from his angle, sitting quietly among his bears at Hallo Bay, watching them, now and then sharing some intimate moment as one of his favorites passes nearby or lies down by his tent. In roars a garishly painted Otter on floats and disgorges a knot of brightly colored, noisy intruders who galumph across the field, pointing and peering. An hour later, a group of four in a Cessna, and later on, yet another plane from a different company. Even as the bears continue to feed, all but the most relaxed shift away from human pressure or change their chosen paths to avoid the hubbub. The shyest are outright displaced and fade into the brush. Most visitors are respectful and maintain the prescribed distances; some, intent on photography or pursuing personal experience, crowd the animals repeatedly or follow them.

Timothy, watching from the bushes, becomes more and more agitated. *That's Windy, and she's scared. That's Mr. Chocolate's spot; he shouldn't have to move.* While he may have a point, he does lack authority. But that lack is superseded by the badge tattooed on his heart. Timothy is determined and tenacious as always, and his tactics vary with the day. Sometimes—especially early on in his sojourn—he approaches the viewers straight out, introduces himself, and offers to guide them. As the seasons go on, he becomes more withdrawn and evasive, as if overwhelmed, or attempting to mimic, as he so often does, the behavior of his self-appointed charges. In fact, guides observe him bounding off on all fours, right through concentrations of bears, woofing and huffing like some sort of ursine Paul Revere. He habitually wears black clothing, following the theory that it makes him resemble the animals he loves. Bear-viewing guide Chris Day, who witnessed such behavior, says, "He didn't look or move anything like a bear. It was ridiculous." But what Timothy feels and what others see are no doubt two different things.

On occasion, Timothy opts for head-on, guerrilla-theater confrontation—especially when it comes to his hole in the wall, Kaflia, his beloved Grizzly Maze. Pilot and guide Dan Doorman recalls an incident at Lower Kaflia Lake. He'd pulled up on his floatplane with several clients, planning to use the plane as a viewing platform—standard procedure for the place, safe for bears and visitors alike. Timothy suddenly appeared out of the bushes and swam out to Doorman's floatplane, fully clothed, holding a video camera over his head, "record" light on, and demanded to know if Doorman "intended to displace those bears." Doorman, having never met Timothy, was nonplussed. He remembers, "The guy was struggling. The water was cold and he was holding up that camera, his chin barely above the surface. I was worried he was going to drown." He finally convinced Timothy to take his hand, and pulled him up onto the floats to talk things over. Shivering, Timothy informed Doorman that he was working for and supplied by the Park Service. After a conciliatory conversation, Timothy seemed satisfied, erased his tape "evidence," swam back to shore, and disappeared into the brush. Doorman muses, "It was hard to be mad at him. He was kind of a strange duck, but just full of enthusiasm for bears."

Most often Timothy merely lurks and films. The video camera is turned not on the bears, but on the human viewers. Sometimes he wears full camouflage gear and face paint and slithers around in the shrubbery, apparently trying to document the transgressions, real or imaginary, of the visitors.

"That's what he did," says Perry Mollan, a guide with twenty-five years of experience in the park, much of it in the same places Timothy frequented. "He hid in the bushes and filmed you. It irked me more than anything he did. You'd be out in the middle of nowhere, singing a stupid song to yourself, picking your nose or something, and look up, and there'd be this guy and his camera." Guide John Bartolino adds, "He often wore a bandana on his head and another over his lower face. He was always running around in the bushes and taking pictures, doing some sort of ninja thing."

Needless to say, none of this is what the customers paid to see. *Who's the weirdo, Doris?* Way out here, in the heart of Alaska wilderness, there's this guy. All around, Timothy Treadwell is bad for business.

But Timothy doesn't stop there. He keeps the Park Service informed of violations he perceives—sometimes against the very people who have helped him over the years. He writes in a 2000 letter to Park Superintendent Deb Liggett that he's repeatedly witnessed "unsavory human behavior" and that his presence has protected the bears. His "unconditional love" for the animals is his "greatest gift"—and he manifests it by raising complaints against ex- and would-be friends.

Some operators, as you might expect, find Timothy's presence less than quiet. John Rogers, operator of Katmai Coastal Tours, locks horns with Timothy on several occasions in 2000 at Lower Kaflia Lake. Each has his own versions of events; Rogers, guiding two different professional film crews at the time, accuses Timothy of harassment (screaming incoherently, in fact) and of misrepresenting himself—claiming, as he did with Dan Doorman, that he has National Park Service authority. Rogers, who once picked up Timothy in his skiff in dangerously high seas between Kukak and Hallo Bay, also maintains that Timothy informed his guide, Buck Wilde, that he was officially barred from operating at Kaflia. Timothy, meanwhile, accuses the film crews of violating minimum viewing distances, and creating unsafe conditions for both bears and humans. Rogers—incensed, to put it mildly—says he's done nothing wrong, and that Timothy is interfering with his lawfully conducted business. "Something needs to be done about you," he writes in a pointed note that stops short of threat but clearly indicates that he's done sitting on his hands. Of course, this brouhaha ends up squarely on Katmai Park Superintendent Liggett's plate; and Timothy pens contrite letters of apology and retraction to both Rogers and the Park Service.

While Timothy frets about everyone else's proximity to bears, he seems to have little concern about his own. Though he claims to follow all viewing guidelines, both the camera and eyewitnesses repeatedly indicate otherwise.

"He touched the bears, you know," asserts Kathleen Parker, who, as a loyal, devoted friend, scarcely has an ax to grind. "Not all of them, just certain ones." Accounts by a double handful of bear-viewing guides place Timothy at arm's length from bears throughout his thirteen seasons on the coast—distances initiated not only by the bears (quite a different matter) but by him. Though supporters claim that professional wildlife photographers and filmmakers habitually violate the 50/100 yard rule, there is a notable difference: Timothy's transgressions are showcased on national television, where they can't be ignored, with him featured in the same frame as the animals. There is also a huge difference between crowding a bear (unethical though it is) and courting physical relationships. And Timothy's proximity to the bears is the whole reason the footage is there.

A series of letters to an independent television producer in September 1998 offers insight into the contradictoy world in which Timothy operates. With by far his biggest feature to date on the line—The Discovery Channel special, *The Grizzly Diaries*—he's deeply concerned (obsessed might be a better word) with protecting the secret identity of his locations. He even insists on not showing floatplane logos, lest they be used to identify Kodiak, the town of departure. Worried sick about his animals, Timothy frets about pressure from "tourists," and makes it clear he's not interested in attracting more—especially not to the Grizzly Maze, which he calls "magical" and his "favorite." He's a man of principle, with only bears at heart. Yet, in the same letters, he asks for an advance of the production money and a hotel room back in Kodiak, and even asks if the company's medical insurance will cover treating a gash on his face. Timothy also seems totally willing to evade Park Service regulations requiring a commercial permit, and instructs the producers to disguise their professional identity even from the Andrew Airways pilot who will carry them. He wants to avoid, he explains, "increased scrutiny" and urges them to "keep this . . . quiet." He goes on to all but promise point-blank footage of himself with his charges, obviously much closer than Park Service regulations dictate. And Timothy makes several mentions of a "secret" surveillance camera he's set up on an apparently empty tent, attempting to get images of a bear tearing it up. But though there are "no takers" so far, he's hopeful. Apparently, working close with no one looking, dodging required permits, and hoping to attract bears into tents is no big deal, as long as it's him and nobody else.

"It was Don't do as I do, but as I say," says Tom Walters. Joe

Allen, once framed as Timothy's cameo poacher, adds, "He felt he was the chosen one, and everyone else was supposed to just stay home and watch his videos, I guess."

Other incidents involving Timothy Treadwell, most of them trickling down through unofficial channels, further ratchet up the level of concern. Reports of what can only be described as bizarre behavior, just in case what's already before them doesn't qualify. A brief sampler of such incidents: Chris Day of Emerald Air Service reports Timothy walking around among the bears of Hallo Bay wearing a black tuxedo—the full prom-quality regalia, complete with white shirt, bow tie, and tails. Chuck Keim of Coastal Expeditions confirms a similar sighting. Keim also tells of watching Timothy through binoculars as he dances alone on a beach, holding circular metallic photographic light reflectors in each hand—one silver, one gold—whirling like a dervish in his own impromptu fan dance as the bears dig clams. Nothing illegal, to be sure, and maybe not even enough to turn heads on Venice Beach. But this is the Katmai Coast, where rational behavior is held in high regard. "I saw him now and then," says Keim, with a quizzical grin on his weathered face, "but I kept my distance." *Who knows,* he seems to say as he drains his beer, *what the guy might do?*

A definitive Treadwell event, if there is such a thing, takes place at Lower Kaflia Lake several years before his death. It's witnessed by bear-viewing guides Perry and Angela Mollan and John Bartolino. They're kayaking near the creek that rises steeply to the upper lake; it's summer, and the salmon are running strong—a fact hardly lost on the bears. There's a knot of them feasting on the easy pickings in the shallow, boulder-strewn waterway. Given that this is Kaflia and the bears are thick, the three guides figure Timothy must be around somewhere. Bartolino, who's always wanted to talk to Timothy, calls out, inviting him to come out and talk. "I was always curious," he says, "and had a certain admiration for the guy because he survived for so many years doing what he was doing without being mauled or killed. . . . I saw him at a distance a few times, but was never able to speak with him. I wanted to know what he was doing, and why."

There's no response to John's repeated calls. Then Bartolino notices a bear staring into the alders. There, he guesses, is Timothy. He paddles around a rocky point out of sight, beaches his kayak, and sneaks ashore. Picking his way through the brush, he creeps up on the spot, and sure enough, there Tim is, hunkered down, video camera at the ready. At John's tap on the shoulder, Timothy goes into a violent startle reflex, like anyone would. But on turning to see John there, he does something inexplicable. Bartolino recalls, "He dropped down on all fours and started making bear noises, similar to a female calling to her cubs, trying to warn them. I tried to talk to him and told him we wouldn't hurt him, but all he would do was make those bear sounds."

Mollan says, "We were wondering what all that noise was." Timothy, still on all fours, keeps trying to scramble past, but John, barring his way with an alder branch and his own body, holds him up, all the while trying to reassure him that he just wants to talk. Finally Timothy blurts out, almost a wail, "I just want to be left alone!" And he scrambles off into the Maze.

"It was quite a sight," says Mollan. "Tim just ran up the creek, mostly on all fours, right through the middle of a bunch of bears, zigzagging between them and the rocks, bouncing off boulders and bears. Some got a little startled, but most just ignored him."

Bartolino muses, "Those are the only words I ever got out of him. To this day I'm still curious about him, and I guess now I always will be."

Whether this incident, and the tuxedo, the fan dance, and a dozen others were manifestations of Timothy the hopeless loony, Timothy the irrepressible flake, or Timothy the conscious manipulator is anybody's guess. Says Perry Mollan of the Kaflia incident,

"I think about that a lot. It almost had to be an act. Otherwise it was almost too weird." He shrugs like someone trying to convince himself as much as me. In almost all instances, Timothy must have been aware of an audience—people watching, someone to play to and perhaps mess with. I suspect a motivational combination plate, so to speak. On the other hand, who ever really knew what made Timothy Treadwell tick, including maybe himself? And what was that desperate cry to Bartolino—was it Timothy speaking as himself, or as the perennially lonely inner child, or as the bear he was trying to become (in his mind, perhaps already was)? *I just want to be left alone.* When I think of Timothy Treadwell, these words reverberate when others have faded.

The glacial reaction of the Park Service to the Treadwell conundrum might strike an outside observer as curious. However, that pace is shaped by a number of factors. First, the revolving-door culture of the agency means that every three or four years, tops, there's a new superintendent in Katmai National Park. Just when one is getting a handle on things, there's a transfer to a different park. Unless an administrator hits the ground running, someone like Timothy Treadwell slips through the cracks. It's easier to pass on a problem to someone else than deal with it yourself.

Superintendent Deb Liggett, the third to hold the position since Timothy arrived, hardly sits on her hands. She comes on in 1999, and over the course of her first year, she hears enough to focus her concern. The *Dateline* NBC feature, televised in 2000, tweaks her enough that she refers the matter to the NPS legal department. Liggett is sure there's grounds for prosecution and argues strenuously in favor of action, but, as she puts it, "our solicitor was unwilling to go to court."

As one might expect, the paper trail between Timothy Treadwell and the Park Service is as well-marked as bear tracks on a mud flat. The letters back and forth, the permit applications, ranger incident reports and notes are a story in themselves, and the volume of correspondence generated by Timothy and duly logged by the Park Service is impressive—fourteen separate hand-written letters between May and October of 2000 alone. While clearly the relationship is often strained, Timothy, especially in later years, spends far more time and letter space courting the Park Service than wrangling with them. His wooing of Superintendent Deb Liggett is especially persistent. In one of these letters he tells her that his "work" and her "judgment" mean "everything" to him. Above all, Timothy seems to crave some form of official recognition. He suggests thast he could function in an unpaid but official capacity as Katmai's "bear keeper"; he'd have no law-enforcement powers, but would "be a witness" for the bears, clean up beach flotsam, and give reports of comings, goings, and violations, plus provide weather observations. He'll sign a waiver, freeing the NPS of any potential liability if something happens to him in the park (though he incorrectly tells them he has no living kin).

Timothy is just one manifestation of a growing concern: people in growing numbers interacting with bears in all manner of ways on the Katmai coast. "It became apparent to me we had a huge snowball rolling down the hill toward us," Liggett says. "The National Park Service doesn't manage wildlife; we manage people." But Timothy is at least a single target to focus upon. She requests him (summons might be a more accurate term) to meet her in Anchorage on his way south at the end of the 2000 season—the equivalent, you might say, of being called into the principal's office. She doesn't characterize the meeting as confrontational; in fact, to extend the simile, it's more a heart-to-heart with an errant child. When she tells him that she won't forgive him if he or any bears die on her watch, she recalls, "He almost broke into tears when I told him I was worried about him. Timothy was just a big kid who wanted so desperately to be wanted."

But Liggett throws some tough love into the mix too. She

expresses concern about the media message being projected and about his behavior. She also knows that mere concern won't cut it. "The only thing that would make Tim pay attention would be no more access," Liggett says. In kind but direct words, she threatens to petition the federal magistrate in charge of such matters to have him banned from the park. Customary sentences of exile range from one year to three. What he must improve, she says, is both his attention to personal safety and the public image that he projects. Not to mention adherence to Park Service regulations. And enough of this bugging commercial operators, already. Then there's this matter of claiming you represent the Park Service. . . .

Deb Liggett definitely has captured Timothy's attention. Being barred from the park and from his bears would be an emotional sledgehammer, not to mention a serious ding to his credibility among supporters. Timothy does, in fact, make a strong attempt to clean things up, at least on the PR end of things. On Liggett's advice, he consults with a nonprofit Montana organization called the Center for Wildlife Information, which works for responsible wildlife viewing and public education. Director Chuck Bartlebaugh, a prior outspoken critic of Timothy's previous media image, works with Timothy, as the NPS suggested, to "finesse" his presentation, integrating the Center's bear safety materials. Bartlebaugh also tries to involve Timothy in their national Be Bear Aware campaign as a spokesman, and Timothy is at first all for the idea. A fifty-thousand-dollar grant from benefactor Roland Dixon is tied in, as well as large-scale planning. In the end, though, Timothy backs out, pulling his grant with him, and accuses Bartlebaugh of "fear mongering." "As far as our goal of spreading a message of responsible behavior around bears," Bartlebaugh sighs, "I see Timothy as an unfortunate, lost, brilliant opportunity. He had the charisma we needed to help reach an ignorant public gone wildlife crazy."

Liggett echoes the sentiment: "Timothy had the opportunity to do great good. I felt we'd made a little bit of headway."

Even with Timothy's backing out of Be Bear Aware, the Letterman appearances in 2001 and 2002 feature a new, improved bear safety message, as do his classroom presentations. Timothy even goes so far as to buy a portable electric bear fence (though he apparently erects it just once the following season, claims he can't get it to work, and puts it on permanent file in Kathleen Parker's Kodiak basement).

Timothy also tries another angle toward legitimizing his presence in the park. In 2001 he applies for a scientific research permit, titled "Alaska Animal Education Project." His entire project description, forty-six words in all, ends in the ringing but vague statement "It is imperative for Treadwell to continue these studies for the benefit of the educational work." Regarding the permit, which was summarily rejected for lack of substance, Liggett makes her stance abundantly clear: "He was an insult to the real scientists who work out there."

Timothy, meanwhile, is not beyond applying a little pressure of his own. In his schoolboy scrawl he informs Liggett in a 2001 letter that he is organizing a "campaign" that will demonstrate to the Park Service the "value" of his "work." It will include testimonial letters from "credible ecology leaders" (among them representatives of the Sierra Club, the Great Bear Foundation, and the Leakey Foundation, all of which apparently buy into both the poaching story and support Timothy's very real enthusiasm for bears and volunteerism); scads of notes from school children; an impassioned letter of support from Amie Huguenard; and videos of himself preaching bear safety. He apologizes for the *Dateline* footage, calling it "old work" and begging not to be "punished" for it. And, though he doesn't bring it up this time, he has repeatedly played the celebrity card, claiming "an increasing list" of well-known supporters, some that wield influence in the "executive branch"—an implied threat, but a threat nonetheless: *I know people, and you need to remember that.* And over the top of all this subtext, he is unrelentingly respectful to the point of fawning— "humbly offer[ing]" his voluntary service to the Park Service and the entire country, and thanking Liggett for her "consideration and kindness." In short, this is an astute political critter, and no one's fool. He shucks and jives with the best of them. No wonder Liggett will later say, "No rule or regulation could ever contain a Timothy Treadwell."

And Timmy the fox goes right on being himself.

The Last Trip Out There

For Timothy Treadwell, the summer of 2003 is much the same as any of the twelve that have gone before. He shows up June 1 at Kathleen Parker's house in Kodiak and prepares his gear for the usual four months in the field. Parker recalls, "He was cheerful and upbeat. He told me he 'felt so good'—he didn't have any girl-friend, no worries. He was free and very happy." Timothy has a contract with Disney to be an advisor for the animated feature *Brother Bear* and to star in a short film that will introduce it in movie theaters. The deal is a chance to reach his favorite audi-ence, on a Disney scale. Joel Bennett of Juneau, his friend for ten years, will do the filming honors, as he has so often done. All around, it's a huge deal: Timothy on the big screen for the first time, with millions of kids out there, an international audience. The shoot will be on Kodiak Island, a nod to easier logistics and abundant bears fishing an early salmon run at Frazier Lake.

But while officials grant a permit to the small Disney crew to work there with Timothy, his own commercial permit to work in the Kodiak National Wildlife Refuge for 2003 is refused out-right. Says Leslie Kerr, manager of the refuge, "We were extremely concerned about his presence. Some of the stuff he did [on the Katmai Coast] as a matter of public record amounted to wildlife harassment, and some of what was reported was clearly off the chart." The rejection is a long step short of Timothy's worst fear—banishment from Katmai National Park—but a portent nonetheless. Still, it really doesn't affect his plans; he can work on Kodiak under the Disney permit, and anyway, he's planned to spend most of his season in Katmai, as usual. Due to the Disney gig and his usual pattern of splitting time between Hallo and Kaflia, he'll be chartering several trips out to the coast and back by floatplane. Due to the financial support Grizzly People now enjoys, he can handle the added cost.

As he sets out for Expedition 2003 to Hallo Bay, he tells Parker the same thing he has every year, part of a ritual between them: "I love you. This is going to be the best year ever out there. If I don't come back, it's where I want to be." There's no doubt, she says, that he had fully accepted the possibility of his death. One thing he also tells Parker, almost as an afterthought—oh, Amie's coming up in September. Could she stay at the house instead of the hotel? Given the big talk-up about no girlfriend, this comes as a major surprise. Of course, Parker has met Amie Huguenard before; she came up not only in 2001, but also for part of the 2002 season. She's even now listed on the Grizzly People Web page as "expedition coordinator and consultant." The number of active members has risen to three.

Obviously, Timothy considers Amie to be in some ambiguous subcategory in the relationship continuum. Considering that she's quit her post as a physician's assistant in Boulder and found one in L.A. at Cedars-Sinai Medical Center—just to be with Timothy—obviously Parker isn't the only one confused. Timothy has known this woman for seven years, and this is her third season visiting him on the coast. And now she's uprooting to live with him—yet he tells one of his closest friends that he's unencumbered? Then later on that summer, working with Joel Bennett, on the Disney project, he doesn't ever mention her.

Timothy obviously deploys some sort of denial airbag on this issue, which should, given his past penchant for consistent inconsistency, come as no surprise. It's doubtful that Amie Huguenard has made such a sweeping and life-altering decision unilaterally; whatever else she may be, she's no head case. However, she may well be the one doing all the emotional and physical work here, and Timothy is floating along, passive but uncomfortable with the reality and unsure of what to do about it. Amie is a great person, as well as a loyal friend and backer; clearly a deeper relationship is a possibility he's entertained. He may understand that it's the right thing to do. Here, after all, is a woman who is committed to wildlife as he is, educated and professionally successful, willing to share his life both in and out of Alaska. And she loves him.

Yet Timothy Treadwell can't bring himself to take that next step. Understandable, since love isn't, most would agree, a matter of choice. That could be it—she's cool, she's great, but he just isn't in love with her; and now that reality has sunk in, he's getting cold feet. Most of us have been there before and can accept that explanation. But as before, Timothy Treadwell seems to have an internal barrier, some sort of fail-safe switch that bars interpersonal commitment beyond a certain point, pushes away those who reach out to him, asking, or seeming to ask, for love in return. This rationale could explain his lack of close childhood friends some have commented on; his leaving his family and changing his name; his abrupt drifting in and out of certain friendships; and the fact that, well into his forties, he's never married. So, even if he's agreed to some arrangement with Amie, he may well be unable to admit it to any of his friends, or even to himself.

If Amie were the love of his life, the story would make the poetic, Romeo-and-Juliet sense of the sort we all yearn for: star-crossed lovers die together. But the bitter irony of the truth seems all the more suited to the enigmatic, contradictory being that was

Timothy Treadwell—and small consolation to those who knew and loved Amie Huguenard. Though she herself loves this man and, by extension, the bears in a general, collective sort of way, she has no deep and abiding connection to either the animals by name or the landscape, in all its subtle detail—she simply hasn't spent the time on the coast to develop that sort of relationship. And she certainly hasn't embraced the possibility of her own death in this far and strange country. The final and most unkind twist of all is that this man to whom she's quite literally entrusted her life seems unable or unwilling to return her emotion. She, more than Timothy, is the one fated to meet her end alone—while he, in the best nineteenth-century folk-song tradition, will indeed die in the arms of his own true love.

The month at Hallo Bay goes without notable incident—bears galore, of course, mating and feeding and occasionally scuffling violently, doing their usual early summer thing. After an extended camping trip in the middle of this, most of us would come back red eyed and emotionally frayed; for Timothy, it's just another season on the coast. In July Timothy returns from Hallo to Kodiak for the Disney shoot, and it all goes off without a hitch. Joel Bennett, though, who's filmed Timothy among his bears five times now, broaches the subject—haven't they done enough work with bears? What's left to say or do? It's not just a matter of artistic limitation. Joel, despite his abiding fondness for these animals and decades of experience, has still never lost the certain, unquiet knowledge of what can happen. The uneasiness swells and fades, but never entirely goes away. Eight years before, Japanese wildlife photographer Michio Hoshino—his friend as well as mine—was killed and eaten by a bear in the Russian Far East, a place not unlike Katmai. Maybe we've pushed our luck far enough, Joel murmurs. But Timothy just nods and smiles, brushing off Joel's concern as he's dismissed the fretting and warnings of so many others. Everything will be all right. He knows what he's doing, and intends to keep on doing it.

The Disney filming over, Timothy heads out to the Grizzly Maze in late July. He'll stay there alone until late September, when Amie will come out again, accompanied by Kathleen Parker. Though Parker admits she fears bears—she says she'd carry a shotgun in Katmai if it were allowed—she's traveled the Maze with Timothy more than once, crawling headfirst through those shadowy tunnels, bears around any bend, putting her faith in his experience. After being schooled on the tough streets of L.A., just as he was, that's saying something. That she's invited along may say something else about the relationship between Timothy and Amie.

Six weeks alone in the Grizzly Maze—one of the toughest and most volatile places to camp alone on the entire Katmai Coast—and once more, Timothy pulls it off. He has, without doubt, come far in this rough, primeval world for which his upbringing has so poorly prepared him. By now, he knows every curve of every trail in the Maze, and understands things he can scarcely articulate: vague stirrings on the wind, the subtle messages conveyed by a bear's shifting posture, and the distinctive mark left by a certain clawed print. Maybe he knows a bit too much. Intellect—and Timothy is certainly quick minded—is its own trap. Experience is another. It inevitably leads to generalizations, which all too often lead to certainty.

Still, Timothy Treadwell, by simple dint of his own survival over thirteen seasons among the bears of the Katmai Coast, has earned, if anyone has, the right to call his shots in the field. Who better knows the bears of Hallo Bay or Kaflia, or those chunks of terrain, than he does? Not the biologists who study there, nor the photographers who come and go, nor the bear guides who fly home every night to a dry, quiet, bear-free home, complete with a hot shower and a cold beer. Conditions at Kaflia, though, seem even more unsettled than the norm. Timothy's journals, examined later by the state troopers, reflect this—more bear fights than usual, and the presence of three "killer bears." He gives Demon and other huge males space (which they themselves generally seek when it comes to humans), and spends time close to more tolerant bears, including those he's known since cubhood. Of course, unknown bears wander through as well, animals that are more difficult to predict.

His campsite, tucked back into a far corner of the Maze, is away from the prime feeding areas where the big males dominate. But it still lies just a few paces from a major thoroughfare, a pounded groove a foot wide and three inches deep. Lying within twenty yards of the camp are a dozen lesser trails. By accident of topography and conscious decision, Timothy is situated at the throat of a funnel, a place where the lake on one side and a small, swampy drainage on the other lead the bears up the inviting curve of the knoll, straight to the prime feeding area along the outlet stream. The same conditions that make the knoll a good campsite—a well-drained, elevated spot with decent sun and lots of soft grass, protection from prevailing winds—also make it a perfect spot for bears to make their daybeds. The camp area is surrounded by their circular nestlike depressions, some of them within several yards of the tents. Timothy is completely aware of all this. It's why he's here.

And though the bears seem more stirred up than usual, Timothy Treadwell doesn't call for a pickup after a few run-ins, as he might have done in his early years. He doesn't panic. He can't even count the times he's faced an uneasy or outright aggressive bear head-on and stood down the threat. He's like a seasoned bush pilot who's flown for years in bad weather; each time he rides it through and lands safely, his confidence grows, along with a belief that he can meet and beat any challenge. Timothy Treadwell is at the top of his game. So are most good pilots when they finally fly out into the fog one last time.

*   *   *

It's mid-September. Amie has just arrived in Kodiak from a month back and forth between Colorado and Malibu, finishing moving chores and working on the simple apartment she and Timothy will share down there. Kathleen Parker, instead of being home, is down in California on unexpected private business and won't be joining them at the Maze after all. Amie ends up staying at what's locally known simply as the KI—the Best Western Kodiak Inn. The KI is a haunt familiar to Timothy, less so to her: the remote Alaska version of a chain hotel, decorated (as one might expect, given both the locale and the clientele) with hides and skulls on the walls and a front window case inhabited by a stuffed bear the size of a steroid-fed quarter horse, huge even by Kodiak standards.

Due to a snotty band of weather sweeping through, Amie's stuck here for several days, staring at the walls. Timothy, meanwhile, is hunkered in the Maze, up to the usual: soggy clothes day after day, no cooking or drying fire, a long procession of candy bars and peanut butter sandwiches, and the steady passing of bears at arm's length. The Sony digital camcorder hums. Even when physically exhausted, he never gets tired of it. This is where he's supposed to be.

Back in Kodiak at the KI, Amie kills time hanging around in the restaurant and bar upstairs—a low-ceilinged room pleasantly lit by a bank of picture windows overlooking the harbor. No one cares if you hang at a back table all day, nursing a cup of coffee and reading. The ambience beats the dim, cavelike room she's signed into. So Amie sits and waits here, goes for walks or runs, makes occasional phone calls down to Andrew Airways to see if anything's changed, and gets antsy. She's supposed to be out there and she has things to do back in California. Waiting for weather, at least on this scale, is a distinctly Alaskan pastime. It sure as hell doesn't happen in Malibu.

Dan Eubank tends bar and waits tables at the KI when he's not crafting gold jewelry writing country music lyrics, or teaching karate. Over the years he's watched Timothy come and go; even when he stayed at Kathleen Parker's, the KI is one of the few all-day dining options in town, and a popular waiting spot for bush flights—so here Timothy often sat, nursing a procession of Cokes and yakking with whoever was around. Eubank, like any bartender, enjoys a special role as fly on the wall and occasional father confessor; he knows a little of everyone's business. It's an occupational blessing or hazard, depending on the day.

"Amie," says Eubank, "was almost the exact opposite of Timothy. He'd be talking to everyone, and she'd be in the corner with a book. She wasn't shy, really, but just quiet in a strong way. Hard to read. Anyway, she was sitting there waiting and seemed pensive—something was just a bit different, I can't say exactly what. And then she told me quietly, 'This is the last trip out there.' Now that I look back, I think about the way she said it. What did she mean? Did she know something?"

Whether visited by a moment of prescience or not, when the weather clears, Amie Huguenard flies out to Kaflia just the same. It's her third visit to the Maze in three years (she's spent a week there in each of the preceding seasons), but she's never camped here this late, when the weather is turning sour and the bears are running out of fish. Instead of glowing green and lush, the Maze increasingly resembles the monochromatic, fog-shrouded set of a cheap horror flick. The dismal, rain-swept weather and that landscape set the tone for the next two weeks.

While she's athletic and tomboyish, trail hiking in Colorado isn't bushwhacking in Alaska. Take a quick glance at the snapshot Willy Fulton took of her the season before, holding hands with Timothy at Kaflia (on the back cover). There she is, out in the middle of nowhere, wearing black leather lace-up elevator soles and some sort of fleece cardigan over a scoop neck top, capped off by some stylish but definitely impractical sunglasses, her long hair flowing free around her shoulders. She looks more Eddie Bauer suburban than Alaska modern; where are the rubber knee boots, the baggy layers of fleece and nylon or canvas jeans and caps everyone wears—with good reason? What, no hair tie or braids? That one image by itself is a fair indicator that she's in over her head, and it makes you wonder what Timothy (whose own dress often seems dictated more by quirky, personal style than function) is thinking by not advising her better. If you don't know how to dress—and the shoes are truly inexplicable—there's no way you're ready to deal with the bush in all its grubby, chilly, bug-and-rain-splattered glory, and surely not Upper Kaflia Lake. But from another angle, it all makes sense: She's just arrived, and isn't dressing for the country, but for Timothy, trying to look her best. This is a date first, expedition second. Timothy may appreciate her efforts but no doubt sees their situation the other way around.

If outdoor experiences were numbered like college courses, the Maze in late September is Ph.D. stuff, 600-level-plus. Let's not forget about keeping warm and dry while cold-camping in autumn rains, with the first snows just around the corner. Then there's the matter of the bears. Timothy may take them almost for granted; there's no way Amie is going to relax, whether or not she's been here before. Maybe she senses, too, that things are different at this time of year: Shortening days. Dim light. The rattle of dying leaves. Anxious bears. Big, scary males woofing and huffing in the alders. Her own angst shows on the video the investigating troopers will later see. In one sequence, she sits in the brush with a female bear and cubs ten feet away. Then the bears shift even closer. Her face is taut and unsmiling. This is just a few minutes of her trip, and the bears, while close, seem completely unconcerned. In another sequence, which Amie must have filmed, a monster male rises out of the brush behind Timothy as he gapes.

What else goes on off camera? They witness at least one terrific fight between a big male and a female, not far from camp. Timothy's and Amie's journals percolate with tension. She wants to pull back. Not push to get so close. She's frightened. He tries to reassure her. They argue, it goes badly, and they end up, according to Parker, who later examined their journals, sleeping in separate tents at one point. Considering how nervous Amie must be, lying there in the dark alone, things must be really bad. *What?* You can practically hear Timothy saying. *Everything's fine. It's only Tabitha. What's wrong?*

In fact, something is wrong—or at least, very different. Five miles away as the crow flies, at the next bay down the coast, Matthias Breiter is camped out with a small party of photographers he's guiding. Breiter is not only a seasoned Katmai hand and a highly regarded professional photographer; he's a bear biologist, his vision shaped more by science than by his heart. He notices wider environmental factors that Timothy, homed in on his bears almost to the exclusion of everything else, might not. For example, if Timothy doesn't know or care if it's a razorback clam or a razor clam, a spruce or a pine, Breiter certainly does. And the bear dynamics Matthias Breiter observes are both chaotic and unique. In a normal year, the half mile of creek before him might have fifteen bears working for fish; this year, more than sixty show up. The creek, meanwhile, is the same length that it ever was. Even tolerant coastal bears have their limits, and crowding leads to conflict. "You'd usually see four fights a week," says Breiter. "It was ten a day. Real, all-out fights. The level of aggression was far above normal." Needless to say, the conditions mean a photographer's dream—but a tenuous and violent environment. Still, hardly the same as Kaflia. The lower expanse of Breiter's creek is in wide open country, allowing bears who want to avoid close encounters with people ample opportunity to do so; also, Breiter's camp is some distance from the feeding area, well off bear trails, and surrounded by an electric bear fence. The men also carry large projectile flares with which to repel aggressive bears. In other words, they've taken standard precautions—the kind Timothy has rejected for years.

According to data compiled by Dr. Tom Smith and Stephen Herrero, both specialists in bear–human interaction, there are two major factors in predicting the likelihood of a brown/grizzly attack. Their conclusions are based on a century's worth of Alaska bear-attack data, compiled and organized into a statistical base that breaks down and categorizes incidents according to specific who-what-when-where information. According to Smith and Herrero, most brown/grizzly attacks occur when a lone person surprises a bear in heavy cover. Two people are safer, but three or more seems to be the magic threshold. In open areas, with larger groups, plus defensive measures in place, the likelihood of attack plummets to near zero. In reality, there's no comparison of the risk levels assumed by Breiter's group and the duo of Timothy and Amie. From a rational point of view, Timothy's long experience and his bond with certain bears must afford some measure of additional safety. But from a scientific perspective, these factors offer no protection whatsoever. And a century's worth of exhaustively analyzed data backs up that latter point of view.

The question begs: why the fourfold increase of bears that Breiter witnesses in the fall of 2003? Sixty-plus bears instead of fifteen—what could explain such a congregation, beyond a population explosion or a mass migration? The answer is deceptively simple: Due to freak weather conditions—probably a combination of frost and drought at the wrong times—the entire berry crop along the Katmai Coast has failed. At the same time, the salmon runs are at least average, or even above normal. Even when fish are available, berries of several varieties (blueberry, crowberry, highbush cranberry, salmon berry, and lingonberry) are vital and much sought-after mid- and late-season food sources. Some bears even select abundant berry patches over fish, as counterintuitive as the choice may seem. But if the berries aren't there, the bears don't have much choice.

At this time of the season, bears are in the final throes of hyperphagia—a genetically programmed metabolic overdrive that short-circuits the body's normal tendency to stop eating when full. The need to pack on winter fat is overpowering, especially for animals that are a bit underweight. Bears with two or three inches of fat on their rumps eat as though they're starving—as if they can sense their own caloric budget over six months of lying in a den, eating or drinking absolutely nothing. An average adult, even in the depth of hibernation, with pulse slowed to under ten beats a minute and body temperature lowered by eight degrees, still needs roughly four thousand calories a day. If it's not in the bank, the bear will waken to a cold, white world where starvation is a bleak certainty.

Mere survival, though, isn't enough. A bred female must have sufficient fat reserves or her eggs, fertilized last spring and waiting, won't be implanted in her uterus. Breeding males must have the strength and size to compete for mates in June. To bears at the end of the season, food isn't the main thing; it's the only thing. At the peak of hyperphagia, a bear consuming twenty thousand calories per day is more the rule than the exception. Eating to the point of button-bursting excess isn't slothful indulgence, but a matter of desperate necessity. Being the ultimate survivalists, bears march until they find something to eat. With plenty of salmon on hand, everyone ends up working the creeks where fish are present. Food is available, but space at the best runs and pools is limited, and turmoil results.

The run in Breiter's valley peters out the third week of September. When most of the bears depart, so do the photographers. But unlike the humans, the animals don't leave the coast. They merely set out on a short hike, several hours at the most, over the pass to the next drainage: Kaflia, where due to local factors, the run is slightly later and more prolonged. At the very least, Timothy and Amie have a couple of dozen hungry bears headed their way—and Kaflia already has more than its share wrangling along the creek just three hundred yards from Timothy's camp. It's not, by any stretch of the imagination, the attack of the killer bears looming, but it's a stress-adding factor—another spoon stirring an already boiling pot.

Meanwhile, fair or foul, the days pass at the Maze for Timothy and Amie. Some bears are on edge, to be sure, but being Katmai bears, they're far easier on humans than each other, and there's no real trouble. When the sun breaks out, which it does occasionally, the tension between the erstwhile lovers relaxes somewhat. Amie starts getting the hang of things out here. Timothy is contrite. They patch things up, just in time for the plane to arrive on September 26. The only real regret that Timothy has is that he hasn't spotted his favorite bear in the world, a female named Downy—a bear he can almost literally put his arm around and hug. He's worried about her. Is she all right? Has she been killed or injured in a fight? Could a poacher have gotten her?

An hour later, Timothy and Amie are back on Kodiak, sorting and drying equipment in the cavernous Andrew Airways hangar, getting ready to pull out and head south for the year. Tents, sleeping bags, bear-proof containers, and so on get ferried in the van over to Kathleen Parker's basement, where he stashes them for the winter. Camera equipment and personal gear goes in another pile, bound for California. The work takes a few hours of concerted effort.

With everything squared away, Tim and Amie head for the nearby Alaska Airlines terminal to make the connection to Anchorage and on to Seattle and L.A. But there's a hitch at the counter. The agent tells Timothy he has to pay far more than he expected to change his tickets, and the discussion turns into an argument. Timothy, who still has the soul of a hothead burning within him, gets so pissed he marches out of there, Amie swept along in his backwash. They stand around, blowing off steam, discussing what to do. And somehow they decide they're going back out to Kaflia.

The decision is one everyone who knew Timothy still wonders about. "He was very methodical about coming and going," says Joel Bennett. "Once his gear was put away, he was out of there." Kathleen Parker and Willy Fulton say almost exactly the same thing. It wasn't like him. Fulton recalls, "They told me they hadn't said their proper good-byes to the bears." There's the matter of Downy missing; Timothy is worried about that. But there's more. The previous two weeks have been an emotional ripsaw for both Timothy and Amie. After getting so far apart as sleeping in separate tents, the only way they're going back out there together is if they've made up. They don't want to remember their experience that way, and from here they're headed for sharing a cramped Malibu apartment; the only way to fix things is to go back and put the right end mark on the season—to say, as they insisted, their proper good-byes to the bears.

So Timothy and Amie dig their gear out of Parker's basement (she's still in California), pick up a few things at the store, and stack everything on a couple of pallets in the big Andrew Airways hangar, as is the custom. Then you sit and drink coffee and shoot the breeze in the adjacent office; when your gear is gone, it means your plane is being loaded. When Stan Divine, the operations manager, taps you on the shoulder, it's time to fly. Willy Fulton is the pilot of choice, as usual these past several years. But the gear sits and sits. So do Timothy and Amie, getting increasingly buggy with the inactivity. The culprit is the weather, of course. It's pouring rain and fog down on the deck—nothing to do but wait. It's as if even the country is trying to tell Timothy something.

The storm lasts three days. On September 29, there's a slight break in the weather, known to pilots as a "sucker hole"—that is, a false clearing you get suckered into. But for a good pilot in a good plane (and Fulton in his Beaver are certainly that), it's enough. Flying low over the leaden waters of Shelikof Strait, weaving around patches of scud, Willy makes the hour-long trip, helps unload, and promises to pick them up in a week. Time to go—the weather is closing down again.

Tim and Amie set up camp at the familiar spot, tucked back into the alders just fifteen feet from a little cliff that drops to the lake. The tents fit right back in their cleared pockets of ground, and in an hour it's like they'd never left. Both sleeping bags go in one tent; the second, staggered slightly back, for gear; the steel BRFCs (cleaned-out thirty-gallon fuel drums) in which their food is stored are piled a few feet beyond. The main bear trail leading to the salmon creek is several paces at most from the sleeping tent entrance, marked here and there with circular puddles dimpled by rain—the depressions formed by generations of bears stepping in the same measured stride. More leaves have fallen; the grass, shoulder high in places, sags. The rain continues, pounding in. It doesn't stop, but neither does Timothy. In the overcast, soggy gloom, he and Amie make daily pilgrimages into the skeletal remains of the Maze. And the bears are still there—more than ever, unusual numbers for this late in the year, attracted by a late surge of cohos. Normally the rocky creek bed would be littered with fish parts—tails, gills, skeletons, entire carcasses with a bite or two removed. But there are none to be seen. The bears, scrounging desperately, have eaten every scrap of every fish they catch. Tensions continue to run high as resident bears clash with interlopers and each other, vying for the calories that may spell survival until next May, when the sedge grasses begin to green again. The big, older "killer bears" like Demon are increasingly irritable as they compete for whatever's left. Their size and aggression are what made them dominant, and are all that keep them so. The tolerance that characterizes the gathering of summer's bounty is evaporating by the day—and some of the Maze bears didn't have much to begin with. But if Timothy senses the ramping peril, he gives little sign. One of his last videos, taken at the camp, features him explaining to the camera that this is a dangerous place, but they'll be safe here. He knows these bears.

After three days of storm and fog, the ceiling lifts and the sky clears. The yellow leaves of willows reflect in the dark, clear water of the lake, and the mountains soar upward on either side, cradling the valley in its autumn glory. The brush steams dry in the warming sun. It's almost balmy. On October 4, Timothy uses his satellite phone to call Stan Divine at Andrew Airways, then Willy Fulton. Timothy is bursting at the seams, enthusiastic and rambling. All's well. Everything's great. Lots of bears, crazy, unbelievable action. Downy showed up too. Best choice of their lives, says Timothy. He confirms their pickup on the sixth. Sure, Willy will be there—as long as there's a crack in the sky big enough to fly through.

Final Darkness

Timothy Treadwell makes his last contact with the outside world at noon on October 5—a satellite phone call to his longtime friend and cofounder of Grizzly People, Jewel Palovak. She's in Malibu; he's three thousand miles north, camped on a brushy knoll above Kaflia Lake, surrounded by some of the wildest terrain on the planet. On one end, palm trees, asphalt, and warm breezes; on the other, glacier-draped mountains wrapped in low clouds, an intensifying storm spattering cold rain, and a brush-choked knoll crisscrossed by bear trails. By the miracle of modern technology, Tim and Jewel speak to each other for the last time. Satellite phones often clip and echo, and white noise may drift in and out. The cost per minute, compared to regular phone service, is horrendous—close to a dollar a minute. Still, two people, separated by an incomprehensible heave of geography, joined only by the fact that they sit within a mile or so of the same vast ocean, can communicate instantaneously. Almost certainly this creates a false sense of both proximity and security for Timothy and Jewel. It's not as if these few minutes of contact change anything, but they do get to have one last conversation—fitting and right considering they've known each other for nineteen years, sharing

THE GRIZZLY MAZE · 93

a common passion and cause. The distance that separates them evaporates.

Timothy, as always, is effusive and enthusiastic. Jewel always loved this about him. He tells her that he found Downy, that she's fine, and that the bear and he connected, as they had from the first. The trip has been a success. The weather is getting worse, though; he hopes that Willy Fulton will make it in tomorrow. He and Amie are ready to come home to Malibu. The season is coming to a close. Snow coats the high country, and that last burst of salmon is petering out. Soon the bears will be getting sleepy, beginning to wander off toward their den sites. From Kodiak, home is just two hops away on Alaska Airlines 737s—to Anchorage and on to L.A. After weeks of typical Katmai Coast fall weather—rain, fog, sleet, and wind, broken by all-too-brief interludes of sun—Tim and Amie are looking forward to southern California, smog, Santa Ana winds, and all. No one could possibly guess that Timothy and Amie have just two hours to live.

An hour earlier Timothy had also called Andrew Airways in Kodiak to confirm the floatplane pickup. If the weather gets too grungy, they'll have to reschedule for another day, and their Alaska Airlines reservations will be shot—again. Cooled down from his earlier snit, Timothy's probably resigned to the worst-case scenario, while hoping for the best. If you can't cultivate that sort of mindset, you aren't cut out for bush Alaska. The storm is stiffening—wind gusts to thirty knots forecast, heavy fog, and rain hammering in. But these fronts move fast. Willy will take a look in the morning, which is about all any honest bush pilot can promise.

After the calls, Timothy and Amie no doubt settle back into the soggy, somewhat threatening world before them, which demands constant attention of the most practical sort. Anyone who's spent much time camping for extended periods knows the general drill—there's water to haul, food to prepare and eat, and they probably need to make sure the tents and covering flies and tarps are secure. Over the years, Timothy's had his share of tents flattened and shredded. By now he's a seasoned long-term camper, and he takes little for granted. If you don't have a bombproof shelter in a cold autumn blow, you don't have a damn thing. Of course, they're leaving tomorrow, or at least hoping they are—so sorting and packing is certainly high on the punch list. No doubt both tents, one for sleeping and one for gear, are by now cluttered with camera equipment, waterproof dry bags, damp clothing, and so on. The stuff they won't use again gets stowed; sleeping bags, food for the next three meals, headlamps, and journals stay handy.

The main priority, beyond packing up, is staying dry and comfortable—which means as little outside time as possible. Good rain gear, while certainly preferable to nothing, still doesn't keep you dry, especially when you're moving through dense, wet brush, hauling camera gear. Condensation and sweat soak you from the inside. Timothy and Amie have been doing this for three weeks with only a slight break (and for him, a dozen or so weeks tacked on to that), and must be worn down. Tim's toughness in cold and wet is remarked upon by those who've spent time with him along the coast; through nearly constant exposure, he's acclimated to conditions that would send the average person spiraling into hypothermia. Amie, with far less experience and her petite build, is much more vulnerable. If there's any outside work, Timothy will be the one to do it.

They'll certainly need water for lunch, dinner, and breakfast—which could mean, if the water jug is empty, a seventy-yard trip to the lake, down the knoll on one of those winding, alder-choked bear trails. Timothy probably doesn't even think twice about tromping to the water's edge and back. Since the pair of them set up camp, bears have walked past dozens of times, traveling the ancient trails to the outlet creek, and he fully expects, even relishes, encounters. But the attack doesn't occur then. One small detail—a pair of shoes—indicates the circumstances.

Most likely, he and Amie are in the sleeping tent, doing what damp, tired campers are most likely to do in a cold autumn storm—hunkering, passing the time, and trying to keep warm in their sleeping bags. They've either just eaten lunch or are about to; the rescue team will find Ziploc bags of sausage and cheese inside the tent, as well as a candy bar and other odds and ends—standard Treadwell camp fare. The sausage is Amie's; he's a junk food vegetarian. Maybe Timothy and Amie are talking, reading, or writing in the journals they've kept each day, or carefully drying off camera gear, stowing away precious film and videotape. Given the weather, it's almost dark enough inside to require headlamps for writing.

Besides filtering light, the double layers of nylon flex and pop in the wind, and rain spatters down, rattling like handfuls of buckshot. It would be difficult under these circumstances to hear anything. A bear, even a big one, simply walking along one of several trails that converge within twenty feet of camp would be almost undetectable. So the bear, agitated by the scent and sound of the tents, must make some sort of noise—perhaps a series of sharp, low woofs, breathy snorts, or growls. Maybe he makes actual contact with the tent, brushing against it, or even knocks the gear tent down. Timothy would respond almost instantly. He's always believed that it's crucial to confront a bear that comes into camp, meet it outside with firmness, and bluff it into leaving. Waiting in the tent for a bear to come through the wall is asking for disaster—an opinion supported by both biologist Stephen Herrero and Canadian bear-defense consultant James Shelton. Once a brown/grizzly takes down or rips into a tent, predatory instincts seem to be triggered by the struggling shapes and cries of the people inside. It's what happened to Michio Hoshino, and Tim knows the story well.

He shifts into action. He doesn't even bother to pull on his shoes (which are later found neatly stowed outside, under the fly, indicating a quick exit). No doubt he gives Amie some rapid-fire instructions—maybe even tells her to get the camcorder, which is still in its bag, lens cover on. They may be able to get some footage if the situation stands down. In the past, Timothy has exchanged that correspondence with a producer who wants footage of an aggressive bear and a tent; Timothy's always on the lookout for dramatic footage, and this may be an opportunity. But this is all speculation. The camcorder is one of those inexplicable mysteries related to the attack; it wouldn't be worth mentioning except for one chilling detail: As the attack is taking place, the digital tape is set into motion and records until the tape runs out—six minutes in all—and the camera's microphone is sensitive enough to capture snatches of the desperate struggle that ensues. And the time-date stamp on the tape is set. It's just a bit after 1:56 P.M. Alaska Standard Time, October 5, 2003.

Timothy Treadwell stands outside his tent as he has many times before. He's not in full fast-forward mode, because he's zipped the tent shut behind him. The first zip captured on tape will be Amie opening it to look out. No doubt his adrenaline-loaded pulse is fluttering like a flock of startled birds. He knows his back is to the wall, and without pepper spray, noisemaking cracker shells, or even a flare gun, his only weapons are his wits and experience. Still, he's as confident as any adrenaline junkie can be. This is what he's lived with, and what he lives for. In all these years, all these close meetings and occasional scrapes, both he and the bears have always emerged unscathed. Why should this time be any different? He loves this bear. Why would it hurt him? He stands tall, opens his jacket and flares his elbows, stares the bear down, and shouts firmly in a low voice. Or he waves his arms in a deliberate shooing motion and shakes the alders as a bear would. He might even make a short bluff charge, a tactic he's employed in the past. There's no backing down here—no place to back down to. The man who's tried so hard to become a bear now needs to convince this one that he's something to be avoided.

The bear perceives Timothy's sudden appearance as a direct threat. It huffs and pops its jaws in agitation, doesn't retreat as it should. Still, Timothy doesn't panic. He's run into thousands of bears; this may even be one he knows. The question is whether it's Demon, or one of the other "killer bears" that have periodically threatened him. Maybe, out of desperation, he switches tactics: backs up toward the tent, averting his eyes and rounding his shoulders as he speaks in that stylized, singsong voice—doing all he can to reassure the animal that he wants no trouble, and that he accepts its higher social rank. The bear keeps coming—on all fours, elbows out, staring intently, head lowered, silent except for an occasional explosive huff or growl. Maybe the rush is instantaneous, a hair-trigger response. Or the bear makes a series of short bluff charges, bouncing forward, stiff legged, then skidding to an abrupt stop and then retreating—only to wheel and charge again. Even at the last instant, there's a chance it will veer and crash off through the brush and vanish as quickly as it appeared. But at some point a nerve synapse crackles, an inner switch is thrown, and the bear switches from threat to attack.

The bear probably isn't bent on killing and eating Treadwell, just neutralizing the threat it perceives—an animal crowding its personal envelope of space. It's what experts call a defensive-aggressive attack, a genetically programmed response that may date back thousands of years, when the barren steppe of the Pleistocene was patrolled by all manner of threatening beasts—saber-toothed cats, lionlike felines, and short-faced bears that stood five feet at the shoulder. Bold bears kept their food and their young, so the theory goes, and lived to breed, thereby passing along that aggressive trait. The same behavior is also useful in dealing with others of its kind. In the bear world such attacks rarely end in serious injury or death—though that depends on the subordinate bear making gestures of appeasement and beating a hasty retreat. A human, though, can neither absorb that level of punishment nor outrun the attacker.

It could be, though, that things happen much faster. Timothy steps out and instantly senses this time *is* different. *He knows this bear. And he knows it means to kill him.* He looks the animal in the eye, six feet away, and understands it's over. There's scarcely time for that realization to blur past before the bear is on him.

Amie, still inside and hearing the struggle, has the presence of mind to reach in the camera bag and turn the video recorder on with the attack in progress. They've been filming for days, and it may be a nearly automatic reaction. Maybe, too, she realizes, *This is it,* and like anyone facing death, wants to reach out toward the living one last time. The camera's tape is her message in a bottle.

Now the horror begins. However Timothy and Amie arrived at this point, the flow chart of possibilities has narrowed into a bleak, brutal funnel.

Come out here, I'm being killed out here! Treadwell screams to Huguenard.

Play dead! she shouts back. Obviously she realizes what Timothy, in his desperation, does not—there is nothing that she can do to help him.

The speed and force of an attacking grizzly is overwhelming. Like being hit by a truck doing sixty. Or an avalanche. What many survivors of a mauling recall is the sheer explosion of power that tears into them, sweeps them along like a scrap of paper. One woman describes being grabbed, shaken, and thrown into a tree; another victim says the most painful and lasting injury he suffered was deep bruising caused by the bear's snout slamming into his chest. One man, charged by a grizzly defending a moose carcass, recalled in a letter to James Shelton, "I remember thinking, just prior to firing, that it would be impossible to stop something coming that fast."

According to Dr. Franc Fallico, Alaska's deputy state medical examiner, "Out of four [brown/grizzly-inflicted] autopsies that I've performed, in two cases the victims were able to place one rifle shot into the bear and were still killed. You draw your own conclusions from that." And in each case the damage was enough to kill them several times over.

The memories and perceptions of mauling victims often bear striking similarities. One common, chillingly vivid recollection is the sound of the bear's teeth scraping against the skull, and the sensation of incredible pressure as the animal tries to crush the head in its jaws. One man likens the sound to "eggshells crunching." Very few survivors of severe maulings escape trauma to the face and scalp; this is where an attack, either defensive-aggressive or predatory, usually focuses. Bear attack expert Stephen Herrero points out that fighting bears typically attack each other's heads, trying to seize and cripple the other's lower jaw; he theorizes the behavior may transfer during attacks on people. In human victims, often entire areas of tissue—a forehead, a nose and cheek, or a jaw—are mangled or ripped free. The gush of blood often makes vision during the attack impossible. Hospital photographs document horrific, stomach-churning damage. Thus the oft-repeated recommendation of experts to protect the head while "playing dead" in a grizzly attack: lie, if possible, facedown, hands clasped behind the skull, elbows wrapped tight on either side. Legs should be spread to make it as difficult as possible for the bear to roll you over—not only to get at the face, but to eviscerate your abdomen. Or roll up in a tight, knee-clasping ball.

Dr. Fallico, describing the progression of an all-out bear attack, deploys the clinical language one might expect of a forensic expert,

a man whose profession requires working backward from mangled remains:

> Basically, the bear can injure first by slapping and hitting
> with the paws; I've had some experience with that, espe-
> cially directed to the face. The bear will knock a person
> down that way. Second, the bear can grab and bite, and
> often what the bear will do is grab around the buttocks
> area and shake. And after the body is thrown about, regrab
> and bite and chew about the head. The teeth will slip into
> the skull bone, which is made of three layers—a hard outer
> layer, a middle spongy layer, and a hard inner layer—and
> the scrape marks will go into that inner layer and some-
> times pierce the skull into the brain. The skull is stripped by
> grabbing and shaking.

Obviously, a great deal is up to the bear. Some attacks are
brief, almost cursory, with comparatively little damage; others are
prolonged, with pauses in the assault; some are so violent and savage that maintaining any sort of position is impossible. Once contact is made by a grizzly, the idea is to weather the storm, pray the
bear is quickly satisfied that it has overcome the perceived threat
and doesn't switch into predatory mode—and leaves.

Some victims feel incredible, excruciating pain as the bear's
claws and teeth rake and tear their bodies; others are blessedly
pain free, only dimly aware of the damage being wreaked—spared
by sliding into shock, the body's final wall of self-defense. Or
perhaps it's a merely a cushion to ease the seemingly inevitable
downward spiral toward death. Many people enduring a mauling
describe a heightened, lucid state that seems remarkably calm and
rational. They may recall thinking, *Well, there goes my arm . . .*
or, *I wish he'd get it over with quickly.* One man recalls thinking
he "was happy there was just crunching and not crunching and
ripping." (Herrero, p. 23) It's not uncommon to wander down the

bright tunnel of a classic near-death experience, or to have thoughts and visions of loved ones. Several survivors report hearing someone screaming and shouting—and then they realize they're listening to themselves. Sometimes, though, victims display unbelievable presence of mind. One woman geologist, while a predatory black bear was eating one arm, managed to use the other to reach her VHF radio and call in a nearby helicopter.

There are also those who fight back—shouting, gouging at eyes, kicking and punching, firing a pistol or rifle, stabbing with a knife—using whatever they have. They often describe enduring the mauling, then suddenly becoming irritated or angry, and lashing out. Improbably, the reaction is sometimes enough to drive away, even kill, the bear. One ten-year-old Canadian girl, attacked by a black bear, first struck it with an ax, momentarily escaped, and threw a pot of boiling water into its face. An older Athabaskan Indian man, his face literally ripped off, stabbed a bear to death with his sheath knife as it stood over him. Though the conventional wisdom is "play dead" during a grizzly attack, Stephen Herrero notes, referring to thirteen instances where people resisted or fought back against grizzlies and successfully "decreased the intensity of attack" in seven cases: "Trying to fight back . . . can't be ruled out as a strategy based on the data." (Herrero, p. 18) Cutting through the science-speak, resisting may not be a bad idea—especially, Herrero explains, if the preferred "play-dead" strategy doesn't seem to be working. At that point, you've got nothing to lose.

In the rare case of a predatory attack, the damage intensifies. Dr. Fallico again:

> The bear will dismember the body, take the limbs off, and preferentially eat the meat off the limbs after death, or even while the person is still dying. Then the bear will strip the meat off the rib cage and eat parts of the ribs, usually

the thinner lateral parts, then strip the meat off the back and the backbone, and eat portions of the leg bones, usually the ends.

It is Fallico who conducted the autopsy of Timothy and Amie's remains; veiled in his impersonal descriptions are horrific details, sifted from the scant remnants.

Though we can only guess at all that's passing through Timothy Treadwell's mind, he's obviously all too aware of his desperate situation. In all these years he's never been so much as scratched by a bear. But he's watched them all these seasons, and no doubt understands the difference between bluff, disciplinary slap, and deadly intent. Even a small bear can drag off a moose carcass; this animal is excited and aggressive, surging with power, and, in its mind, battling a threat. It's intolerant of subordinate creatures—ursine or human. Almost always it's expressed that intolerance by avoiding people. But this time is different.

One of Treadwell's first cries to Amie isn't that he's being attacked and needs help to chase the bear off, but that's he's "getting killed." The phrase isn't to be taken lightly. Treadwell is tough, courageous, and heady, not one to overreact; in fact, he has a long history of underplaying danger. We can guess he's either suffered immediate, terrible damage, or he instantly perceives the bear's intentions from the force of the attack.

The bear almost certainly smashes Treadwell to the ground with its initial charge—either an overpowering blow with a front paw, a snatch of a leg or arm with its jaws, or a rearing, downward lunge that envelops him. A bear of any size is capable of holding him sideways in its mouth and literally shaking him to death the way a terrier would a cat. But Timothy Treadwell doesn't die quickly. The tape runs roughly six minutes, and his cries can be heard two thirds of that time. Clearly he's not one of those people who float off into a shock-induced dream state. He's sharply aware and struggling desperately to survive.

What does he think as he's being ripped apart? Beyond the physical agony, and the despairing awareness of his body's ruin, there must be flashes of disbelief—*This can't be happening, this isn't right*. . . . He had gone so long leading a charmed life he'd stopped believing it could ever happen. *Why this bear? Why now? I must have made a mistake*. . . . And you have to wonder if he senses the extent of the tragedy that's just started, a spiral of destruction set in motion by his own actions. The bear, as is often the case, is nearly silent—no Hollywood roars—which only adds to the horror.

The sound of a zipper is evident on the tape—the sound of the sleeping-tent fly opening. From what seems a great distance away, Treadwell hears the high-pitched, urgent call. Amie screams to Timothy.

Play dead!

Hold absolutely still. Don't even breathe. It must take incredible, almost superhuman discipline to lie there, torn apart and bleeding, with an animal tearing and thrashing you apart. But it works. The bear breaks off the attack and disappears into the brush. Apparently words pass back and forth as they try to see if the bear has gone. Given the density of the alders and the light conditions, it could be standing a few feet away and be invisible. Van Daele's report reads, "It sounds like the bear retreated for a couple minutes. . . ."

At this point, Amie may rush to Treadwell's rescue. She's a surgical physician's assistant—used to seeing things that would make most people blanch, trained to keep cool under pressure and to save lives. And this is the man she loves. He needs her. This is no place for hysterical behavior. She's already shown her courage time and again; it's hard to imagine she wouldn't come to his aid. She may be already fashioning a compression bandage from a piece of clothing. Or maybe she's holding back, getting ready but waiting to make sure the bear is indeed gone.

But the bear returns—a common pattern in defensive-aggressive brown bear attacks, especially if the victim moves too soon. It often remains nearby, watching and waiting. Some survivors report lying still for what seems an eternity, only to look up, crawl, or groan—which triggers a renewed attack. The bear resumes his mauling of Timothy Treadwell, wreaking ghastly damage, biting and ripping chunks of tissue free. Amie is forced to retreat, though she doesn't reenter the tent. Treadwell shrieks that playing dead isn't working, and begs her to get a pan and hit the bear.

Fight back! she screams. A last, desperate move—resisting a bear of any size, even more so after all the damage Treadwell has sustained, is all but impossible. Whether or not Amie attacks the animal herself isn't clear. On the tape, there seems to be the sound of something being thrown. Van Daele's final comment regarding the recording: "The audio ends with his sounds no longer evident and her screams continuing." Dragging sounds and the fading of Timothy's cries seem to indicate he's being pulled off into the brush, still clinging to life but his fate now sealed. Amie Huguenard is alone.

We're uncertain if the bear immediately returns for her at this point. We do know, from the evidence found by the would-be rescuers, that Amie was killed outside the sleeping tent, very possibly right in front of the unzipped door, where her remains are found buried. At just over five feet tall and barely over a hundred pounds, no weapon in hand except maybe the pan Timothy called for, she faces the primal fear that haunts us all—a beast with gore-smeared jaws, in a killing frenzy. She's already witnessed, in the unspeakable horror of Treadwell's death, her own fate. The force of the bear is irresistible. She's next.

Maybe she could have saved herself somehow—either by diving into the tent and lying still while the bear was focused on

Treadwell's body, or by slipping off to hide in the tall grass and brush, slithering over the cliff and hand-over-handing down the alders into knee-deep water, balling up and waiting for morning, for the Andrew Airways floatplane they arranged for just hours ago—in a time that must seem impossibly distant now. She even has the satellite phone in the tent, and could call for help, which would surely come within an hour or two. But she's unable or unwilling to leave.

The last sounds on the tape—Huguenard's repeated, high-pitched screams—sound "eerily like a predator call," writes Van Daele, referring to a device carried by hunters to produce the distress cries of a wounded small animal, which often attracts bears (as well as foxes, wolves, and coyotes). Van Daele theorizes these shrieks "may have prompted the bear to return and kill her." After what she's seen—enough to break anyone—it's easy to envision her rooted to the spot outside the tent, hysterical and paralyzed by fear, perhaps for long minutes until the bear returns.

There is one last possibility. The last, agonizing sounds before the tape mercifully runs out could well be Amie Huguenard's final descent into darkness.

The World of Fears

When Andrew Airways pilot Willy Fulton lands at Upper Kaflia Lake at 2:00 P.M. on October 6, things don't seem right. He's flown Tim Treadwell for years, and is expecting the usual neat pile of gear down by the water's edge, ready for a quick load and fly-out. Neither did Treadwell make his customary contact with his hand-held VHF radio as the plane approached. Fulton taxis the Beaver into the tiny bay below camp. As he steps out onto the floats, he sees movement on the knoll. His view partly blocked by the brush, he figures it's a person shaking out a tarp. Things are all right after all. Tim and Amie were just somehow delayed, maybe the weather, a video opportunity, or a morning hike that went on too long. They'd better hurry; the weather isn't getting any better. Pounding rain and a lowering sky, in Fulton's words, "a dog-shit day."

He calls out their names.

Silence. A little strange, but nothing to worry about.

Unarmed, clumping along in the floatplane pilot's standard footgear—hip waders—he starts the eighty-yard climb up the more direct of two main bear trails that wind toward camp. "About halfway up, I got kind of an odd feeling," he says, "and decided to go back to the plane." He wants to take off, look things over from the air. Tim and Amie will probably be coming along through the brush from the creek, waving to him. The Beaver is moored to a clump of alders against the bank. Pausing to untie, Fulton glances over his shoulder. And behind him is a bear, coming fast and low, eerily silent, twenty feet away. As the pilot leaps to his floats and pushes off, the bear is a body length behind. Fulton scrambles into the cockpit and slams the door. The bear, a big, dark male, skids to a stop at the water's edge, eyes still fixed on him. Huffing, the bear paces the bank as the plane drifts out into the lake. Normally Fulton would have a shotgun in his plane, as per state regulations, but he's left it back in Kodiak.

"I've been charged by a few bears, but this was different," Fulton says. "He wasn't doing that usual bear-of-the-woods thing, acting big and bad. He was crouched down, sneaking on me. That look in his eye was real different too. Right then I felt like he was out to kill me and eat me." Willy's heart is thumping. Now he knows something isn't right. The Beaver's engine rattles to life and the bear fades into the alders.

Willy is shaken by his own near scrape, but this is swept away by waves of dread. *Maybe it happened this time, maybe he went too far. . . . Oh, Jesus . . .* He taxis out into the center of the lake, turns into the wind, and takes off. Circling over the camp, he can see the tents—still staked out but mashed flat. And in front of one he sees a large bear, the same one, he figures, feeding on human remains—a rib cage for certain. But just one body—someone's still alive down there. He makes pass after pass, fifteen or twenty, he figures, swooping lower and lower, trying to drive off the bear and looking for other signs of movement. "I just about knocked him off the body, I was so low," Fulton says. "The floats were maybe two or three feet over his head and I couldn't get any lower because of the brush." His voice has the same tone as if he's talking about the weather, instead of high-stakes, screw-up-and-die flying. But the bear doesn't budge and, by the last few passes, doesn't even look up. "He just crouched down," Fulton remembers, "and ate faster."

There's no sign of anyone. Still, Tim or Amie—he's not sure which—could be hiding somewhere, maybe in one of the tents or out in the brush, maybe even a mile or two away. He taxis to different places on the upper lake, stops the engine, and calls, his voice echoing in the rain-swept silence. Then he takes off, flies to the lower lake and to different places in the bay, stopping and calling again and again. No answer.

Willy Fulton lands, taxis to the west end of the lake, and raises Andrew Airways, back in Kodiak. Operations manager Stan Divine in turn calls the State Troopers in Kodiak and the Park Service in King Salmon, which is on the mainland, a hundred miles west of Kaflia, on the far side of the Alaska Peninsula. Ranger Joel Ellis takes the call at 2:35 P.M. Though he's in his first year in Alaska, just completing his first season at Katmai, he's had twenty years of experience as a ranger, including posts at Yellowstone and Grand Teton—places with grizzlies.

Ellis immediately contacts Allen Gilliland, the Park Service pilot, to get the NPS Cessna 206 floatplane ready. Then Ellis touches base with the Alaska State Troopers, as well as the Alaska Department of Fish and Game. He relays a message through Andrew Airways, asking Fulton to wait where he is. Though it's Sunday afternoon and offices are closed, Ellis is able to make contact with both agencies. He also calls Ranger Derek Dalrymple and tells him to hustle in. The rangers grab first aid gear and two Remington Model 870 pump shotguns—preferred for their sure, nonjamming actions—and boxes of rifled slugs. Ellis is wearing his .40-caliber Smith & Wesson service pistol. There's a strict protocol to be followed. Ellis is medic and operations commander of the rescue effort. With acting park superintendent Joe Fowler out of town, Chief back-country ranger Missy Epping assumes the formal role as incident commander. She'll remain in King Salmon to supervise communication, pass the word up the chain of command, and get the paperwork moving. Unlike Ellis, who is new to Katmai National Park, Epping has a personal stake in all this. She's known Treadwell for years, and considers him a friend.

The Cessna is in the air less than an hour after Ellis takes the initial call. Ellis says, "At this point we were on a rescue mission, not knowing if people were dead or alive." On the other hand, Gilliland, planning for the worst, has brought along a couple of body bags from the King Salmon police department.

The two men accompanying Ellis, though selected by circumstance, might have been hand-picked for what lies ahead. Gilliland is more than just a pilot. He's an avid and skilled hunter who knows the country—as well as a certified firearms instructor. Before he became a Park Service pilot, he was a cop in King Salmon for sixteen years. Dalrymple, though a seasonal ranger, has been involved in investigating three previous bear-mauling incidents in the lower forty-eight. He is, as Gilliland later says, "very experienced—a steady guy to have around."

Eighty miles away in Kodiak, Alaska state troopers Chris Hill and Allan Jones are airborne. The weather between King Salmon and Kaflia is getting iffy, closing down. Another fast-moving coastal storm is forecast, which may force the Park Service plane to turn back. The troopers are in radio contact with them; if everyone makes it, they'll rendezvous after landing at upper Kaflia Lake.

The Park Service plane runs into skeins of fog and rain, ceilings below three hundred feet. Gilliland isn't sure they can make it in. Fulton tells them they damn well better. Someone may be alive, and he's not leaving. With him playing the role of air controller, the Park Service plane makes it through the weather and taxis down the lake. They confer with Fulton, who by now has been waiting for nearly three hours, alone in the world of unspoken fears, unable to help or do anything for his friends. He jumps in the 206 and they taxi the half mile east toward the outlet stream and the knoll. As they coast toward shore, Gilliland points out a bear on the hill, standing by one of the tents.

Ellis recalls, "We got out of the plane, guns ready. We were in a combat-ready situation, yelling for the people." The shouting is also to alert any bears in the area and drive them away. After tying up the plane, they immediately begin to move forward, hands clenched around weapons, still calling out for Treadwell and Huguenard. Ellis, Dalrymple, and Gilliland thread single file along the steep, narrow trail rising through the alders. Fulton, "amped up" as he says, clambers ahead of them, unarmed, and has to be reminded more than once to slow down. They break into the open below the crown of the knoll and pause, spreading out so that they can all fire at once if necessary. At Gilliland's urging, they decide to wait for Hill and Jones, who are just landing. Due to lack of space in the tiny bay and overhanging alders everywhere else, the troopers will have to moor two hundred yards down the shore and muscle their way along the bank through heavy brush. Gilliland suggests the troopers might have a large-caliber rifle, and the extra firepower could make a difference. Tense and dry mouthed, standing in the cold deluge of rain, the four men remain facing uphill toward the crest of the grass-crowned knoll, where they last saw the bear. Off to their right is a marshy, open swale; ahead, a curtain of eight-foot alder brush and chest-high grass that restricts visibility to a few arm lengths. The bear trails that snake through the growth will require them, in places, to bend at the waist.

Gilliland, the pilot, channels his jitters into his eyes, scanning the brush in all directions. The threat, as it turns out, comes from the rear.

"Bear!" he shouts. It's less than twenty feet away, head low, moving silently toward them, its outline blurred by the alders. All four men yell repeatedly, throwing all their pent-up emotion into it, trying to haze the big male away. Instead of retreating—as almost any bear would, from a tightly packed, aggressive, loud group of humans—it stares straight at them and steps forward. In his official Incident Report, Ellis will write, "I perceived the bear was well aware of our presence and was stalking us. I believe that."

Gilliland concurs. "We were between the bear and its carcass, but it didn't charge us to defend it like most bears would do. It had circled around us and was coming quietly from the rear."

Fulton adds, "He had that same look in his eye. I think he meant to kill all of us."

The first movement toward them is enough of a signal to the men, whose nerves are stretched like piano wire. Ellis says, "We didn't confer. We all just started shooting." Fulton, who is between the men and the bear, finds himself literally in the crossfire.

"I just remember gun barrels swinging toward me," he says. With the bear a dozen feet away, he dives to the ground and the fusillade explodes overhead.

A half-ton brown bear, as experienced hunters know, can be almost impossible to stop, especially worked up, coming straight in. There are tales of magnum-caliber rounds—slugs damn near the size of a thumb—deflecting off the thick, sloped forehead, and charging animals absorbing incredible punishment, dead on their feet but still coming. Gilliland says he never saw one go down once and stay down. But the barrage unleashed by the rangers is staggering: five rounds each of one-ounce rifled shotgun slugs from Dalrymple and Gilliland, and eleven soft points from Ellis's .40 caliber semiautomatic handgun—nineteen shots in under fifteen seconds, the booming crash of shotguns overlaid with the sharp, rapid crack of pistol fire.

Troopers Jones and Hill are just tying off their plane when they hear the volley. "I thought it was some sort of fancy multiple-report cracker shell the Park Service guys had," recalls Jones, referring to the shotgun-fired noisemakers often used to scare off aggressive bears. "It was a continuous series of shots, quite a racket."

Gilliland's report reads, "I fired five rounds . . . with one hit to the head below the eye and four hits to the neck and shoulder." In retrospect, Gilliland feels his first shot killed the bear instantly. But giving his past experience and the extreme close range, he didn't take chances.

Ranger Dalrymple's version is more laconic: "I shot until the threat was stopped."

The big bear drops in his tracks, twitches, sighs out one last breath, and is dead. The men stand stunned in the rain, wrapped in a cloud of acrid powder smoke, their ears ringing and their breath steaming into the air. They're alive. Ellis paces off the distance separating him and the bear: twelve feet. Gilliland says later, "If it was an all-out charge, he would have taken down one of us."

Pilot Willy Fulton is back on his feet. "I want to look that bear in the eyes," he says. He studies the blood-spattered face, the small, rapidly glazing pupils, and says he's sure it's the same bear that chased him to the plane, the same one he saw on the knoll. The four men continue the last thirty yards to the campsite, no less on edge. Below, the troopers are in sight, making their way through the brush along the lakeshore.

The tents are tucked back in the alders, both crushed down but intact; either a bear has walked over them or someone has fallen against them, but the fabric's neither ripped up nor bloody. In front of the sleeping tent is a large mound of mud, grass, and sticks. Several metal BRFCs are scattered on the north side of the camp in some disarray, but sealed and unmarked by claws or teeth. However, it's the mound in front of the first tent, where the bear had stood, that captures the would-be rescuers' attention. There in the muck is what lead ranger Ellis later calls, his voice tight, "fresh flesh"—fingers and an arm protruding from the pile.

There is also a chunk of organ Gilliland believes is a kidney. Digging into the bear's cache will reveal further horror. At least one person is gone, but there's still the possibility of a survivor.

While Gilliland goes down to the lake to meet Troopers Hill and Jones, Fulton and Ellis explore the tents. Dalrymple stands guard with his shotgun. Since both tents are flattened, Ellis decides the quickest way in is to slash the fabric with his knife. Someone could still be inside, unconscious and torn up, but alive. But they find only clothing, and camping and camera gear, most of it stowed neatly. Food in small Ziploc bags, ready to be eaten, as if lunch had been interrupted. Sleeping tent unzipped. Gear tent zipped shut.

By this time, Jones and Hill are on the scene. With unmistakable evidence of at least one fatality, the investigation is officially handed over to the Alaska State Troopers. Hill is the officer in charge. The troopers brief everyone on crime scene protocol—the same rules apply here—and begin documenting the area. Hill takes a couple of minutes of shaky videotape of the wreckage. Ellis and Dalrymple backtrack to the Park Service plane to bring up notebooks and cameras as well. Meanwhile, Gilliland, ever vigilant, spots a bear—an enormous dark male drifting silently up the same trail he and the troopers have just used. Vision screened by the brush and grass, Gilliland doesn't see it until it's practically on top of them. The animal seems equally unaware—just traveling the same trail it has for years, every step locked in memory. This guy is bigger than the last one. Just prior to denning, his muscular frame sheathed in fat, he's at his maximum weight, maybe twelve hundred pounds. *Bear!* Gilliland shouts.

Jangled as everyone's nerves are, it's a miracle no one shoots. Fulton, Gilliland, and the troopers shout and wave. The bear seems nonplussed by the commotion. He considers briefly and shifts into a lumbering lope, off down the hill—leaving, but with his dignity intact. Just another Katmai bear. Gilliland shouts a heads-up to Ellis and Dalrymple. They stand on the Cessna's floats and watch the bear stroll off to the west, then walk up the hill to join the others. For a time, everyone is busy with shooting photos and jotting notes, freezing the scene in time. Ellis asks if someone should do a perimeter check. Gilliland volunteers. He backtracks to where the dead bear lies in the alders. Skirting the edge of the knoll, weaving on a search pattern through the brush, he's a stone's toss from the others, yet totally cut off.

Gilliland is about halfway around his circle when he finds what's left of Timothy Treadwell—a head missing most of its scalp; part of a shoulder, some connecting tissue, and two forearms. The face, recognizable and uncrushed, is caught in a grimace. Fulton accompanies Hill down to photograph and collect the remains. Washed by the steady rain, everything is surprisingly bloodless. The wrists and face are pale, like wax. While they're working, Gilliland hears a bear popping its jaws, a clear signal of stress and possible aggression. The animal is close, but the brush is too thick to see anything. Fulton and Hill make their way up the knoll with the body bag, and Gilliland, despite the bear, continues his circling of the knoll. He finds nothing more and returns to the camp. The others, excavating the cache, have discovered another head with face intact—Amie seems peacefully asleep—as well as some flesh-stripped bones, miscellaneous scraps, and portions of a torso.

Describing the remains, Ellis sounds like he's struggling for the right words, something to mitigate the horror. "It was way past the initial stages," he tells me. "One or more bears had time to eat most of two bodies and cache the remains. There was no clothing attached to any part. There wasn't much left of anything. We could not tell male from female." When I ask for more detail, he repeats, "We could not tell male from female." Then he says, after a pause, "One part had a watch on it."

Four men break camp and collect Timothy and Amie's gear.

A portion of the 400-mile-long Katmai Coast, home to an estimated 1,500 brown bears. This aerial is of Kukak Bay, at the center of Timothy's operating area— between Hallo and Kaflia bays. (Nick Jans)

Timothy Treadwell dressed for field work, at Hallo Bay. He believed dark clothing made him appear more like a bear. (Joel Bennett)

Upper Kaflia Lake on aerial approach. Timothy's campsite and the Grizzly Maze are top center, where the land appears to be thinnest; a sliver of Lower Kaflia Lake is visible beyond; and past that, Kaflia Bay and the waters of Shelikof Strait. (Nick Jans)

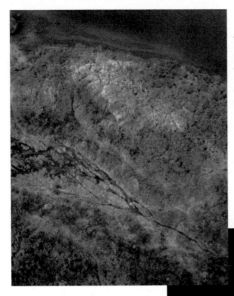

The knoll at Upper Kaflia, furrowed by bear trails. The Treadwell campsite is at top center, near the shoreline. (Nick Jans)

Side aerial view of knoll. From this angle, Treadwell's campsite is at crest of knoll, just left of center. (Nick Jans)

Bear 141 at Lower Kaflia, 2001. His distinctive drooping lip and skewed ears are evident. (Willy Fulton)

Baby Letterman, the second of the bears killed in the rescue-recovery mission; taken in 2002, when he was two years old. (Willy Fulton)

Timothy Treadwell and the fox named Timmy, at Hallo Bay.
(Joel Bennett)

Timothy Treadwell at work in the heart of the Grizzly Maze. A total of five bears are visible, all feeding on salmon. (Joel Bennett)

The main bear trail leading to the Treadwell camp, Upper Kaflia Lake, October 11, 2003, five days after the fatal attack. (Nick Jans)

The ruin of the Treadwell camp, taken by a member of the rescue-recovery mission on October 6, 2003. (courtesy of National Park Service)

Bear 141, less than two hours after he was killed. Shotgun slug wound is evident below his eye. Ranger Joel Ellis kneels to the right. (courtesy of Alaska State Troopers)

The food found inside, laid out on the collapsed tent. (courtesy of National Park Service)

Closure signs posted by National Park Service at Upper Kaflia Lake near the Treadwell campsite. (Nick Jans)

DANGER
Bear-Caused Fatality
Under Investigation

-CLOSURE-
From Cape Chiniak (Hallo Bay) to
Cape Ilktugitak (Amalik Bay)
All Areas, Extending Inland 15 Miles,
Are Closed Through Dec. 1, 2003

Entering a closed area or approaching an
is punishable by fine up to $5000 or
imprisonment up to 6 months or both.

U.S. Department of the Interior
Katmai National Park & Preserve

Katmai National Park   Case 03-109
6 OCT 2003
Fatality - Attack by Bear
Incident Site Diagram

Approximate Distances

b-d	80m
b-c	20m
b-g	18m
c-d	68m
d-e	2m
d-f	6m
d-h	30m

Upper Kaflia Lake

Bear cache with
Huguenard's remains

Best access to camp

Airplane parked

(A)   (B)   (d) (e) (f)   "gear" tent

Bear trail

Stream

Sleeping tent

Small bear killed   (8)   Bear trail   (C)   Bear trail

Large Bear killed   Bear trail   Bear trail

to outlet Stream

(h)   Bear trail   ≈ 300 m

Open marsh

Treadwell remains

Kaflia Bay, Upper Lake   58°14'50.63"N   154°15'24.68" E

Joel Ellis   10/20/03   Not to Scale

Map of the Treadwell campsite drawn by Joel Ellis, lead ranger, NPS. Not drawn to scale; the addition of the worded labels for the remains of Treadwell and Huguenard are the author's own, replacing "blacked out" wording. (courtesy of National Park Service)

Cleared tent site photographed on Oct. 8, 2003 by necropsy team. Upper Kaflia Lake is visible in background. (courtesy of National Park Service)

A large male found feeding on the remains of Bear 141, October 11, 2003. (Nick Jans)

Bear leg bones from the smaller bear shot by the recovery team, scattered on a bear cache, October 11, 2003.
(Nick Jans)

The view from the Kaflia knoll near Treadwell's campsite.
(courtesy of National Park Service)

DeHavilland Beaver at Upper Kaflia Lake, at the landing for
Treadwell's campsite. (Nick Jans)

Each makes several trips down the now-familiar bear trail to the lake. Meanwhile, Gilliland taxis Fulton back to his plane at the other end of the lake. His Beaver will carry the remains and gear to Kodiak, where the Troopers will continue the investigation. (The body bags are so light—forty pounds at the most between them—that the medical examiner meeting the plane will ask for the rest.)

While Fulton is warming up his plane, Gilliland taxis back.

As he's hiking up the knoll one last time, he hears Trooper Hill yell, *Bear!* Gilliland can see it moving in the brush, circling from the right toward Ellis and Hill, who are to his left. Darymple and Jones are to the right and behind, standing by the pile of gear on the lake shore. About thirty feet separates the three men in front and the bear. It's a much smaller animal, probably a three-year-old—the kind of bear that most often gets in trouble with people. Driven off by their mothers and on their own for the first time, some are timid and uncertain; others curious and apparently eager for company; a few aggressive, testing the boundaries, seeing how far they can push things. Teenagers, in other words. There's nothing abnormal about the bear's approach, but its timing couldn't be worse. The men have all had enough—all of them tired and raw-nerved. Still, they hold off. Everyone waves and yells the by now familiar mantra, their voices low and forceful: *Hey, bear! Ahhh! Get outta here!*

Vision obscured by a clump of alder, Gilliland circles to his right. He yells to the others that he's going to take a warning shot. There is little reaction from the bear, which continues closing the distance between itself and Ellis—then turns to go, but circles back, ears forward and staring. It's far too persistent—either overly curious or aggressive. That's it. Ellis shouts for Gilliland to take a shot if he has one. Gilliland replies that he doesn't. The bear moves into a window in the brush, still closing the distance, and Hill and Ellis open fire with their slug-loaded 12-gauge pump guns—once each. The bear turns, giving Gilliland a momentary opening. He shoots twice. The bear falls and struggles to get up. Gilliland moves in and makes a killing shot to the base of the skull. Four dead now—two people, two bears. No one takes comfort in the grim mathematical symmetry.

It's now after 6:00 P.M., the light fading and the weather deteriorating. Wind rattles in the alders, scattering leaves and ruffling the dark water of Kaflia Lake. All three planes have an hour of flying ahead, and will be landing on the water in near darkness. There's no time to do a necropsy on the dead bears—open them up and see what's in the gastrointestinal tract, discover if they even have the bears involved in the predation. That job will have to wait for Fish and Game tomorrow, weather willing. It's a task better suited to trained biologists, anyway.

One by one, the three planes taxi east, turn, and roar down the lake in the dusk—Ellis, Dalrymple, and Gilliland in the Park Service Cessna 206, bound for King Salmon; Troopers Jones and Hill in their Supercub headed for Kodiak; and Willy Fulton in the Andrew Airways Beaver, alone with his gruesome load and his thoughts. Six men ride the currents of the sky, rising away from this place of darkness and death. But Kaflia will stir on its haunches and follow them the rest of their lives.

Bear 141

The weather on Tuesday, October 7, matches the forecast exactly—
a wall of low pressure screaming out of the North Pacific, across
the Kodiak archipelago and the current-swept waters of Shelikof
Strait. It slams into the Alaska Peninsula's south side and beats its
wet fists against the jagged, glacier-draped mountains, dumping
close to an inch of rain and, higher up, a splatter of wet snow. In
narrow passes and valleys, places like Kaflia, the funneled wind
tops forty knots. The chest-high grass on the knoll, tawny with
autumn, is beaten flat; the alders thrash and flex, surrendering
their dark, half-dead leaves grudgingly. The two dead bears lie less
than thirty yards apart, bloating. Blood fades into the soil. Other
bears walk past in the rain, patrolling the edge of the lake. Some
drift around the campsite, drawn by the scent of death. Ravens,
wings beating against the storm, swoop and veer, look down, and
shout hoarse announcements.

In Kodiak, Larry Van Daele looks out the window, sighs, and
shrugs. There will be no flying today. As the regional biologist for
the Alaska Department of Fish and Game, he's in charge of the
next stage of the investigation—the necropsy on the two dead
bears. He knows his job is becoming more unpleasant and difficult

by the minute, but that can't be helped. Meanwhile, he and Troopers Jones and Hill sort through Treadwell and Huguenard's effects, looking for anything that might shed light. Besides Tim and Amie's daily journals, they find the Sony digital camcorder neatly stowed in its case, laden with its dark secret—six minutes of agony etched on a thin ribbon of magnetic tape. But buried at the end of a cassette, without accompanying video and buffered by a few blank seconds, it's overlooked.

By Wednesday morning the storm has blown itself out. An hour before noon the necropsy team, headed by Van Daele, arrives at Kaflia. The weather is pleasant for this time of year—overcast skies, temperatures in the forties, and ten-knot winds. In the plane are Trooper Jones, pilot Butch Patterson of the Kodiak National Wildlife Refuge, KNWR enforcement officer Greg Wilker, and Fish and Game technician John Crye. Meanwhile, the Park Service plane and a Bell Jet Ranger helicopter are en route from King Salmon.

Passing low over what is now officially designated as the "incident site," Van Daele's crew spots two bears in the immediate area—both dark-colored adults. The larger one, a mature male, is guarding a fresh food cache near the base of the knoll. The other animal seems to be waiting for an opportunity. Patterson swoops low over the bears, trying to scare them off. Neither seems inclined to leave, but finally, after the third or fourth pass, the big male moves off a few yards. But he stays within range of protecting what's his. All considered—limited visibility and two dead bears acting as a magnet—these are less than ideal working conditions. A bear defending a carcass is as dangerous as it gets. The team lands on the next knoll over and makes a careful approach. Patterson stays with the plane, in radio contact. The team fires a volley of cracker shells toward the bears, and much to their relief, the animals respond as they should—by running off. Jones and Crye stand lookout on the crest of the knoll while Wilker and Van Daele approach the first bear's carcass, lying in the alders. The big, dark-furred male lies on one side, swollen and already rotting, the insulation of his fat and fur holding in the tremendous inner furnace. The ravens have pecked at the one exposed eye, but other bears haven't touched him. Even in death, his dominant scent and bulk is enough to hold scavengers at bay. It's not uncommon for the bodies of such males to lie undisturbed for a time like pharaohs, despite the wealth of calories they represent—an indication of how wary other, lesser bears are in the presence of a superior.

Van Daele goes to work. Besides cutting into the distended gut in search of human remains, he needs to conduct a thorough examination of the animal, to be on the alert for anything that might offer a clue as to what happened, and why. At this point this bear is, in human terms, the prime suspect in a double homicide. With Wilker's help, he wrestles the male over onto its back, takes photos, and makes preliminary observations. The male is large but not huge by Katmai standards—one thousand pounds, he estimates. Many males never pass eight hundred, and adult females are often half that. Despite initial observations from the rangers that the bear appeared to be gaunt and in poor condition, Van Daele finds both the bear's coat and fat thickness (four centimeters on the rump) indicate a reasonably healthy animal— "a little light for this time of year," he allows, "but not unusual." The animal certainly wasn't starving. Broken canines and teeth worn to the gum line suggest it's over twenty-five years old—near the upper limit of life expectancy for a male in the wild. Still, the animal could have lasted another season or two. It doesn't appear to have had any crippling injuries; in fact, there is no sign that this bear is in any sort of desperate condition that might explain why it would have engaged in behavior so abnormal that it represents a statistical asterisk.

Pierced by Van Daele's sharpened knife, the abdominal cavity emits a whoosh of pent-up gas, fluid, and stench. Holding his breath, Van Daele leans in. Tight below the wall of diaphragm muscle, which separates heart and lungs from the digestive organs, lies the swollen, gray-white stomach, and lower yet, the coil of intestine. Off to the left in the open body cavity, the liver and gall bladder. Mesenteric fat—skeins that overlie the intestines, a key indicator of overall condition—is "abundant."

Inside the digestive tract they find proof that they have, at least in some sense, the right bear. Even in the purely descriptive language of a scientist, what he finds is ghastly enough. This section of Van Daele's report reads:

> The stomach was distended and full. Contents were exclusively human body parts and clothing. Approximately 25 pounds of muscle, adipose tissue, and skin were removed. Bone fragments were prevalent. Rib, foot, pelvis, and vertebrae fragments were identifiable, but most was too small for gross identification. Much dark blonde hair about 45 cm long was present as was an esophagus and trachea. I also removed most of a white undershirt and some unidentifiable dark material. Intestines also had material in them, but it was too digested to make positive identification.

Van Daele bags the stomach contents in gallon-size Ziplocs, then goes on to take samples from the bear's heart, liver, and lungs, preserving them in formalin for further study. The two front paws and head are also removed to be taken back, as part of standard Fish and Game procedure. It's possible, too, that they might provide more information—and as it turns out, the head indeed offers up a secret.

Van Daele and Wilker move on to the second bear—or more accurately, what's left of it. Digging into the new cache, they find just a head, scraps of hide, and nearly skeletal remains. There's not enough left to determine what sex the bear was was. Without any digestive organs, there certainly won't be a necropsy. Still, the men examine the mouth and esophagus. It's a long shot, but all that they have left. There's nothing to indicate it fed on the bodies. From the teeth and size of the skull, Van Daele determines the animal to have been three years old, probably a male. Again, they salvage the head to carry back with them.

As they're preparing to work on the second bear, the Jet Ranger from King Salmon makes its raucous arrival. The two live bears Van Daele's crew hazed off the knoll—who have been watching wistfully from a distance—make an undignified exit from the area, dark rumps flouncing through the brush. Aboard the Jet Ranger are Joel Ellis and pilot Sam Egli. Both walk over from the landing site.

Egli recalls, "Van Daele was kneeling down, up to his elbows in the cache, holding his breath and gagging as he hit the dead bear. Between it and the other one, all cut open and pulled apart, the smell was pretty nauseating. I was just sort of standing there, taking in the smell and the ambience. We all had guns and were keeping a sharp eye out for bears, but I didn't see anybody really stressed out—just sort of professional and doing their jobs." The Park Service 206, piloted by Gilliland, arrives twenty minutes later, carrying Bruce Bartley of Fish and Game. Necropsy completed, the entire crew organizes for a last sweep through the area. Aside from a few more fragments of bone recovered from the cache that held Huguenard, all they find is a thermometer and a lone sock. Ellis posts closure signs, effective for the entire Katmai Coast into December, when all the bears will be denned up; one by one the aircraft depart, leaving Kaflia to the bears.

Back in Kodiak, Trooper Hill calls in Jones and Van Daele; running through the tape one more time, reviewing the footage of Timothy, Amie, and bears, he's discovered the chilling audio sequence. The men play it again and again, pause and rewind, taking notes, blocking out scenarios, all the while trying to decipher sounds muffled by the tent walls, the camera case itself, and the incessant spatter of rain on the tent. Over and over they listen to the screams and are unable to help. Later, when I ask Van Daele about the tape, he simply says, "Believe me—you don't want to hear it."

Van Daele continues his written report, which he started in the plane on the way home—a department memorandum that will focus on summarizing events and drawing conclusions from a biologist's perspective. Meanwhile, state troopers Hill and Jones continue their own investigation—standard procedure in any violent or accidental death. The remains of Treadwell and Huguenard have already been flown to the medical examiner's office in Anchorage, where a coroner's report from Dr. Fallico is under way. And of course the National Park Service is working on its own inquiry. Some information will be shared between agencies and some released to the public; some will remain confidential. Bear maulings and predation always attract an inordinate amount of attention, and Treadwell's celebrity will magnify the incident further. Factors need to be weighed and considered rapid-fire: freedom of information versus privacy and respect for the victims and families; informing and protecting the public without creating a firestorm of antibear hysteria; and in the case of all agencies, but certainly the Park Service (on whose ground and watch this occurred), guarding against potential litigation. Also, given that Treadwell had repeatedly claimed to be under death threat from poachers, rumors of foul play need to be addressed.

The Alaska State Troopers make their first press release on Monday morning, October 7, less than twenty hours after Willy Fulton landed at Kaflia and made his grim discovery. Spokesperson Greg Wilkinson has never heard of Timothy Treadwell until now. But a woman in his office, obviously shaken, gives Wilkinson a hint of what lies ahead. I was just reading his book, she says. With his long background in media, Wilkinson decides not to deviate from his usual open-gate philosophy—"to get out as much good, accurate information as quickly as possible." His second press release of the day includes the transcribed summary of the tape's contents (delivered by phone from Trooper Hill), as well as an account of the rescue attempt.

Wilkinson's counterpart at the National Park Service offices in Anchorage, John Quinley, knows from the start what kind of shadow this story will cast. As the officer in charge of public affairs for Alaska's National Parks, Treadwell's name has crossed Quinley's desk dozens of times, though the two never met. Both the AP and local Alaska media, including the *Anchorage Daily News*, are onto the story by Sunday evening—before Quinley is even free to confirm or deny the identity of the victims. But his approach is the same as Wilkinson's, as befits the most public of the involved agencies.

"There was no reason not to be putting out all the information," says Quinley. Except for the more lurid details, the story emerges with almost startling rapidity. And since the Troopers have the tape, there are no decisions to be made regarding its release. Quinley observes, "The increments of real news became awfully small after about a day." Except for a misinterpretation that Ellis had single-handedly shot the larger bear with his handgun (an inaccuracy that was quickly corrected, but nonetheless seized upon and repeated in several major news stories, and later in *Outside* magazine) and details revolving around the videotape, the story remains largely the same.

"We tried not to comment on Timothy's motivations, which we couldn't pretend to know," says Quinley. "We just stuck to the physical evidence and the policy piece—basically, that this was an unfortunate tragedy connected to what Mr. Treadwell chose to do."

However, the free flow of information lasts just a few days; Jewel Palovak hires a lawyer to level a cease-and-desist complaint to stop any further release of the tape's content, and to secure all effects belonging to Timothy and Amie—including the Sony camcorder and the tape. Palovak wants to ensure the audio of the attack doesn't slip into the public domain. There are rumblings of legal action over the insensitive and unnecessary release of information—from a tape that is private property. Litigation in cases like this is every agency's worst nightmare. Farfetched as it sounds, there's plenty of precedent for filing suit against the Park Service for negligence in case of animal attacks, or against the State Troopers or Fish and Game for divulging private information that results in emotional duress for the surviving families.

Suddenly, no one wants to talk. Missy Epping, the chief back-country ranger at Katmai National Park, refers me to NPS spokes-person John Quinley. She'll speak only with his approval, and is obviously nervous. The Alaska Department of Fish and Game puts out a general gag order regarding the case to all employees. When I call Kodiak biologist Larry Van Daele for a follow-up interview, he's apologetic, but tells me if only I'd contacted him a few hours earlier, he could have talked to me. I need to go higher up the ladder; he suggests his supervisor, or even the state's deputy director of wildlife conservation, Matt Robus (I choose him, since my wife cleans his teeth—but no luck). It will turn out that Van Daele's report on the incident, briefly available on request, will not again be available through official channels. Only a cautiously edited "redacted" ver-sion will be offered—and that one takes over a month to arrive. The State Troopers are the most tight lipped of all; after a terse conversa-tion with Trooper Jones, I don't even bother contacting his partner at the scene, Trooper Hill. They're under orders not to release fur-ther details, and everyone's watching his or her back. But the fact re-mains that most of the useful information was out in the first hours, as NPS spokesman John Quinley had observed.

Meanwhile, Alaska Fish and Game biologist Larry Van Daele, six hundred miles away, submits his report. It will become the de-finitive document in the case, tying together elements of the Park Service incident reports, the State Troopers' investigation, and his own findings. Through roundabout channels—Alaska is, after all, a paradoxically small state—I obtain an unauthorized copy. Written in the cautious, unadorned prose of a biologist, yet remarkable for its grounded clarity, the report projects almost an eerie calm over the horror it describes:

> Part of Mr. Treadwell's body was found down a bear trail near camp, and parts of Ms. Huguenard's body were found in a fresh bear cache next to the tent. The tent was collapsed but not torn up. Bear-proof containers were strewn about, but did not appear to be tested by the bear. . . .

He goes on to observe that

> the audio ends with his sounds no longer evident and her screams continuing.

But there is a thread of laconic wit that runs through the narrative as well. For example, Van Daele notes that Fulton tried to walk up the knoll to camp "but was dissuaded by the bear." And, in his examination of the first bear's carcass, he dryly comments,

> There were no overt signs of recent injury other than the numerous bullet holes in the head and chest cavity.

The most significant part of the four-page report is the last section, simply entitled "Speculation About What May Have Happened." Like any good biologist, Van Daele is clearly uncomfortable relying on circumstantial evidence. He cautions,

> We will never know exactly what happened, and it is somewhat risky to speculate. My thoughts on this are just an effort to put the pieces together to the best of my ability. . . .

Van Daele points to an earlier videotape recovered from the Kaflia camp showing Treadwell on the knoll—the one where Treadwell tells the camera that they're safe here because he knows these bears. Another tape includes that footage of Amie hunkered in the brush with the female and cubs at arm's length. Then there are the journals recording earlier squabbles, frozen in time. One of Treadwell's last journal entries recounts a large adult male attacking one of his favorite females, not far from camp. He laments the punishment she took and wishes he could have gone to her rescue. While Van Daele is careful to qualify his interpretation as guesswork, he assembles the various fragments of evidence into a possible scenario.

There's a large, old bear in the immediate area of the Treadwell camp. The salmon run is fading, and it's getting late in the season. He's not starving, but his instincts tell him he needs to pack on more fat before denning. The fight with the female suggests the sort of testiness that's evident when food runs short. The bear walks past camp on the main trail on Sunday evening and, somehow encountering Treadwell, attacks. The bear leaves, as they often do when someone plays dead, but returns, maybe when he moves or Huguenard tries to help him. Van Daele rather safely surmises that "at this time, for some reason, the bear killed and ate him." Then he goes on to make the chilling suggestion about Huguenard's cries' resembling a predator call, which "may have prompted the bear to return and kill her."

Van Daele is at a loss when it comes to the key question— exactly why this particular bear not only attacked humans (virtually unheard of in the Katmai Park area) but engaged in predatory behavior. Mauling deaths from brown/grizzlies are rare enough in all of Alaska, averaging under one every two years over the past century. Predation is rarer still, to the point of anomaly; Van Daele later calls it, "for lack of a better term, a strange taboo that seems to exist in brown bear culture." In the entire history of the state, there are just six confirmed cases of *Ursus arctos* killing a person and consuming flesh (if cases from the lower forty-eight, Canada, Europe, and Asia are included, the numbers of course rise, but reflect the same extreme rarity of predatory behavior). In the light of this statistic, Van Daele is understandably reluctant to label the deaths of Treadwell and Huguenard as being the result of intentional stalking and killing for food. Rather, he speculates that the predation at Kaflia falls into the category of "opportunistic"—in other words, the attack was due to a chance encounter; sometime during the struggle, or perhaps after Treadwell was dead, the bear switched from its defensive-aggressive behavior, realized it had meat in front of it, and began to feed.

Though he stops short of making the call, Van Daele's implication regarding Huguenard's screams is that they triggered a predatory response—that the bear, already excited by the taste of blood, may have been stimulated by the cries to attack and kill her as food. This sort of escalating, switchover response from one mode to another is accepted by most bear-attack experts as an explanation for most cases where brown/grizzlies ended up eating people, not only in Alaska, but wherever the bears are found, including Canada and the lower forty-eight.

Incidentally, the Kaflia incident also may be an example of what's known as "surplus killing"—an animal in predatory mode killing more animals than it can eat at once. Again, Van Daele doesn't directly state this but he does suggest that the bear "cached [Huguenard's] body to be eaten later." An interesting further speculation (not Van Daele's) is that the bear's response to the rescue team—not a standard carcass-defense charge but a stealthy approach from behind, so quiet they didn't sense the animal until it was within several paces—was, as Fulton, Ellis, and Gilliland felt, stalking behavior. Perhaps to neutralize a threat to its kill, but it isn't unreasonable to interpret this as the same predatory intent bears sometimes show toward caribou or moose. Possibly the bear, on the basis of a successful hunt, had already come to recognize people as food.

Though the odds of being killed and eaten by a Katmai bear were statistically zero before October 5, Van Daele still concludes,

> I saw no evidence that this was anything other than a very isolated incident and not something that would have occurred in any other situation. I am confident that there is no strange bear behavior occurring in the area.

Instead, he lays the responsibility squarely at the feet of Timothy Treadwell—not for any specific behavior, but for his choice of campsite:

> The most evident discovery during the search was the preponderance of bear sign throughout the vicinity. Numerous fresh trails (both major thoroughfares and smaller spurs) crisscrossed the site. Salmon spawning areas surrounded it and thick alders surround the campsite. The camp was set up in such a way that bears wishing to traverse the area would have had to either wade in the lake or walk right next to the tent. A person could not have designed a more dangerous location to set up a camp.

There were simply too many chances for point-blank encounters between people and bears. In fact, the location made such dangerous, surprise contacts inevitable and exponentially raised the possibility of conflict. Bear-wise people who know Kaflia agree. Bruce Bartley, late-arriving member of the necropsy team, says, "If I were shipwrecked and that hill was the only land in sight, I wouldn't stay five minutes." My friend, wildlife photographer Tom Walker, who's been close to more Katmai bears than he can count over three decades and has walked the Kaflia knoll, tells me he wouldn't spend a night there for a million bucks. And when bear-viewing guide Gary Porter and I land at the site—Porter a man who sits unarmed on beaches with nervous tourists as bears stroll past, sometimes close enough to touch—he just shakes his head. "Not me," he says. "I wouldn't get a wink of sleep here, even with a loaded shotgun across my chest."

Yet Timothy Treadwell somehow managed to camp on that knoll, crisscrossed by a maze of ancient trails, weeks at a time, season after season, as the bears padded past. He learned to recognize dozens, knew their personalities and gave them names, passed by them on their tunneled trails, watched them fish and suckle their cubs, sometimes even swam and played with them. And he slept where perhaps no one else could or would have, wrapped in little more than his own faith. Whether you subscribe to biologist Sterling Miller, who once called Timothy Treadwell's longevity "a testament to the tolerance of the bears," or to bear conservation advocate Louisa Wilcox, who labeled Timothy a "bear whisperer," the fact of his singular determination stands free and clear above any dispute.

Equally thought provoking is the bear that circumstances label Treadwell's killer. When Van Daele first examined the big bear's mouth in the opening stages of the necropsy, he found incontrovertible evidence that this animal had had previous human contact, though of a quite different sort—a tattoo inside its lip, a simple number: 141. It had been placed there in May 1990 by a Fish and Game team led by internationally recognized bear biologists Sterling Miller (Van Daele's predecessor) and Dick Sellers. As part of the massive post–*Exxon Valdez* oil spill studies, this animal was captured by tranquilizer dart, inspected, marked with ear tags, tattooed, and released—just over the hill from Kaflia, in Kukak Bay. Chances are good, then, he was a local, rather than a transient, bear. He was estimated to weigh eight hundred pounds then, and examination of an extracted tooth (growth rings similar to those on a tree provide reliable measurement) gave an age of fifteen years—a mature male in his prime. He was then, as at the time of his death, in solid shape, without notable injury or scarring. The biologists rated his body condition a 3 (average) on a scale to 5, not unusual considering it was early in the season. As is normal, his ear tags wore away—so at the time of his death, he had no outwardly apparent distinguishing marks.

Bear 141 went on to live another thirteen years before he died at Kaflia. Over the twenty-eight years of his life, he wandered untold miles with the seasons, moving each year from his den in the high country to the coastal rye grass flats where he fed and mated each spring, and on to the salmon streams and berry fields of summer and fall, where he gorged, then wandered back up into the nearby mountains to dig his den and drift off to sleep. He spent at least half of each year curled against the cold in absolute solitude, drifting through dreams we can scarcely imagine as his body consumed itself, until the gnawing of his flesh stirred him awake. Nearly three decades of this—a rare survivor, a patriarch. How many young did this bear sire? How many still walk the country, expressions of his genetic message, shaped on the uncompromising lathe of centuries? The roots of his being stretch back into a far landscape where mammoths and ground sloths wandered, and men clad in skins stood watching, small on the skyline. No doubt his ancestors crossed paths with these puny beings. Some of these bears felt the sting of arrows and spears in their flanks, and those that survived learned fear.

Somehow that lesson was momentarily forgotten, perhaps overridden by the very impulses that had carried his species so far—the instinct to defend personal space and hard-won food. And the bitter irony is that his death resulted from the actions of someone who hoped, above all, to protect creatures like this bear from others of his own kind. It's almost certain Timothy Treadwell and this bear had known each other for years and passed each other on the beach at Kukak or the funneled trails of Kaflia. If so, Treadwell almost certainly gave the animal one of those whimsical names, spoke to it, even sang its praises. Could it have been one of the "killer bears" that terrorized him on and off over the years but still never harmed him? Or was it one of his favorites, or a total stranger? The tragedy reverberates—no less one for the bears than for Timothy and Amie.

Though the case seems open and shut, the debate over which bear killed Timothy Treadwell and Amie Huguenard is far from settled. No doubt the big male killed by Ellis and his team fed on the remains of both people. Matching its bite radius—the pattern and size of its toothmarks—to what was left of the victims was therefore a pointless exercise. And there was too little left of either body to determine exact details. But, coupled with the evidence of the tape, there's more than enough for Dr. Fallico of the state medical examiner's office to establish the official cause of death as "blunt trauma"—a brutally telling phrase in itself—inflicted by a brown bear. The question remains: which bear? There's compelling evidence pointing to the big male, and an equally plausible argument supporting a different killer.

Katmai bear expert Dr. Tom Smith, for one, believes that another bear probably killed Treadwell and Huguenard. He points out that under normal circumstances, big, old males almost always go to great lengths to avoid contact with people (one of the reasons, by the way, that they live to such great age and size). Only a handful of the forty-seven—formerly forty-five—confirmed brown/grizzly-caused human fatalities recorded over the past century in Alaska were caused by older males. In violent bear–human encounters, females with cubs and subadults were commonly involved. The females were invariably defending their cubs against the sudden appearance of an intruder; the "teenage" bears were displaying the rash aggressiveness or bold curiosity of youth. Smith reasons it's likely that one of these younger animals killed Treadwell and Huguenard in a defensive-aggressive attack. Perhaps Amie was killed as she attempted to protect Timothy. Then the larger bear happened along, discovered carrion, and began to feed, as bears will. From here on, his bold response to humans was simply a classic case of carcass defense—one of those instances where any bear, certainly a dominant male, seldom backs down. This scenario neatly resolves both the rarity of human predation by brown bears and the statistical improbability of a large, older male attacking humans without provocation.

An interesting theory, and one that everyone involved in the case considers plausible. Larry Van Daele is the first to admit that the version of events contained in his report is—as he carefully indicated by the title of that section—speculation. It might even account for the strangely aggressive behavior of the second, smaller bear that was shot. Maybe that bear wasn't just an innocent bystander but the killer after all.

Another piece of circumstantial evidence that might support the idea of a smaller bear being involved in the actual attacks is the amount of time on the tape (around four minutes) that Treadwell survived. As Smith points out, a thousand-pound bear like 141 is capable of delivering a single swift, killing bite or swat. And in the two most recent, well-documented cases of human fatality involving a very large bear, that's exactly what occurred. The first was an Alaskan seismic worker in 1999 who, with headphones on, preoccupied by work, stumbled on a big male in his den. The animal, clearly reacting defensively, bit him just twice—once on the arm and once on the head—and then ran off. As Smith points out, it doesn't sound that bad, until you discover that the second bite removed the top of the skull at eyebrow level. In the case of Russian bear expert Vitaly Nikolayenko, who was killed by a huge male in December 2003 in Kamchatka after he apparently followed it into a dense thicket, the result was similar: a massive, crushing swat to the skull. Then the bear fled. One could make the case that bear 141, bad teeth and all, would have killed Tim Treadwell in similar rapid fashion. But to claim that, or anything else for a certainty, would be crawling too far out on a slender limb.

People who know Kaflia and its bears firsthand have their own information to add, and it's not stuff that makes its way into the final reports. Tom Walters of Katmai Wilderness Lodge says, "Everyone knew there was a bad old bear up there at Kaflia. Some of the guides called him Satan."

Willy Fulton, who often took bear-viewing clients to Lower Kaflia Lake, says flatly, "I knew the bear that ate Timothy and Amie. I'd known him for years and I recognized him that day, alive and dead. Timothy knew him, too, and was scared of him. So was I. That bear didn't like people and he let you know it." He was easy to identify: a big, rangy bear with a scraggly coat, a pendulous lower lip, and ears that skewed in different directions—the right tagged over, the left facing outward, probably the result of an old fighting injury. He was so dominant that other bears steered clear of him; he kept his distance from people but nonetheless expressed his intolerance through body language and stares. Early on in his Kaflia days, Timothy called the bear Mr. Vicious, and in fact wrote that name on a picture of the animal he gave to Fulton. Later on, Timothy amended the name to The Big Red Machine, perhaps in an attempt to wax less judgmental. But Fulton says Timothy's assessment of the bear's essential nature remained the same. Timothy gave another image of the bear to Jeff Slaughter, a mutual friend of his and Fulton's, jokingly telling Slaughter, who was a bear hunter, that if he wanted to shoot a bear, that was the one he should go after. This from a man who loved bears above all. "Pretty ironic," muses Fulton, "how that worked out." He himself, the only person who knew the bear and saw him both alive and dead, has a clear opinion about what happened at Kaflia. "I respect bear biologists and what they do," Fulton says. "I'm no expert on bears. I just go look at them sometimes. But my common sense tells me that that bear was the killer all the way. Personally, I'm not sorry he's dead. Not one bit."

Matthias Breiter, the photographer and biologist who was camped one bay away, concurs with Fulton on the big bear's identity. "Timmy, Willy, and I all knew that bear. That was a bear who would stare you down. Timmy had problems with him." Breiter makes the point that while ursine tolerance is the rule along the coast, a few big males see people as competition and respond to them as a big bear would toward another—a fact which Timothy knew well, one that shaped his actions. "Timmy was by no means a careless person around bears," says Breiter. "He knew which ones to approach and which ones weren't safe. He knew there was real danger, but he also thought it was relatively small and manageable. Bears were his whole life, his obsession, so he wasn't going to change or back down."

"Timmy," Breiter continues, "counted on things being always the same with bears. And they aren't. I see the circumstances of the attack entirely in the unusual conditions on the coast last fall." His theory is supported by what the investigators read in Timothy's and Amie's journals, and the last satellite phone call Willy received from Timothy, pointing to an incredible level of bear activity in the days preceding their deaths. Breiter adds that the more time he spends among bears, the less he's sure of them. "If someone asks me why a bear did something, I'll say I don't know. Years ago I would have known."

German filmmaker Andreas Kieling also recognizes the big bear from pictures I e-mail him, taken by Willy Fulton the previous year at Kaflia; quite definitely, he says, that's the bear he knew as "Baba"—or "Bubba," after Forrest Gump's slack-lipped sidekick. He points to not only the dangling lower lip, but a cyst at the outside corner of the right eye as positive identifying marks. Kieling had returned to Kaflia in 2004 and noted the old bear, a fixture in the area for years, was inexplicably missing. But he didn't make the connection between that absence and the Treadwell incident until now. When I explain what Fulton and Breiter had to say about the bear's menacing temperament and Treadwell's own label of "Mr. Vicious," Kieling is surprised. That's not the way he saw the bear at all. But yes, he's sure we're talking about the same bear. If Fulton says that's the one that ate Timothy, it's also Bubba. Kieling tells me to see for myself—in his film *Grizzly Encounters* (previously released as *Searching for Brown Giants*). There's a sequence where he's fishing for pinks at the mouth of the Kaflia stream; he has two fish on the bank, with Bubba lurking behind in the brush. When the big bear strolls up inside of ten feet, obviously hoping for a hand-out, Kieling, unarmed, shakes his fishing pole and tells the bear to scram, and Bubba—aka Mr. Vicious, the Big Red Machine, and Satan, not to mention Bear 141—shambles off like a disappointed old dog. Watching, you get the impression the whole scene was staged, with more than one take. I run the tape back several times; not only the lower lip and cyst, but the skewed ears are distinctive. I, too, am sure it's the same bear. And no, Kieling says, he never heard Timothy complain about that bear. As far as he knows, Bubba was never, ever aggressive. He hints that Timothy may have been helping the drama along just a bit, as he was so fond of doing.

Kieling's version of the bear is a curious wrinkle in the story, but one that can't be dismissed. No doubt the bear that he saw as gentle also acted in an aggressive, quite possibly predatory manner toward Fulton and the recovery team. Given that, it certainly still could have been Timothy's and Amie's killer. Or not. As a final grace note, add in Larry Van Daele's judgment, informed by decades of experience. He doesn't think the bear in Fulton's pictures is the same bear he dissected at Kaflia. Then again, he allows that bloating and disfigurement made a positive identification difficult. In the end, all the varying perspectives only add to the mystery.

Fulton has something to add about the smaller dead bear too. He was prepping his plane for loading when the shooting broke out, and arrived in the aftermath. In the fading light, he lifted the animal's head and, for a second time, looked into the dead eyes of a bear he knew. But this time there was no grim satisfaction—instead, an inner sigh and a shrug. The luxuriant, coffee-toned coat, petite facial features, and claws left little doubt in his mind: It was the bear Timothy called Baby Letterman, named in honor of the talk show host. "He was a friendly little guy," says Fulton. "He'd come right up and sit practically next to you. I'll bet he was just coming over to say hello and to see what the fuss was all about in Tim's camp." A killer? "No way," says Willy Fulton.

I study the pictures he took the previous summer at lower Kaflia. In one, Baby Letterman—an incongruous name given his appearance—stands at the water's edge, a two-year-old fluff-ball. He's one of those bears that seems as long as they are tall, his face growing straight out of his body, his round ears perked up. He stands frozen in time, one paw raised, water glistening on his claws, eyes bright as they seem to peer straight into my own. The light collar of fur around his neck is haloed with sunlight. If he can survive another year or two, chances are he'll live to see twenty or more. He'll quadruple in size, and take his place among the dominant bears of the Maze.

In Fulton's other image, Bear 141 stands in nearly the same spot at the creek mouth, as battered and homely as the little bear was beautiful. His body is gaunt despite its bulk; a purplish scar mars one sun-bleached, ragged flank. The skewed ears, drooping lip, and all but toothless lower gum offer testament to nearly three hard decades, and to the sheer vitality, the incredible force of life, that beats within that cavernous chest. His eyes, cast in shadow, are fixed in a cold, wild stare. I think of Oedipus or Lear, beaten down but imperious, daring the world to do its worst.

In the end, any of the various scenarios and explanations offered for Timothy and Amie's deaths are possible, singly or in combination. Of course, exactly what happened at Kaflia or why will never be known—though there's little doubt the story will be retold around campfires, bars, and boardrooms, discussed, argued, and altered until it passes into the pantheon of Alaskan mythology. Aside from the stylized, vague language that suits such tales, though, no one will ever say much about the two dead bears. At this moment, their faces are all I see.

Monkey Pajamas

Gary and Jeannie Porter and I banked inland on the sunlit afternoon of October 10, continuing our journey in the wake of Timothy's death, away from Kaflia and the torn remains of the bears, through a craggy, glacier-draped pass, and a funnel of austere peaks where the first snow lay spackled on dark rock. Then a land of sparsely forested valleys, crystal rivers and lakes, that in turn was replaced by a volcanic moonscape—the Valley of Ten Thousand Smokes. First came the Novarupta Crater, site of the massive 1912 blast that remains one of the most violent single volcanic eruptions in recorded history. Then we passed low over a mountainside where fumaroles vented steam into the air; shortly after the eruption there had been thousands of such "smokes," which gave the place its name. Beyond lay a vast, undulating plain of volcanic ash, the Valley itself, which more resembled a stretch of Arabian desert than anything Alaskan. Once-lush forests of birch, balsam poplar, and spruce had stood there, now blasted flat and buried, perhaps to be unearthed and marveled over by geologists in some future world. Across the face of this desolation the River Lethe carved its own stark canyon. The valley gave way to a line of trees and brush; the world became itself again, and beyond, the blue-tinged glacial waters of thirty-five-mile-long Naknek Lake.

*   *   *

Brooks Camp is by far the most popular destination in Katmai National Park. At peak season (mid-June through mid-August) up to three hundred visitors a day, carried by a small air force of float-planes, make the pilgrimage to watch one of the great wildlife spectacles in the world: dozens of brown bears gathered to feed on a living tide of spawning salmon. The viewing area, perched on an isthmus between Naknek Lake and the much smaller Lake Brooks, is supported by a nearby lodge and campground. Thousands of yards of trails and elevated boardwalks lead to two viewing platforms overlooking the lower pool and the upper falls of the Brooks River, which connects the two lakes. Squads of park rangers preside over this traffic jam of bears, fish, and people, enforcing a protocol designed to minimize conflict. The prime directive is that bears have the right of way—with the important exception of the guardrailed and gated viewing platforms, large enough to hold seventy-five visitors each. Any bruin attempting to enter these is immediately discouraged. Of equal importance are regulations designed to prohibit bears from associating people with food in any way.

And despite dozens of close-range encounters between bears and humans daily—sometimes just short of physical contact—only two bear-caused injuries have been recorded over five decades. Both amounted to ursine love taps—a nipped hand and a punctured buttock. Considering that most visitors are tourists with virtually no bear experience, the safety record is truly remarkable, a testament to several factors: the incredible tolerance of the bears; the soundness of a time-tested management plan; and an occasional wink from lady luck.

Brooks, like its sister to the northeast, the McNeil River State Game Sanctuary, is one of those magical places where brown bears gather in staggering numbers to take advantage of a rich food source—spawning salmon concentrated at a waterfall. If we want to wax anthropomorphic, as we're so often tempted to do when describing bear behavior, we'd say a truce was in effect. Or perhaps some sort of cooperative understanding that dealing with a crowd and sharing is in everyone's best interest. On some genetic level, that may be a reasonable, if unscientific, explanation.

In the complex, dynamic, highly structured world of bear society, the rationale is less romantic. Basically, the most dominant, aggressive bears claim whatever feeding spot they want, usually without so much as a growl, instead relying on subtle physical signals—staring, lowering the head, or ignoring a competitor. Bears of lesser rank either wait their turn, or move to a slightly different feeding area, and so on down to the bottom rungs, occupied by adolescents and younger females. But there's plenty to go around. If there is a disagreement about rank, or if a sow feels her cubs are threatened, there may be a row—still often more bluster and threat than actual contact. Despite appearances, a fairly high level of stress runs right beneath the surface at all times, and the peace depends on all bears watching each other carefully and reacting to slight cues.

In rare instances, neither bear backs down. The ensuing battle can be spectacular, accompanied by savage roars, clashing jaws, gouts of fur, fat, and blood flying, and horrific injuries. In extreme cases, the loser is killed on the spot and may be eaten by the victor—a case of opportunistic predation. And there are certainly all-out attempts by large males to kill and eat cubs, sometimes with appalled viewers as witnesses. Whether motivated by an acquired taste or a genetically programmed response to control population, certain bears seem to specialize in such cannibalistic behavior.

Generally, though, such aggregations of bears seem—and are— remarkably peaceful. In cases where the food source is both seasonal and predictable, as it is at Brooks, the knowledge of the place is ancient, passed down across centuries through generations of bears. Females teach their cubs to find food, locate resting places, behave properly, and to avoid certain bears. And last but not least, cubs learn that people are of no consequence. Each bear grows into adulthood with a cognitive map of the area, knowledge of the bears that share it, and of the strange, two-legged things that stand watching. And though social rank is in constant flux (young bears grow larger as older ones fade and die; fights and injuries shuffle the deck), the system is inherently stable provided one factor remains constant—the force that brought this mob of inherently antisocial creatures together in the first place: food.

So it is that the crowds of people on the viewing platforms at Brooks Falls, oohing and ahing, jabbering in a myriad of languages and brandishing the menacing dark eyes of telephoto lenses, are totally ignored by the bears below. They know, through years of contact or, in the case of cubs, the examples of their mothers, that these strange creatures are neither food nor threat. In this and other protected areas like McNeil River, where no hunting is allowed, bears clearly become safely habituated to human presence over time—provided the contact is predictable and managed for minimal impact. Even with the runaway escalation of bear viewing in Katmai, one's tempted to conclude that all is well. Bear numbers are stable or on the rise, and the visitors come and go.

This particular day at Brooks, the lower viewing platform is all but empty. The lodge and campsite are closed, the tourists long gone. So are most of the bears and salmon. A Park Service biologist peers into her spotting scope, observing a half-dozen animals, making cryptic, coded comments to an assistant who dutifully jots them down and snaps photos. Each bear has an assigned letter, each behavior a number. Typical scientific fieldwork—businesslike, mechanical bean-counting, with little space for chitchat, let alone emotional projections and interactions of the sort Timothy indulged in. Our presence is acknowledged, then all but ignored by the biologist, whom Gary knows. The assistant, a young, outdoorsy woman, is more outgoing.

"Why don't you two get off this stand and walk around out there, where you really can learn something?" Gary grins, but I can tell he's only half joking. Two hundred yards upstream, hindquarters sprawled in the icy river, front end hauled out in the grass, an enormous male bear dozes in the sun, his sun-bleached fur caught in stunning sidelight. He's attended by an entourage of gulls picking at the scraps of a coho he's left on the bank. The bear seems to be struggling and failing to stay awake, sliding into hibernation right before our eyes. Watching the biologist, intent on her task, I wonder what the official code for catching a snooze might be.

Closer in, a medium-sized female cautiously leads her two grown cubs into the river, right below the platform. She's clearly more concerned about a different male off to her left in the brush than she is about us. She and her cubs are here to scrounge dead and dying cohos that drift along the pool's bottom. While far less preferable than fresh fish, which are bursting with eggs and fatty oils, they make a fine, easily gathered, late-season meal. The female wades along, ducking her head underwater from time to time, and within minutes has her first salmon. Clutching it between her front paws, she deftly strips and eats the choice parts— brain and skin—and leaves the carcass for the mewing crowd of gulls. The cubs, in their third season, seem to have the technique down, and are finding their own fish. But being cubs, they get distracted and engage in the sort of shenanigans viewers love to watch—play fighting and (you'd swear) mugging for the camera.

At times it's impossible not to read human emotions into their faces. Meanwhile, their mother is continuing the lesson of where to eat safely—close to the viewing stand, in the shadow of people, where traffic from dominant males is less frequent. They'll carry this lesson for a lifetime—and, if they're female, teach it to their own cubs. This tendency of habituated females to use humans as protective buffers for their cubs, and even to leave their young near groups of viewers, is hardly the magic of a bear whisperer;

it's a frequently reported phenomenon not only along the Katmai Coast, but wherever similar conditions exist.

Upstream, the big male is in stately slow motion. Drifting along the bank with the current, so buoyed up by his stored blanket of fat that he scarcely has to paddle, he watches salmon eddy past with the air of a full-bellied Thanksgiving diner eyeing a last piece of pie. Apparently even a bear's late-season gluttony, upon which its survival depends, has its limits. Watching through the lens, snapping an occasional image, I forget about actual distance—and am startled, when I lift my eye, to find the bear twenty feet away. His head is so enormous that his eyes and ears seem minuscule, ill-fitting parts somehow borrowed from a much smaller bear. He lazily shakes the water from his fur and, just for a moment, looks upward at me. I can read no menace or curiosity in his expression—just an undeniable, overwhelming presence that dismisses my puny being, let alone any notion of my own superiority.

Standing here on this platform with the autumn sun slanting in, the grass golden and the river tinged with blue chrome, the silence broken only by the cry of gulls, the swirl of fish, and the occasional grunt of a feeding bear, I found myself once again unable to grasp the fact of Tim and Amie's deaths. Though the printed notices and stench at Kaflia, and physical contact with the ground there, had made the tragedy briefly concrete, it was again slipping into abstraction—something that happened to someone else, far away. If looking into the eyes of this great bear before me, and brushing close to three others, all inside of two hours, hadn't fixed the reality in my mind, what would? Even my mad dash down the hill remained surreal and disconnected, though the crusted blood inside my lip and the throb of my ankle insisted on the truth of events, and on my body's twig-snapping frailty. It's said we aren't able to dream our own deaths; we waken the instant before the fatal blow. But in the end, coming to grips with death—any death—

is a personal matter. If we truly own its shape and taste, it becomes, in a sense, our own. And so I stood on the lower platform at Brooks River, wanting only light and life.

Gary nudged me. Ellis, the ranger we were looking for, wasn't here. He was at Park Headquarters in King Salmon, forty miles away. And the chief back-country ranger for the park, Missy Epping, with whom I'd spoken on the phone two days before, was there too. If I wanted to interview anyone and still get back to Homer before nightfall, we'd better get going. While I fumbled with collapsing my tripod and putting away gear, trying to watch the bears at the same time and meanwhile attempting to set my mind straight of tangled thoughts, Gary and Jeannie strode ahead, leaving me to peg-leg along in the rear, on an ankle that now felt as if a tennis ball had been surgically implanted in the joint. The gate to the viewing stand was, I noted, gouged with claw and tooth marks. Walking the trail to the lakeshore, where the plane and the Porters waited, I followed a set of fresh bear tracks, the claw marks crisp in the sand.

Another half hour of flying, this time over rolling tundra hills with patchy timber, brought us to King Salmon, population fifteen hundred. Spread along the banks of the Naknek River, it's a jumping-off point for sport hunters, fishermen, and Katmai Park visitors. The outsized airport and runway is a vestige of Cold War era, when a wing of Air Force interceptors was stationed here, to challenge marauding Russian pilots to games of supersonic tag. Though connected to the outside world by daily jet service, and definitely a town rather than a village, there's an undeniable sense that King Salmon is an outpost, drifting on the edge of an immense ocean of land. The nearest highway is roughly two hundred miles away.

We pull into a local flying service's floatplane dock, where Gary has permission to tie up for a couple of hours. As is common in the Alaska bush, people are relaxed and friendly. A pretty young woman in the Branch River Air office smiles, offers us coffee, and asks what brings us to town. Without going into much detail, I mention Treadwell's name. Her lip curls into an immediate sneer.

"Oh," she says. "The dork." It's a viewpoint that seems widespread in these parts. Asked if she ever met him, the woman shrugs shakes her head.

A few phone calls from the office come up empty. It's Saturday, of course, and the Park Service is closed. I figured in a town this size it would be easy to find individual listings, but neither Ellis nor Epping is in the book. There are tracts of housing for federal employees, the woman suggests. I could try knocking on a few doors. We hitch a ride to town; while Gary and Jeannie grab a sandwich at one of the two local restaurants, I wander into a block of prefab houses, pick one at random, and ask directions. No luck. But as I stand in the road, scratching my head, a pickup truck slows. The man rolls down a window, gives a friendly smile, and asks who I'm looking for.

"Well, Missy's my wife," he offers. "I can give you a ride to our place, but I'm not sure she'll talk to you. You'll have to ask her yourself."

A mile down the road, we pull into another set of neat prefabs. I follow the guy through a doorway, and he calls upstairs, announcing my presence. Despite the bright blue day—an anomaly for southwest Alaska at any time of year, let alone autumn—the blinds are all pulled, and my eyes struggle to adjust to the dim interior.

"I can't come down," calls a strained voice from the second floor. "I'm in my pajamas." I identify myself, and haltingly explain that I've come a thousand miles. I'd called a couple days before, remember? She'd promised that we could talk.

"I'm sorry, I just can't do this," the voice continues, but I can hear the halting pad of feet on stairs. The outline of a person appears on the landing. I fumble for words—something about how I understand, without being quite clear what I'm claiming to grasp. I repeat that I've come a long way, then sigh and turn to go.

"I'm in my monkey pajamas, I can't talk now, I can't. . . ." she says, but continues to move down the stairs, one at a time, until we end up as bookends on the living room couch.

To put it mildly, Missy Epping is out of uniform. She is, as advertised, clad in flannel pajamas emblazoned with what seem to be minute semblances of Curious George. Her hair is askew, her eyes red rimmed. She's the head back-country ranger for Katmai National Park—a person who's traveled the jagged spill of the Katmai Coast by inflatable skiff, plane, and on foot for years, a competent, tough outdoorswoman. She is, by virtue of seniority and position, the lead incident ranger for the Treadwell case. But at this point, professional involvement has clearly been overwhelmed; I'm not talking to an official representative of the United States Park Service, but to a person struggling with shock and loss. I put away my notebook and don't even think of bringing out my recorder.

For an hour we sit in the dim light, trading information and sounding out opinions, asking questions back and forth. Though perhaps I come across as more confident, I don't feel that way. Neither of us has any real answers, or is able to reassure the other. I feel more like an ill-prepared grief counselor than a writer on assignment. She offers to show me pictures taken at the site, and though it's the sort of thing I came for, I shake my head.

"I know he did things that were wrong—I know he got too close to bears, took chances, did things that were against regulations," Missy murmurs. "But he helped us out too. He reported things he saw and gave us advice. And besides, he was my friend. We sat around the fire and laughed together. He was my friend. . . ."

Her voice trails off, and she stares out at nothing. I decide it's time for me to go.

Joel Ellis, the ranger who led the rescue and recovery missions, happens to live next door. I rap knuckles and wait, but get no answer. I'm out of time anyway. The afternoon sun continues to spill down, and the air is unnaturally warm and still. On the two-mile walk back to the plane, my ankle is doing its best impression of a ball and chain. I'd figured on catching a ride.

Twenty-five sweaty minutes later, I'm still stumping along the roadside. I've walked right through the heart of King Salmon and out the main road past the airport on a Saturday afternoon, and not one vehicle has passed. Finally, a pickup truck full of workers slows, and I clamber over the tailgate. It beats walking the last quarter mile. Gary and Jeannie are waiting. We have two hours to fly, and only an hour and a half of light—normally no big deal, but we're landing on a lake back in Homer, not a lighted runway.

The ride back is spectacular—sky, earth, and water glowing in incandescent shades of pink, orange, and red that have no earthly name. Just out of King Salmon, as we skim along, following the contours of the land, the tundra, carpeted in blueberry and dwarf birch, seems on fire. We indulge Gary's second passion to watching bears—spotting moose—and he circles an enormous bull in a clump of alder. It's near the world record, he claims, and I see little reason to doubt him. Farther on, a distant volcano is lit by the sunset, cast in such sharp relief it seems a perfect miniature, close enough to reach out and touch. And as we roar over a snowbound pass, so low it seems the Beaver's floats might furrow the drifts, a lone caribou bull stands, up to its brisket in snow, hoarfrost coating his antlers, the steam of his breath pulsing out into the cold. It's one of those visions that flash past, but remain fused in memory. A thousand feet lower, the world is still green, food available, the walking easier—yet here he is. I recall an apocryphal Zen riddle from Hemingway, about a frozen leopard found high on the slopes of Kilimanjaro. What was the leopard seeking at that altitude? And suddenly I wish Timothy Treadwell were here beside me, leaning over to see for himself. And I want to ask him the same question.

A Mighty Lightning Rod

Far from bush Alaska, the story forges its own trail. Of course, the AP picks it up, and thanks to Timothy Treadwell's Malibu connection, the *L.A. Times* provides both extensive coverage and commentary. The editorial slant is generally less than positive. Treadwell's friends and supporters, especially Grizzly People cofounder Jewel Palovak, provide staunch, if not always effective, counterfire. Palovak makes the statement that Treadwell's being killed and eaten is "the culmination of his life's work"—a comment that is pounced on by USGS research ecologist Tom Smith, among others.

"Culmination?" Smith asks. "If you consider yourself a friend to bears, and want to project a positive image about them, how is getting two bears and yourself and your girlfriend killed a culmination of your life's work?"

Captain Paul Watson of the Sea Shepherd Society, who knew Treadwell from a voyage to northern Canada to film and protect baby harp seals, makes a vehement response to a blunt anti-Treadwell piece by *Anchorage Daily News* columnist Mike Doogan. In a lengthy and rambling e-mail retort, Watson intones,

> Were you aware, Mr. Doogan, that Tim and Amie were
> scheduled to have left Katmai but had to stay to keep an

eye on a poacher in the area? Are you aware, Mr. Doogan, that this case is still under investigation and all the facts are not yet in? There is the possibility that the offending bear may have been wounded. And if so, by who or what? Like Dian Fossey, it may turn out that it was a poacher that brought down Tim and Amie by wounding a bear. We don't yet know all the facts. What we do know is that this bear acted contrary to any bear in Timothy's thirteen years of experience and this suggests that there is more here than meets the eye.

The notion that poachers were somehow involved is a persistent rumor among Treadwell supporters. How better to explain, both to themselves and the world, the unexpected horror of their champion being killed by his animal friends? The bear must have been wounded; perhaps Timothy was even trying to help the bear when he was killed. Maybe, too, he and Amie were victims of poachers' bullets, not a bear at all. And from there the stories soar out into the thin air of fantasy. Poachers air-dropped a rogue bear in the camp area; or they baited bears in with food or alluring scents strewn around the camp, driving the animals into a killing frenzy—theories so farfetched that even Jewel Palovak, Timothy's staunchest ally, offers them up as examples of good-hearted but wrongheaded spin control.

"There are a lot of people that I love dearly that are defending him," she says, "but not all of them are thinking clearly."

On the other side of the ideological fence, a growing postmortem lynch mob of actual and self-styled outdoorsmen (not a politically incorrect term here, since it's an accurate report of gender) takes sardonic, even gleeful satisfaction in the deaths of Treadwell and Huguenard. The commentary ranges from the mainstream hook-and-bullet crowd, as personified by Thomas McIntyre's column in *Field and Stream* magazine (subtitled "Brown bears were his life; he was their lunch") to voluminous assaults in Internet Web logs—

arguably the first time such a venue has been used to comment on a fatal bear mauling. The January 2004 interchange on Free Republic.com, labeled as "a conservative news forum," is typical of the more restrained attacks. A sample of the dozens of aliased blog entries:

> Con artist, crook, imposter, he became more than an enigma in death, he became what a bear does in the woods as well.

> [That] Treadwell was killed doing what he loved did not surprise many of those who knew him. Sort of the same way people contract AIDS.

> If Timmy Treadwell doesn't prove that dope fries your brain, what will it take?

Some of the cybercommentary posted by anonymous bloggers ranges far beyond this, into the downright vicious and obscene— crude sexual comments aimed at Huguenard to pronouncements against the "uneducated, effeminate, silly, wreckless [sic], druggie, flake, idiot loser who thought he was some sort of new age Dr. Dolittle but is now know as 'Steaming Grizzlyshit.' " Perhaps the most virulent attack (including the preceding quote and a number of far cruder sexual and scatalogical comments) seems to have been generated by an anonymous British animal rights activist, who criticizes Treadwell for "harassing" and "patronizing" wildlife. The writer fumes, "Treadwell killed these bears! He didn't care about bears! He harassed them! Now they . . . are dead. . . . These animals should have been respected and left alone." Hunters and those most opposed to killing animals for sport are ironically united in their criticism.

Neither is the National Park Service safe from the outcry following the incident; Treadwell supporters and animal lovers launch a spate of calls and messages, some of them approaching what Katmai ranger Missy Epping calls "hate mail" for what some consider the rangers' unwarranted killing of the two bears. Even the Alaska Department of Fish and Game, which was in no way involved in the shooting, receives angry calls and e-mail, blaming them for destroying, without cause, the animals they were supposed to protect. In fact, the bears were technically in the jurisdiction of the National Park Service.

The Grizzly People Web site is of course barraged by e-mail, over eight hundred messages in the several weeks following Timothy's death. Roughly half of it is negative or mean spirited—a request for a public appearance by Treadwell's corpse, for example. There are also hundreds of heartfelt expressions of condolence, and praise for Timothy's brave sacrifice while protecting bears.

The Treadwell fallout pervades places you wouldn't normally think of—Amazon.com, for one. Here, a witty but vicious prankster writes an online review of a forthcoming book ostensibly by Treadwell—a cookbook for bears, offering such recipes as "quadricep tartar, served on the bone."

While the response is national, even international, the collective reaction of Alaskans, which would be easy to lump into the general anti-Treadwell landslide, is in fact unique on several counts. They feel they have a personal stake in this. As far as they're concerned, this happened on their turf, with their bears. Even if the majority of Alaskans live semiurban lives tied to shopping malls, SUVs, and foraging at McDonald's, they think of themselves as closer to nature and generally more savvy in the outdoors than their lower-forty-eight counterparts. And as a whole, they're probably right, even though most Alaskans, when it comes right down to it, don't know diddly about bears. Having seen a few, fished near some, or even plugged one with your .338 magnum doesn't mean you have any idea of what they're about. Still, their sense of ownership and knowledge gives them, they feel, special right to comment.

Alaskans as a group also pride themselves on their independence, to the point where many consider themselves, on at least an unconscious level, to be as separate politically and ideologically from the rest of America (which they collectively lump into the term "Outside") as they are geographically. The notion that someone from that netherworld has pulled a double-dumb-ass on their turf causes an outburst of righteous, proprietary anger. Such behavior amounts to disrespecting the land and, by extension, Alaska itself. Memories of Chris McCandless, the hapless pilgrim glorified in Jon Krakauer's best-seller *Into the Wild*, come flooding back. Not too many Alaskans liked what he did or stood for, either, and some Outsider grabbed the controls and made him into a hero. Here we go again, they grumble. It's only a matter of time.

There's another, more subtle undercurrent to the vehement reaction to Timothy's death, which seems more subliminal than overt—and Alaskans probably don't have the market cornered on this one. Timothy Treadwell, by virtue of being killed and eaten by a bear as a direct product of risky (most casual commentators would say foolish) behavior, becomes a negative archetype of some sort. *Og get eaten by bear. Him stupid,* the Gary Larsen cartoon caption might read. We all remember, on some level, buried deep in the double helix of our being, a time when such mishaps were more commonplace, and an instrument of natural selection. Rather than pity, we feel a vague disdain for Timothy Treadwell's unfavorable phenotype—which we wouldn't, if he'd died in a socially more acceptable risky manner, such as in a NASCAR wreck or while climbing Everest.

*   *   *

In short, Timothy Treadwell in death becomes a mighty lightning rod crackling with emotion—one that encompasses an amazing spectrum of human attitudes and ideologies. To some, Timothy is a martyr; to others, a fool; some cast him as a cynical, self-serving narcissist, even a menace to wildlife. All the same man, the same basic set of circumstances. If nothing else, the death of Timothy Treadwell reflects the extent to which we project our own beliefs upon the universe. But more so, the sometimes shocking vehemence and sheer volume of response indicates the depth of our profound, ambivalent connection to bears—and to the deep-rooted fear we carry of being not only attacked but eaten by a beast so much like ourselves.

Standing alone at the center of this vortex is Jewel Palovak. Given Treadwell's long-standing disconnection from both his family and his past, she is the "next of kin" the authorities contact, and the one who makes arrangements for the cremation of Timothy's remains, and the recovery of his personal effects. She also fills the role of his oldest friend, and (as cofounder of Grizzly People) his closest professional associate—the spokesperson everyone wants to mine for a sound bite. From the moment the story first broke she's been inundated by strangers who all want something from her. And I'm just one more in the line. Reluctant to intrude, I don't even attempt to call for several weeks; and even then it feels like an imposition. I'm also unsure of what sort of person she might be—a flake? A crystal hugger? It turns out, when we finally speak over the phone in November 2003, a month after the tragedy, that she's relaxed, honest, intelligent, well spoken, and, considering the circumstances, remarkably focused. Within a matter of minutes, I feel at ease; an interview becomes a friendly conversation—one that goes on for nearly two hours, then continues for an equal duration the next morning.

"When I got that first phone call, I almost got on the next plane to Alaska, to fly up and see the remains. Then I thought, what good would that do?" She sighs and says she can't remember much from that first week. She recalls the TV studio lights, two interviews at least, but can't remember a thing she said. No doubt some things she'd like to take back. The shock—the disbelief and numbness—still hasn't worn off.

The whole thing's ironic, she tells me. The timing. Just a day before Timothy was scheduled for pickup. I reply that yes, if he'd left Kaflia a day earlier, he and Amie would still be alive.

"That's true," she replies, "but I mean if the *attack* had happened a couple of days earlier, Timothy would have just disappeared." People would have come looking for him, she explains, and no doubt found signs of predation, but the bear would have finished off the bodies and moved on, disappeared into the brush, indistinguishable from any of a dozen or more bears wandering the Kaflia area. If Timothy could have written the script, that's what should have happened. But as it was, Willie Fulton was called and showed up on time, setting in motion the aborted rescue and the killing of the two bears.

"Timothy would have felt just terrible," Jewel says, "if he'd known that two bears would die because of him . . . those bears became his family." Especially, she adds, given his own estrangement from his parents. The connection Timothy felt, she said, surely crossed the boundaries between species.

I bring up the negative press and hate mail. "I just don't understand the level of hatred, the meanness . . ." She trails off. She's especially appalled by the vehement reactions of so many Alaskans, including columnists like Craig Medred and Mike Doogan of the *Anchorage Daily News*. I allow that while most Alaskans do seem downright negative when they hear Treadwell's name, not everyone feels that way.

Then there's the issue of the nearly unanimous condemnation by bear biologists. Jewel freely admits that Timothy was no scientist, and didn't pretend to be. But again she's bitter that he was given so little of a chance. Someone could have acted as a mentor. All those hours in the field with the bears, those pages and pages of notes on behavior and genealogy, the years of knowledge he carried in his head—he had so much to offer. What stings most is that so few bear scientists (Dr. Stephen Stringham a notable exception) took Timothy seriously. And now they never will.

In the background, as Jewel and I speak, I hear someone knocking and entering. Far to the south, in Malibu, a friend is returning a kayak. Jewel explains to this person that she's on the phone—*again*—with some reporter, and I can hear her voice change tone, start to fray. Hand over the phone, she's half-shouting about something, and it's obvious I'm part of the problem. Look, I tell her, I should be going. I'm sorry.

Jewel fights a brief battle for self-control, then teeters off the edge. She's sorry too, she half-shouts, her voice rising and breaking. Timothy's dead, and everyone seems to be tearing at his corpse. She's struggling to hold herself together, to respond with dignity, to protect his memory. Day after day, she's been stumbling along, exhausted. And there seems to be no end in sight. The words pour out of her in a torrent. I don't have a thing to say, beyond my own awkward apology. Uneasy from the start with this journalistic errand, I'm ready to sign off for good. But as I'm about to hang up, Jewel collects herself and promises to call tomorrow. She proves as good as her word.

At nine A.M. the following day the phone rings, and we continue. I purposefully steer away from Kaflia, and Jewel tells me about the relationship between her and Timothy, which stretches back more than two decades—how two young, surf-and-party-hearty waiters at a hip southern California restaurant made the unlikely transformation into Alaska bear activists funded by movie stars and big corporations; how their friendship outlived their live-together romance, and all the rest. Without question, Timothy was protecting the bears from poachers, conducting important research, and reaching tens of thousands of people, spreading love, knowledge, and respect for bears. It was something to live for, something to believe in. As she speaks, Timothy Treadwell comes alive—good humored, driven, naïve, shrewd, tough, sensitive, flaky, charismatic, and percolating with boundless enthusiasm and energy.

But inevitably, the conversation turns toward the present, and the immediate past that shaped it. I ask Jewel about what she knows of Kaflia, and it turns out she can offer few details—little more than what was carried in the newspapers. What would change, at this point, if she knew more? Timothy, Amie, and the two bears are gone, irrevocably. If there's one thing she wonders about, it's the identity of the larger bear. Was it one that Timothy knew and named? Was it disfigured in any way—a torn ear or a blind eye—or did it have any identifying marks? Jewel wants to try to match it up to the huge library of photos Timothy had taken over the years. I tell her about the lip tattoo and agree to inquire with the Park Service and Fish and Game to see if they have anything useful, perhaps a telling photo of the dead bear. At this point, my conversations with Fulton and Breiter are months away, and the identity is an enigma that seems without solution.

We merge into the matter of the mysteriously recording camcorder and the audiotape of the attack. She's as puzzled as anyone. Timothy, always conscious of saving batteries, wouldn't have turned on the camera and left it in the tent, and never once, in all the thousands of feet of tape he shot, did he ever forget to remove the lens cap. She also rejects the notion that Treadwell was, as the investigating troopers originally speculated, wearing a switched-on remote microphone at the time of the attack. If they were setting up to film, then the camera would be out of its bag. The whole thing just doesn't sound like Timothy, she tells me. Yet she concedes that the camera, in its case, could not have been turned on and the Record button pushed by accident. That means Amie turned it on. The unanswered and unanswerable question is why. Something seems strange and unresolved here. I wonder to myself if there is an alternate explanation—a clue everyone has either missed, or an untold secret.

Meanwhile, Jewel has the tape. "I'm determined not to listen to it," she says. "It's like the telltale heart, ticking away in my closet for the past few days." Though I don't even come close to asking, she volunteers that she has no plans to release it—ever, to anyone. Her resolve rings clear and true. Why not, then, I ask, destroy it now, to prevent it from falling into the wrong hands? She agrees its not a bad idea, but I don't have the impression she intends to burn it today, or next week. Time has a way of changing things, I reflect to myself. One day that tape will find its way into her hands, and her ears will be filled with the cries of ghosts.

Reflecting on the past four weeks, and the abrupt implosion of her world, the incredible flood of attention, scrutiny, questions, and judgmental statements, Jewel murmurs, "I kind of forgot this would ever happen, and what a big impact it would create . . . I think maybe Timothy didn't realize it either." Where will Grizzly People go from here? I ask. Without Timothy Treadwell out there among the bears, flashing charm to schoolkids and sponsors and talk-show hosts, how can the organization survive? What can it hope to accomplish? Jewel is resolute. Grizzly People will carry on. There's no replacing Timothy, but she'll do her best to continue programs of bear education and find ways to protect the bears. She has countless feet of videotape to catalog and organize, and what she guesses is the largest collection of bear photos in the world. More immediately, she's just moving on instinct, trying to meet the incessant demands for interviews and sound bites from dozens of strangers like me. One foot in front of the other is about all she can manage. And, as if to remind herself of the fact she knows all too well, she murmurs, "Meanwhile, my best friend is dead." There are hundreds of questions I still want to ask, but this simple last statement swallows them all. We trade final pleasantries and agree to keep in touch. Then, with a metallic click and the hiss of distance, we return to our separate worlds.

What Sort of Man . . .

Interviewing Alaska bear scientists for this book was a curious experience. All had active opinions, but they weren't about to give me the uncensored version. And you can hardly blame them. Bear scientists, from Alaska to the tip of Tierra del Fuego and the farthest reaches of Romania, are all part of a fraternity where reputation is everything, and word gets around fast. Also, most are cogs in a bureaucratic entity of one sort or another—generally the state or the federal government—where any words spoken can't help but reflect on the agency itself. So, though all these professionals have a personal stake in the turmoil wrought by Timothy Treadwell's life and death, almost everyone qualifies their words down to emotion-free pablum. Even so, there are deep-running currents percolating beneath many conversations. It's telling—I'm not sure of what, but nonetheless of something—that the only way I could convince one of them to say what he really meant was by airbrushing out his identity. There is, in fact, no biologist named Marc Davis. Nonetheless, the conversation below is entirely accurate, as "Marc" confirmed . . . too accurate for

comfort. I changed his name and dodged details that might identify him.

Marc Davis is angry. Furious might be more accurate. I'd been
working down a list of phone interviews a few days after Tim
Treadwell's death—Park Service officials, Alaska State Troopers,
and bear biologists, and getting the sort of polite, helpful, but
carefully guarded comments you'd expect them to make to a writer
who's busily jotting down every word on the record. Then I come
to Davis, a respected biologist, and all I had to do was mention
Tim Treadwell to trigger a spontaneous combustion. Actually, it
starts out as a slow burn, then escalates into a four-alarm wildfire.
I'm reminded of that Three Stooges episode, when every time Moe
hears "Niagara Falls" he goes crazy. Anyway, halfway through the
call, there's this guy practically leaping through the phone line; I
can imagine a clenched jaw, spittle flying, and index finger jabbing
the air.

First off, I manage to make the error of framing a question that
uses the words *Tim Treadwell* and *bear expert* in conjunction.

"Expert?" Davis sputters. "Oh, please . . . well, whatever. Give
me a break. Call him that if you want to." That sets the tone, and
it doesn't take too much persuasion to keep Davis talking. He has
a personal stake in this—bears are his life. Davis begins his litany,
speaking in precisely worded sentences that cut like a hot razor.
"For starters, what Tim Treadwell did was patently illegal. His
mission was absolutely at odds with the National Park Service's
stated goal of preserving and protecting wildlife. . . . The question
to ask is, how do we justify his ignoring rules?" Davis points out
that regulations for Katmai stipulate viewing distances of no less
than fifty yards for brown bears, and at least a hundred yards for
a "family group"—a female with cubs. Both Treadwell's personal
videos and professional productions featuring him document distances far closer than the minimum half a football field. Then

there was that business about the fox that routinely slept in his tent. "The videos," Davis fumes, "are all of outrageous behavior . . . completely unethical from a scientific point of view . . . a bunch of cheap theatrics, the most absurd, cockamamie crap." As Davis pauses for breath, I allow that he's being pretty hard on Treadwell.

"What do you mean I'm hard on him? . . . Why are we trying to water this down? I don't want to disrespect dead people, but what he was doing was illegal and absolutely selfish," he says, and reminds me that all the bears Treadwell named and followed around, including the two bears that were killed following his death, were wildlife belonging to the American people that Treadwell basically hijacked to satisfy his own agenda. "We have no right," intones Davis, "to impose our own stupid little personal mission on the universe."

I offer that with all that field time concentrated in just a few areas, and all that face time with bears, more than some field biologists might amass in twenty years, Treadwell must have produced something of value to the scientific community. My comment elicits another exasperated snort. "You show me the science. . . . There was no science to him. . . . From where I stand as a biologist, he made a mockery of the word." Davis points out that Treadwell never once submitted material or a paper for peer review—an essential component of scientific inquiry. The one study proposal Treadwell submitted to the Park Service was rejected, Davis says, due to vague objectives and virtually nonexistent design. At the one professional bear conference Treadwell attended, Davis, who was also there, states, "He just sat there. He did not take part in the debate—refused, in fact, to debate anything. He had nothing at all to offer except his touchy-feely Beanie Baby approach. . . . That might work with fifth graders, but you can't advance a good science agenda on public relations and hyperbole."

Davis goes on to slam-dance Treadwell's get-close field methodology. "He systematically failed to acknowledge basic biological principles, including that of generalized habituation. Bears get used to him, they're likely to approach other people, maybe far less experienced, and get in trouble when those people freak out and react inappropriately. Katmai is a national park, and Treadwell hung around areas that see a fair to heavy amount of use. In light of that fact, his behavior was especially irresponsible." Davis also points out that by such close association with the objects of his supposed study, Treadwell was violating a prime biological directive—altering the behavior of his subjects, therefore tainting any results and rendering them useless to researchers. Not to mention permanently altering the behavior of entire populations of bears.

Shifting to a different tack, I observe that, if not an expert in scientific terms, Treadwell must have been a pretty astute student of bear behavior to have lasted as long as he did among the bears of Katmai. This just serves to set Davis off again. This time he's less like a fire than a human bomb.

"You must be joking! He was an absolute disaster with bears. You've been to Katmai—you've seen it yourself. Those bears are so tolerant, so laid back, you could have a day care center out there. No one's ever been killed in Katmai, not ever. I don't know how he managed, but he finally goaded a bear into it. . . . Did Tim Treadwell teach me anything about bears? Yeah, it was an incredible testament to their patience. Look, there are only two reasons, from a mature bear's point of view, why any creature would approach it closely—to mate with it or displace it. That's the message he was constantly sending bears: I want to hump you or I want to chase you off."

Everyone says he was a nice guy, I say. It's my final card, but by now I'm braced for the retort. "Nice?" Davis sputters. "Nice? Everybody's nice. That's not the point here. The measure of a person isn't how nice they are—it's what they actually do in the world. A bank robber might be pleasant and funny if you meet him on the street."

Then abruptly, Marc Davis is quiet. It seems his quarter has run out. "Look," he says, "I apologize for all this venting. I'm sorry to dump all this on you. This incident has been very, very frustrating from a professional standpoint. It's done tremendous damage to our mission of promoting brown bear conservation and education. There's lots of anger among professionals. . . . Still, I wouldn't ever say Treadwell deserved what happened to him. Nobody I know wished ill on those two. It's a tragedy for bears and humans alike. The sad part is, these deaths were predictable and totally preventable." Davis sighs. "We can go right down the list of errors he made. It didn't have to happen. He was warned and warned and warned and warned. Yet he negated, defied, and ignored all common sense."

For a time, Davis and I wander on different subjects, chatting about things I can't remember. After the force and emotion of our conversation, the mad scribbling on my part, it's pleasant and re-laxed. I tell him sincerely that I respect his honesty and forthright attitude, when so many seem to be guarding their words. We cir-cle back to the subject at hand, and though his voice is lower, Davis's anger and the force of his conviction carry through.

"The hypocrisy here is what really gripes a lot of us. . . . The internal inconsistencies in his life's stated mission make you won-der, really, if Treadwell was mentally well. Protect bears by putting them at risk. Study them by crowding. Export widely to the world a book and endless streams of videotape that basically says if you act like I do, then you, too, can be close to bears, which influences people to put bears and themselves at risk. Tell thousands and thousands of kids—how many—forty thousand or fifty—that bears are huggable and lovable, then get yourself, your girlfriend, and two bears killed and plastered all over the news. What are those kids supposed to think? I just don't get it," Davis says, and I can sense his bitter shrug from five hundred miles away. "Tell me, what kind of legacy is that?"

II.

Joel Bennett is the sort of guy you might overlook in a crowd—quiet, bespectacled, and silver haired, not especially tall or broad shouldered, perennially clad in the local southeast Alaska uniform of polyester fleece, denim, and rubber knee boots. If someone told you he was a retired lawyer, you'd believe it. And in fact, he is—but Joel's a still-waters-run-deep sort of guy. Besides having been an influential member on Alaska's State Board of Game for fourteen years, on a first-name basis with four Alaska governors, over the past three decades he's established himself as a top nature filmmaker, shooting, directing, and sometimes producing for the likes of Disney, the Discovery Channel, and Audubon. He's traveled as far as Mongolia and Nepal, and captured the first footage ever of a snow leopard in the wild. I first met Joel in the Upper Kobuk Valley when he came up to do a film on caribou, and somewhere along the way we became friends.

A dozen years ago, he mentioned over the phone, in a casual, unassuming, Joel kind of way, that he'd just come back from doing a film with some Californian who crawled around with brown bears, gave them names, and sang to them. Like most Alaskans who'd lived close to wildlife, I snorted. Joel went on, saying, really, this guy was pretty remarkable. That was the first I heard of Timothy Treadwell, who was, through Joel's work on the 1992 Audubon/Turner Broadcasting feature "In the Land of the Grizzlies," about to emerge on the national stage—a limited celebrity, perhaps, but one that would clearly outlast the fifteen minutes we've all been promised.

At that point I was still living in an arctic Eskimo village, and had yet to meet my wife, Sherrie. But Alaska being the paradoxically small place that it is, it turned out that one of her best friends, Lynne Grandvionet, had been the sound technician for Joel's film; and a photography guide and then-aspiring writer named Lynn

Schooler had been the outfitter for the shoot. All of them, like Joel, lived in Juneau, where I eventually moved, and all of us ended up in the same social circle. So it was, through some strange synergy, that my life and Tim Treadwell's somehow overlapped through Joel Bennett—both then and now.

Over the years, Joel ended up shooting a grand total of five film projects involving Timothy Treadwell and, in the process, ended up spending far more time with him in the field than any-one else. By his own reckoning, "thousands of hours"—weeks at a time camping out in the notorious southwest Alaska coastal weather, following and filming Timothy's daily life among the bears of Kodiak Island and Katmai. The two weren't just friends in the casual way most people use the word, but what Eskimo elders might call traveling partners—a relationship forged in the land. Over the years, they'd shivered and laughed together, shared lousy food and wet gear, sweated out rough rides in bush planes, and spent endless hours waiting and watching for the right shot. They'd seen the light shift in strange, slanted magic on the hills. Those things don't go away. When Joel says quietly, "Tim Treadwell was my friend," he means it in the fullest sense.

Joel and I were driving out Juneau's Douglas Highway on a blustery, unseasonably warm December morning, on the way to one of his favorite deer hunting areas—a stand of old growth and brushy muskegs where it was easy to forget there was a city nearby. The sky spattered rain; our guns and packs lay in the back-seat. Treadwell and Huguenard's deaths were just twelve weeks past. The media was still abuzz, from local radio talk shows to lurid tabloid nonsense to Associated Press features. And in all of them, kind words for Timothy Treadwell were hard to come by. At the news of Treadwell's death, Joel had anticipated the gather-ing firestorm of negativity, and had sent out a letter describing and defending the Tim Treadwell he knew. As we drove, our conversa-tion followed that path.

"All these people who've criticized Tim—they didn't know him at all. They may have met him once or twice, written letters, talked to him on the phone. Only a few ever saw him in the field. They didn't see him interacting with bears day after day," said Joel, his voice betraying an uncharacteristic edge. "I did. And I can tell you, I never once saw him behave in what I considered an inappropriate or dangerous manner. He didn't get any closer to bears than most wildlife photographers do. Bear-viewing guides and tourists get close every day. So do field biologists and fishermen. What was the difference?"

I pointed out that we weren't the ones on the Discovery Channel. And in the Treadwell video clips people saw—including in footage Joel had shot—the proximity between human and bear, and the potential for things to go wrong, seemed pretty alarming. Then there was Timothy's manner and dress, which at times appeared decidedly goofy.

"I think those sequences and images give the wrong impression," Joel replied. "It's all people pay any attention to, and out of context, they can be deceiving. Look, I was there, and I can tell you what I saw. When I was with Tim in the field, he exercised the same sort of judgment that you or I would use. He was always paying attention, taking cues from behavior. He'd look over a bear and tell us, 'This one's OK,' or give us orders to back off. And he was always right." Joel pointed out, too, that a telephoto lens or lens angle distorts the distance between objects, sometimes creating the illusion of greater proximity—an effect commonly used to heighten dramatic effect. He explained, "In some clips I shot, it looks like Tim is practically touching a bear, but in fact was thirty or forty feet away."

Joel continued. When they were out filming, Timothy used techniques common among wildlife photographers and naturalists. Often he didn't approach bears. Instead, he set up in a given location, often in the open, allowing the animals to become aware of his presence at a distance. Or he'd make a gradual, meandering approach, sitting for periods, then moving forward or back, reading the mood of the bears. Along streams and other brushy areas, he'd set up, stay put, and wait for animals to appear. Some bears avoided him; a rare few put on aggressive displays that stopped short of contact. Some seemed curious, even social. Most simply went on with their daily affairs and, in the process, often passed close by, providing the footage that was signature Treadwell—bears and people in the same frame, both obviously at ease.

Things didn't always go smoothly. "Tim didn't think he could handle every bear in the universe," Joel said, and told a story about one particular time at lower Kaflia Lake—less than a half mile from the fatal campsite—shooting footage for the French film. A big male, approaching rapidly down a brushy hill, thrashing willows as he came, set off Treadwell's instincts. He'd ordered everyone to run for their skiff, which luckily was nearby. "He was just as alarmed as any of us," Joel recalled. "He was saying stuff like 'My God, don't stop for that tripod—get in the boat, now!' " The film crew, which included Joel's wife, Luisa, shoved off to safety as the bear broke out of the brush. With the crew at a safe distance, the animal channeled his aggression into running off another bear, then wandered away.

"Tim was always concerned with safety," Joel continued, "and I personally never felt he put us in danger beyond what's usual with bears anywhere." This is from a man who's put in close to four decades around Alaska brown bears and, despite having no desire to kill one, carries a Ruger .45/70 on this deer hunting trip—a cannon by any standard—in unspoken homage to ursine power. He seldom walks the woods without it. He also packs a 12-gauge flare pistol as a nonlethal first line of defense. Yet, in Katmai National Park, where no firearms are allowed, Joel put his faith in Treadwell's judgment—the equivalent of trusting someone to pack your parachute, or belay you down a cliff. However, Joel never took the inherent risk for granted. He shakes his head. "First Michio, now Tim. It makes me wonder if it's worth it. I might be done with bear films." But, addressing the personal risks Treadwell assumed over years of bear exposure, for which he was roundly—and after his death, sometimes rabidly—criticized, Joel pointed out that extreme skiers and other adventurers are often widely admired for routinely putting their lives on the line. He also argued that Treadwell not only understood and accepted the danger, but demonstrated, over thirteen years, both competence and an undeniable talent for coexisting with the Katmai bears.

"I believe there are some people who have an ability to relate to wild animals and to some extent communicate with them," Joel said a week later, continuing our conversation as we sat on the edge of Mendenhall Lake in near-zero temperatures. Our camera tripods were before us as we waited for a wolf to emerge from the tree line and perhaps step into the sun. Given the odds of success, there was plenty of time for talk. "Jane Goodall and Dian Fossey are examples. Tim had that sort of connection, without a doubt." Joel went on to liken Treadwell's rapport with bears to that of the legendary bear man of Admiralty Island, Stan Price, who lived among brown bears for four decades. It was a bold statement—the rough equivalent of comparing a young, up-and-coming outfielder to Willie Mays—but one Joel, if anyone, was qualified to make. He was close friends with Stan from 1968 until the old man's death in 1989, and frequently stayed in Stan's guest cabin. In fact, Joel shot his first film around Pack Creek, Price's homestead.

"I'm not suggesting that Stan and Tim were similar people. Stan was a rasty old Alaska gold miner; Tim was urban as could be, with a totally different background. But in the end, they were remarkably close in attitude around animals," Joel said. "Maybe more alike than different." Marten and mink walked in and out of Stan's Pack Creek float cabin. Deer curled up in his bunk to rest, and bears sometimes hibernated beneath the building. Tread-well, too, often had bears bedding close to his camp, and Timmy the fox often slept inside his tent at Hallo Bay. Neither man would carry a gun for protection; Stan never carried any more of a weapon than a walking stick. He generally wouldn't use it to thrust or strike blows but, confronted by an unruly bruin, would hold it out at chest level with both hands and swing it rapidly back and forth like a drum major directing a hirsute band of one. Price once instructed Bill Bacon (a cameraman for many of the classic Disney wildlife features such as *Charlie, the Lonesome Cougar*) to whack a problem bear on the nose if it became too aggressive. Of course, in the event of an actual attack, such a defense would have been useless; a tap with a stick, like the thrown rocks favored by Kat-mai bear-viewing guides, served as a signal, and no doubt the mo-tion also served to distract the bear or alter its mindset. When Stan died, he left his stick to Joel, who adorned it with a Buddhist prayer flag and brought it along to set by his tripod when filming bears—partly in homage to the old man, partly to invoke protec-tion of a higher order.

"There's no doubt that Stan had personal relationships with some of the bears that knew him," Joel said. "Bears in the area recognized his body language and voice, and found him non-threatening. They approached on their own and seemed comfort-able around him. Tim was much the same that way." And like Treadwell, Stan gave names to the bears he knew and thought of them as friends.

To illustrate the bond Joel observed between Treadwell and certain bears, he singles out one female that Tim named Downy, one of the Kaflia bears—in fact, the very bear he returned to lo-cate on that last fatal trip. "With a bear like Downy, he had a re-lationship as if it were some kind of pet," Joel recalls. One day they were filming, with Treadwell on one side of the creek and Joel and his assistant on the other. Downy—a wild, potentially dangerous bear as far as Joel was concerned—emerged from the brush and lay down five feet away. "Not ten or fifteen feet," Joel emphasizes. "Five. Close enough to reach out and touch. And we were sitting down." Frozen in place, imagining themselves in dire straits, the two men silently signaled Treadwell and finally caught his eye. Grasping the men's distress, he hurried over to reassure them that it was only Downy. No big deal; she liked hanging around like that. Still, Joel breathed easier when the bear ambled off to a more comfortable distance.

At the end of Stan Price's life, the connection between the man and the bears he loved seemed to verge on the inexplicable. When family and friends gathered at Pack Creek for a memorial service and to erect a plaque, a single bear—what Joel called "a perfect archetypal brown bear"—lay in the grass fifty yards away, its head down between its paws as it quietly watched the ceremony. Even the installation of the plaque, which involved a pneumatic jackhammer and cement work, didn't drive it off. "Very unbearlike behavior," Joel said. "I can't explain it." And later, when he returned alone to visit the site, he found two bears prostrate on the roof of Stan's empty cabin, looking out toward the sea like sentinel totems. These sound like those stories people love, the facts blurring with each retelling into the haze of myth, but Joel has witnesses to support the first event, and a photograph that documents the second.

What to make of such a bond, whether between Stan Price and his bears or between Timothy Treadwell and Downy, Booble, or Mr. Chocolate? That's a larger question that spirals off on its own. More immediately, is Joel Bennett, with his prayer-flag bear stick and decidedly unscientific leanings in matters of the spirit, a reliable narrator? When I tried to explain Joel's views on Tim Treadwell to one well-known Alaska bear expert, the man muttered, "What's wrong with him? He should know better." I can only say that in the years I've known him, Joel is as careful with words as you'd expect an ex-lawyer to be. And unlike some practitioners of law, I've never known him to fabricate, exaggerate, or misrepresent an opinion as fact.

It's tempting to shrug off Joel Bennett as an apologist; certainly some friends and followers have cast a death mask of Timothy in faultless, idealized features. Joel, however, speaks of a complex, often contradictory character that, despite their years of friendship, he still is struggling to understand. "There's no doubt that Tim enjoyed the spotlight," he says. "He was a showman, and clearly enjoyed his notoriety; you could see that. I don't doubt that motivated him, in part, to do the things he did." Joel also acknowledges the thrill-seeking aspect of Treadwell's character and describes "disconnects" that trouble him.

"First, he was clearly overweighting the poaching issue," Joel says, referring to Timothy's claim that his presence protected the bears he camped among from illegal hunters. "You couldn't get through to him that it [poaching in Katmai National Park] wasn't really at a statistically significant level." Likewise, Joel finds it odd that Tim felt obliged to justify his presence there as the bears' guardian—a theme he repeated throughout his book, *Among Grizzlies*. "He never argued the point with me," Joel says. "I think he knew better. It was directed largely toward his audience outside of Alaska." Yet Joel also believes that this wasn't a mere tactic designed to garner support. Timothy himself was absolutely convinced of both the rightness and necessity of his role. "I think he just got too emotionally close to those particular animals," Joel says quietly. "Not just at Hallo Bay, but those several other areas he knew along the Katmai Coast."

A second point Joel tried in vain to impress on Timothy was the danger of staying out late in the season—September, even (as the last time) into October. By that time of year, visitation to the park slows to a trickle, and the Park Service shuts down its field stations—for good reason. "Late September is full-on nasty conditions out there," Joel says. "It's not just the bears. Days are getting short and dark, and it rains or snows and blows for days. Hypothermia is a real danger, especially out on your own." And transportation—flying in a bush plane or traveling by boat in marginal weather—is perhaps the greatest hazard of all. Meanwhile, tension builds between feeding bears as the salmon runs thin. "The level of risk just didn't make sense to me," says Joel, "and I was kind of annoyed with him." But Treadwell just brushed off Joel's worries, reminding his friend that he'd been out in late season before, and this was a time when the bears especially needed protection. Besides, this predenning period was a vital part of their world, and he wanted to be there to watch and learn. "I think if he could have hibernated with them he would have," murmurs Joel.

"Finally, I had problems with where he chose to camp," Joel continues. "Especially at Kaflia." He describes the dense, brushy maze of trails there, and the way bears would just suddenly appear at short range. But even at Kaflia, there were other campsite choices with fewer converging bear trails, more distance from the salmon stream, and more open space to camp, he reminded Timothy. Again, Treadwell reassured Joel that he'd done all this before, and that he was there to see and interact with as many bears as possible. He wanted to be close to the center of the action.

Looking back, Joel still refuses to condemn his friend's choices, even given the final, appalling cost for both bears and humans. Perhaps he states it best in his written memoriam of Treadwell, excerpted here:

Stan [Price's] behavior around bears and other animals wasn't by the book, and if he had been killed by a bear, there are those that would have criticized his choices too. There is a heightened risk to living in the middle of bears, but this man embraced it. . . . Tim Treadwell's similar passion to involve himself directly in the bear world was an intensely personal choice. . . . Life out near the edge can be a richer experience for many people—and that is the way it will always be.

In response to the criticism levied by Park Service officials and others, he wrote, "If Katmai National Park or other authorities had a problem and considered Tim a hazard, they should have acted long before now to restrict him. It serves no honorable purpose to condemn a dead man after the fact."

The memoriam concludes:

When all is said and done, Timothy Treadwell will be remembered by those who knew him as caring for the future of bears. At least he did *something* when most people won't or are too busy to bother. His particular approach was not mine and probably not yours. But he had a good heart, was fun to be around, and touched thousands of people across the country with his passion and commitment. That's a pretty good legacy in my book.

And he was my friend.

Joel and I sat before our tripods on that cold, bright December morning; the wolf had appeared briefly an hour before, then faded into the trees. At last we gave up. Working through the sting of cold fingers and toes, our eyelashes coated with frost, we packed our gear and trudged homeward, the crunch of our boots echoing in the snow. Abruptly Joel stopped and turned to me. "Think of Tim out on that coast," he said. "Hunkered in a leaky tent, always wet or damp, no fire to dry clothes or cook on, bug bitten, living on peanut butter. Alone most of the time, no one to talk to—and this was a guy who loved company. And bears everywhere, all kinds, some dangerous, in the brush, sometimes at night, coming into camp. Day after day, weeks at a time, season after season—for thirteen years. What sort of man"—Joel shook his head and looked away as if asking the question of the mountains— "I ask you, what sort of man would do that?"

The Skulls That Are Mine

In 1979 I scrawled in my journal, "I'm going to Alaska because of bears. Bears, Alaska; Alaska, bears. The two are the same." A couple of weeks later, I threw my canoe on the roof of my '66 Plymouth and set out across the continent from eastern Maine, the leading actor in my own personal drama. But though I might put it differently now, I was pretty well bull's-eyed on an essential truth: the two words are damn near interchangeable. So, though Timothy Treadwell and I never met, I guess you could argue that we had something basic in common.

I was scared of bears back then, a deep, unreasoning dread that stopped just short of phobia. They haunted my bedroom when I was six; Lord knows how they got there, since I didn't see my first wild bear until I was seventeen, and I can't point to an evil storybook beast that preyed on my imagination. Just the opposite, in fact—Pooh bear and Kipling's Baloo were favorites in our house. Still, the bears were there, lurking silently in the shadows, and like so many children before me, I relied on the door cracked open to keep them under the bed. But I also loved my fear and drew myself toward it, the way a cabled ferryboat crosses a river. As I got older, I camped out whenever I got the chance—backyard stuff, then Boy Scouts, and finally on my own. Most of the time I was in the heart of black bear country: the mountains of Virginia, the provincial parks of Quebec, and finally Maine, where I went to college. I'd often lie awake at night, listening to the furtive rustle of raccoons or deer, imagining the approach of padded, clawed feet and malevolent eyes. When I did sleep, it was usually a hair-trigger doze.

My first grizzly, like Timothy's was for him, is fused into memory: June 1979. I'd been in Alaska less than two weeks, and was floating down the Upper Kobuk with my friend Peter. As we rounded a bend in the river, a drift log on a gravel bar stirred. There was a bear, fifty yards away. We were drifting with the current, almost noiseless. Stretched out on his belly, the grizzly raised his head to test the air, a relaxed, almost gentle expression on his face. His fur was matted with rain. Then his head snapped around, and his eyes registered the shape and movement of our canoe. From his prone position he leaped up and was gone in a series of bounds, accelerating like a racehorse. Caught up in the rush of the moment—the thrill and surprise at seeing him, utter astonishment at his speed—I forgot, just for a moment, to be afraid.

Timothy Treadwell and I actually did share a pile of similarities—both upper-middle-class white kids of nearly the same age, from good families, attended suburban East Coast high schools, both active and good enough in sports that it shaped our choice of colleges. We both had reckless, impulsive natures, stumbled through self-destructive phases with cars, drugs, and fighting, and both found something lacking in our lives that Alaska—and bears—somehow filled. But at least one important thing was different: I came to Alaska with a rifle. Though I was pretty good at canoeing, camping, and catching fish, I wasn't much of a hunter; as a matter of fact, I'd borrowed a gun from my older brother. A lever-action Marlin .35 Remington carbine, it was really more of a close-quarters deer rifle than anything else, with an effective range of a hundred yards. This idea of shooting things was still new to me and, frankly, made me a bit uneasy. Maybe I'd start off with caribou and work my way up. It's what Alaskans did. Timothy, I'm sure, would have blanched at the idea. While I wanted to become like the people I lived among, Timothy wanted them to become like him.

It was no accident that I ended up working for a Dutch big-game guide in a remote arctic Eskimo village. Surrounded by people who killed as easily as they breathed, I set out to do the same. I learned to skin and butcher, to tan hides, and to eat strangely shaped, wild-tasting chunks of meat. I slept in a vole-infested cabin on caribou skins and wore mukluks, hats, and mitts made from animals I'd killed. My back drenched in blood, I carried haunches of moose and antlers for my guide's clients. And I didn't just learn to do these things; I lived, slept, and dreamed them. I'd played violent contact sports all my life, and this was just another. The difference was that this game was rooted in some distant, collective remembrance—rooted in killing. It only took one season, though, to realize that I couldn't get used to the idea of taking money for helping strangers to shoot animals. Dollars and cents screwed up a transaction that seemed far more personal.

I moved on from the bush-bum/hunting-guide gig, fell back on my college education, and took a teaching job in the village of Noatak, 150 miles to the west. Though I was holding down a real job and living in a larger cabin, in my spare time I was living the same life. I shot my first grizzly in early May of 1982—actually, it was legally a friend's bear; he tagged the animal and took home the skin. But I was the one who fired the two last rounds that killed it. The bear died on the ice of a windblown lake, in a little mountain pass with an almost-forgotten Inupiaq name about sixty miles from the village. He was a big, dark male, at least fifteen years old, and probably knew all about men. Just out of the den, he was moving away from our commotion, and guessed wrong. Five minutes and ten bullets later, he was dead.

I have a picture of that first grizzly. The bear is lying on his side in a dark pool of frozen blood. His eyes are slitted shut, and there's a sheen of more blood spattered on his coat. I'm crouched behind his shoulder, rifle pointed skyward. I'm smiling, but there's something not quite right about my eyes and the corners of my mouth. The photo is underexposed, as much shadow as detail, the background blurred. The bear and I are suspended in space, anchored only by that hard pool of blood.

And soon enough, I shot my own: a big male with a pale blond pelt. Even the actual shooting was an anticlimax—he was dead before he hit the ground, as if the bullet had been guided home. I was often lucky—or you could say unlucky—at killing. I didn't wear this bear or eat it, as I did with caribou or beavers, though I did give its meat to an Eskimo neighbor who commented on its fine flavor. What I gained from this killing I couldn't say—though I looked often and thoughtfully at both the bleached skull and the snarling rug that had become a part of my life. Killing a god, I'd found, was no small matter.

The Inupiaq elders I knew called the grizzly *aklaq*, and often lowered their voices when they spoke of him. More than once I was given gentle but firm advice on matters pertaining to these animals—everything from practical tips on fleshing a hide or averting a charge to matters of spiritual etiquette following a successful hunt. The lower jaw was never detached, and a certain small piece of cartilage known as "the worm" was cut from the underside of the tongue. The head was always to be left in the field, either buried or placed in a tree. The brain was never eaten. And, of course, I learned to *nigiluk*—slit the trachea to let the soul escape. These acts assured that the bear's spirit wouldn't follow or molest the hunter, and that it would be born again. On the other hand, ancient tradition also allowed for a bit of veiled braggadocio, not much different from our own; in centuries past, an Eskimo man who killed a bear (usually with a spear) covered his door with its hide—good insulation, it's true, but also immediate notice to anyone who entered that this was the house of a man who'd bested *aklaq*. Although these ancient ways are fading out, many Inupiaq hunters still observe at least some of these customs—at least the cutting of the worm and *nigiluk*. And I've never seen an Eskimo bring a grizzly's head back to town. When I did just that with my first bear, my old neighbor in Noatak, Ned Howarth, who was rumored to have been an *angetuk* (shaman), scolded me roundly. *How come you try to do that?* he demanded. But my even more elderly neighbor on the other side, Emma Porter, reassured me. *I think Jesus make it all right,* she murmured.

Over the next few years, grizzlies and I continued to cross trails, though seldom enough that each time was a distinct and separate memory. This was the arctic interior, where life was spread thin; I sometimes went weeks at a time without so much as glimpsing a grizzly—even though tracks, scat, and marking trees showed bears roamed everywhere. Without doubt, they worked hard to avoid human contact; in fact, every single one I encountered ran as soon as it sensed what I was—even at a distance. I once watched a bear, nearly a mile away, catch my wind-borne scent and gallop straight up a mountain and over the top.

As I pared away the bear of my childhood bedroom from reality, fear gradually uncoiled; I learned to sleep on gravel bars pockmarked with tracks, and sometimes decided to leave my rifle behind when I hiked or fished, just to see how it felt. But reining in my phobia didn't stop me from still wanting to kill another bear—the bigger, the better. Don't ask me if it was the challenge, the adrenaline rush, or some deep-seated instinct; all these years later, I still can't offer a satisfactory explanation, even to myself. Especially when the bear whose life I would take would first spare mine. The short version of the story goes like this. Riding out in the Kipmiksot Mountains one bright April day in 1984, my companion Norma and I found a fresh den—a mound of dirt and a dark opening clear as a beacon against a smooth white backdrop. I carried only a .22 rifle for ptarmigan. The den was a thousand feet above the tree line, dug into a south-facing sidehill. Apparently the roof, wet with thaw, had caved in, creating a narrow, curving trench about a dozen feet long—open on the downhill side, closed on the upper. Day-old tracks wound from the entrance and down the gully toward a brushy creekbed. The animal was probably miles away. Norma gunned her old Polaris up the slope to look down inside the trench from above. As she left her machine and postholed through the soft snow to the edge, camera in hand, I crossed the second set of tracks, headed back toward the entrance. The realization slammed into me: *The bear was still in there.*

From there, things blurred into fast forward. I roared up the slope, waving frantically and shouting, and slewed to a stop just six feet from the hole as an enormous head erupted from the ground. A paw flashed out, working in quick, hooking jabs. More than two decades later, the visual details are sharp and golden as evening light: the glint of enormous claws, flecks of foam flying from a gaping mouth, a dark scar down the bear's snout, Norma turning and stumbling. There must have been an incredible blur of noise—the intermingled roar of animal and machine, the clashing of jaws—but in my memory, the scene is oddly silent, as it was for me at the time. I only hear my voice shouting, as she gunned her machine's throttle, spinning the track and getting stuck: *You're not going to make it!* I meant on her snowmobile, but Norma later told me she thought I was telling her she was dead. I pulled alongside, grabbing a handful of parka and hauling her onto my machine as I accelerated away, braced for the slamming impact.

Nothing happened. When I finally looked over my shoulder,

the bear was a rapidly vanishing speck headed in the opposite direction. Though he'd had us dead, he'd run out of the den entrance and straight downhill.

And two years later, after weeks of hard hunting, I tracked him down. In that sprawl of mountain terrain and in the bottomless soft snow of late spring, it was an almost impossible task. But I kept at it, heading out into the Kipmiksots, traveling hundreds of miles, much of it in the uncertain twilight of late evening, when the snow was solid and the bears were traveling. Even at the time, I floated out of my body, looked down, and loathed myself, but still went on.

In a snow squall at 2:00 A.M. in the faint arctic twilight of early May, I crossed his unhurried tracks, followed them a quarter mile, and, bracing off my snow machine's seat, shot him dead. It seems so easy, told that way—but at the time, far back in the mountains, alone and so exhausted I was shaking and sick, it was another story. At the first round, which hit him high, he ran; at the second, he turned and charged, and went down at the third, less than fifty yards away, roaring blood and biting at his chest as if his own failing body were the enemy. Then he sighed, sagged downward, and was gone. And I sat there, rocking back and forth, crying as if he were my brother, the valley quiet and white with new snow.

Nearly twenty years have passed. In that time, I've met dozens of bears, a blurred procession that I can no longer count or separate. I wish I could loop back in time, gather my bullets in midair back into my rifle, and watch that enormous old bear shuffle up that snow-quiet valley and fade over the rise—but what's done is done. I brought the head home, and once again Jesus didn't make it all right. Instead, Ned Howarth's admonition rings out—*How come you try to do that?*

Nonhunters and animal huggers can shake their heads at my Neanderthal stupidity; friends who hunt also look at me cockeyed if I talk too much about it, while others tell me I think too hard.

There is finally no condemnation more terrible than my own. Neither is there comfort from any quarter, including those contained in the traditions of my older Inupiaq friends. Cutting out "the worm" or opening the throat—*nigiluk*—might work for someone else; for me, they're empty gestures from another place and time.

I think that in the end, my story is that of many hunters, who, as they went along, discovered that the trail of the quest—the hours and years of moving across the country, watching and listening, waiting and hoping—inevitably leads toward love. Or maybe a hunter one day finds the cumulative weight of souls too heavy. For me, I think, it was both. I still hunt an occasional caribou or deer because I believe that if I eat meat, I should do my own mindful killing. But there are no more bears for me in this lifetime. I keep the hides and skulls that are mine, not as talismans, but to remind me of who I am and what I'm capable of doing. Somehow, Timothy and I traveled opposite trails and ended up at a similar destination: We each loved bears and, driven by our love, brought them to their deaths. The final irony is that because I killed bears legally and by design, somehow I'm guiltless; Timothy, because he did so indirectly and by accident, is vilified.

By the mid-nineties I was past knowing bears by their skulls and hides, and instead turned to camera gear—a tripod and pack heavier than any rifle. Along the way, I met professional photographers like Kim Heacox, Tom Walker, and Michio Hoshino, who, out of a combination of kindness and pity, showed me how to choose equipment, wade through the bewildering technical end of things, and occasionally come out with an image that meant something. In 1995, on an arctic photo trip with Michio, I agreed to write the text for a bear book; Michio would take the pictures. We hoped to somehow capture, or at least brush against, things more spiritual and poetic than scientific. "I want to make beautiful book with beautiful picture," Michio said in his lilting, broken English—a summation of everything he'd ever done. He was a gentle, unassuming, and infinitely patient man, blessed with spiritual grace and hampered by an offsetting physical klutziness. All of his attention seemed to be focused either through his camera's viewfinder or on the simple pleasures of life—a sunset, a well-cooked meal, a joke shared with a friend. We met again in Fairbanks the following spring; as his wife, Naoko, served tea, and his boy, Shoma, played toddler games on their cabin floor, we discussed the shape of our project. He was going to the Kamchatka Peninsula in Siberia that coming August—an unspoiled, bear-filled landscape like Treadwell's Katmai Coast, only more wild still. Michio wanted me to come along. But I'd already planned a sailing trip in Prince William Sound, followed by a camping trip in my Brooks Range backyard with my wife-to-be, Sherrie. I reluctantly turned down the invitation. We'd talk when he got back, and get the book going.

The night my friend Michio Hoshino died, dragged from his tent, screaming in the dark, by a brown bear somewhere in the Russian Far East, I was camped on the Nuna River in Northwest Arctic Alaska, more than a thousand miles away. In the dream I awoke from, photographer Tom Walker and I were surrounded by man-eating Dall sheep, fending them off with our tripods, more surprised than frightened, telling each other this just doesn't happen. They don't eat people. Next to me, Sherrie stirred from her own nightmare, whispering there was a bear out there, a bear. I poked my head out into the arctic twilight, looked around, and tried to reassure her. No bear.

I fell back into a dream-racked sleep, wandering the rest of the night through Russia, invisible to everyone, trying to find my way home. Two days later when Sherrie and I returned to Ambler, Tom called to tell me Michio had died that same night. I don't claim any prescience. But I know I had those dreams, and that now Michio was dead. Only a half page into both our friendship and our book—a few dozen words scrawled by hand—and it was over.

Michio's ghost visits me often. Strange to sense the loss so deeply of one I knew for so comparatively little time, but I know there are others as haunted as I am. All across Alaska, in the telling and retelling of stories among friends, he becomes almost alive again, stumbling over his tripod, telling bad jokes across a campfire, sitting in the rain, waiting. Late at night, we lean in, ask each other if somehow one of us might have been able to save him. I know, if we had traveled together as he hoped, I wouldn't have let him camp where he did. Or maybe I'm wrong. Perhaps we would have died there together, or it would have been me, dragged off into the night, which would have made more sense. There finally is no resting place, and no accounting—just another skull that somehow, I've come to own.

On a surface level, the tragedies of Tim Treadwell and Michio Hoshino are quite similar: unarmed, pacifist bear photographer, camping out in a national park close to a salmon stream, is attacked in camp, killed, and eaten by a large brown bear, at least somewhat habituated to human presence. Bear is then hunted down and killed, and confirmed to contain human remains. Incident is duly investigated and considered a rare, isolated case. But the dissimilarities between the two are more instructive than the parallels.*

From the start, Michio's situation was more dire. The bear, a gaunt, seven-hundred-pound male, had been hanging around the Kurilskoya Lake cabin by which Michio camped. The salmon were late, and the bear had repeatedly tried to break into the storage shed and cabin and been repelled by pepper spray. But even

*The facts in the following account are based on George Bryson's fine Oct. 13, 1996, feature in *The Anchorage Daily News*, "The Final Days of Michio Hoshino."

though there was by then a small crowd of people there—Michio, a Japanese film crew, two Russian guides (one of them Igor Ravenko, a highly competent and respected bear biologist), a young Alaskan photographer named Curtis Hight, and various others coming and going by boats and helicopters—the bear persisted. In fact, he broke out the windows of one landed helicopter in search of food, and was witnessed eating from a can that a Russian television crew placed out for him. He had become the most dangerous and difficult of brown/grizzlies: one that has associated people with food. It was only a small shift between associating and equating— one the bear made in a matter of days. His being a large and hungry male further exacerbated the situation, making him all the more difficult to drive off. And no one in the camp had a gun; as in Katmai National Park, they weren't allowed.

Everyone but Hight and Michio slept in the crowded cabin on the shore of Kurilskoya Lake. Hight would have vastly preferred to be inside, but the film crew's gear filled the only available bunk, and he was too polite to press the matter. Michio simply chose to sleep in his own tent pitched outside, within twenty feet of the cabin. From what I knew of him, he might have done so even if he'd had the whole area to himself. His placid, Zen approach to the natural world was at odds with sleeping inside. Why trade the shifting patterns of light, the view of Ilyinsky Volcano towering over the lake, and the company of passing bears for the boisterous conversation, fetid air, and confining atmosphere of a plywood shack? And, like Timothy Treadwell, he believed in the power of good intentions. Sensing them, no bear would ever harm him. If worse came to worst, the cabin was right there, full of people.

Paradoxically, Michio had a deep-seated fear of bears, much like my own. Over the years, he'd not only learned to control that dread, but embrace it. He once wrote, ". . . when we visit the few remaining scraps of wilderness where bears roam free, we can still feel an instinctive fear. How precious that feeling is."

*   *   *

Hight pitched his tent next to Michio's and lasted there all of one night. After dark the bear made a concerted effort at the nearby storage shed, jumping up and down on the tin roof. In spite of the incredible racket—a seven-hundred-pound bear bouncing on sheet metal—no one but Hight seemed to react. He had to rouse Michio—at this point, the bear was ten feet behind the Japanese photographer's tent—then pound on the cabin door to summon Igor. Despite beating on pots and pans and a blast of pepper spray administered by the Russian, the bear left only grudgingly. The next night, Hight slept on the platform of an observation tower a few hundred yards away—and the bear, distinguished by a wound on his head, slept beneath it. Michio stayed right where he was, though over the next ten days, the bear's aggressive food-seeking behavior continued to escalate. Finally, the last of the pepper spray was gone.

In the early hours of August 8, 1996, the bear tore into Michio's tent. Responding to his screams in the darkness, the men in the cabin scrambled outside and attempted to drive the bear away by beating on pots and pans and shouting; Ravenko came within ten feet of the animal, which was standing over Michio's lifeless form. The bear ignored them, then responded by grabbing the body and dragging it off into dense brush. Without weapons, there was nothing to be done.

In the morning, a professional hunter and a Russian special forces soldier tracked the bear with a helicopter, drove it from a patch of timber into the open, and shot it with military assault rifles. An examination of the bear's stomach contents left no doubt that they had Michio's killer.

Again, the scenario seems eerily familiar. But in Tim Treadwell's case, there's no evidence he was dealing with a food-habituated bear, even under the harsh scrutiny of investigation. Nor was there a crowd of people at the Treadwell campsite to lend a false sense of security. And if Treadwell used poor judgment in camping where he did, Michio's decision to remain outside seems off the chart of common sense, especially considering the bear's increasingly fearless raids. It's doubtful even Tim Treadwell, confident and experienced as he was around bears, would have continued to camp outside under those conditions. In fact, Michio's fate inspired and shaped Timothy's in-camp habit of immediately leaving his tent to confront bears—a good idea in most conditions, but possibly the strategy that led to his own death. There was no sign that bear 141, or any other bear, tore into the tents at Kaflia, though they were apparently collapsed in the struggle. If Timothy had remained inside that one time, he and Amie might still be alive. This is less a second guess than another tinge of irony.

In the end, Michio's death has less in common with Timothy Treadwell's than with that handful of cases from the late sixties and seventies, most from Glacier National Park and Yellowstone, where food-habituated grizzlies who'd clearly lost their fear of humans entered established camping areas at night and attacked people in their tents with clear predatory intent. While fitting Treadwell's case into this category is tempting, the evidence doesn't quite fit; and neither was Michio out to prove anything about bears, either to himself or the world. Despite a number of curious parallels, the two men were false doppelgängers, linked by mere coincidence and fate. But in a sense, Michio and Tim Treadwell died together, as they had lived— kind, gentle, a bit naïve, believing in the goodness of all things.

Did Michio's death change how I looked at bears? I should have, by all rights, retreated into my fears. Yet I continued to move in the opposite direction—not because of or in spite of Michio, I think, but because I had learned to fear myself more than anything external. For a while after Michio died I made a point of carrying a rifle and being more careful, as did most of my photographer friends. But one August after his death there I was, standing my ground on open, fall-bright tundra, leaning into my camera as a blond grizzly moved ever closer, straight in—a hundred yards, then fifty. It was obvious the bear saw me, and this was the Northwest Arctic, where bears fall into two broad categories: shy and problematic. There I stood with no rifle, only a single can of pepper spray at my feet. Sherrie, who was a few yards behind, was getting nervous. I reassured her and kept firing off frames until the bear filled the viewfinder. I was keyed up and ready, but that was about it. At thirty yards, I opened my jacket and raised my tripod over my head to make myself seem larger, then moved a few steps toward the bear—the first time I had tried such a tactic. I don't know where I got the idea, whether someone had told me or it was a spontaneous invention. Without any argument or fanfare, the grizzly turned and ran.

Two autumns later, I'd gotten married and moved twelve hundred miles south, to the island-studded rain forests of southeast Alaska. I was teaching in the Tlingit Indian community of Hoonah, on Chichagof Island—a job I took because the school board member who showed me around swung me by the town dump, where several enormous brown bears rummaged around the burn piles. The island, like its more famous neighbor, Admiralty, averaged more than a bear per square mile—as great a population density of *Ursus arctos* as any in the world. Bears wandered the sides of the runway, the maze of logging roads, mountains, and salmon streams, and sometimes right into town. This was the sort of place I'd come to—one where the question wasn't if you'd run into bears, but how many, and with what result. Just the sort of place I wanted to be.

Early on, a Tlingit man gave me some advice. "If I'm going out to hunt or pick berries," he said, "I always do this: clap two or three times and say, 'Grandfather, I'm coming into your woods.

I won't stay long and I don't want to bother you.' Always let Grandfather know what you're up to, and he'll let you by."

That first fall, a brown bear appeared on the school playground one morning and was driven off by cops firing rubber bullets as a crowd of boisterous, unimpressed students looked on. Most townspeople shrugged and took the incident in stride. Yet in my eighth-grade English classroom sat Cody Mills, whose shaved head bore the fresh, striated scars of a brown bear's claws. It had happened the previous spring on the far end of town. Cody had been cutting through a patch of woods, wearing headphones with the music turned up loud. A female with a yearling cub materialized out the brush; Cody, wrapped in his music, was late to spot them, got too close, and the mother charged. Cody went down, was clawed around his head, and the bear retreated—only to renew the assault when he got up and tried to run. This time Cody drew a knife and stabbed at the bear until it ran off. All considered, Cody got off about as lightly as you could from a mauling; the female was remarkably restrained. But the young man's emotional scars went deeper than the physical. It's a story he has trouble telling.

The bears of Chichagof took some getting used to. Not only did they generally look different from northern interior bears—coarser fur, longer legs, boxier heads, and generally larger—they had a completely different mind-set. Despite the fact that they were hunted in season, they often seemed surprisingly casual about humans; it was nothing strange, I discovered, to cast for salmon at one hole while a bear did his own fishing fifty yards upstream. Several times I saw a bear coming toward me on a trail quietly step off to allow me to pass. And once, walking through dense brush to a favored fishing hole, I glanced to my left and there was a young bear, crouched down and watching just off the path, scarcely more than an arm's length away, but showing no signs of aggression. So I nodded a quick acknowledgment, like you might to a stranger in a supermarket aisle, and continued down the trail.

Of course, they still were bears. Not only Cody, but a timber worker a few miles away, were mauled that first fall; and some bears knew that gunshots often meant fresh meat, and would come loping toward deer hunters on the island, driving them from their kills. A half-dozen times I had bears press in too close for comfort. But I seldom carried a gun on Chichagof; in these brushy close quarters, there was no time to unsling a rifle and shoot, and walking around with one in the chamber was both impractical and risky. The only way to be completely safe from bears was to stay at home—and even there, right across from the school where that one bear had been, I had another twenty feet from my back porch one night. So I shrugged and went out. It was a matter of accepting that what happened was more up to the bears than to me.

Depending on the day, I carried bear spray or a plastic 12-gauge flare pistol, or sometimes both. Occasionally I'd get an odd feeling and drag along my rifle, but the last thing I wanted to do was to kill another bear. More often than not, I found that posturing, standing my ground, and clapping was an effective way to hold serve. And several times, when even a flare didn't do the trick, I gained a bear's temporary respect by bluff-charging a few steps as I had that time up north, with the pepper spray drawn and ready. But mostly I went quietly on my way, and the bears did the same. I can't say I've ever forgotten my fear; instead of an adversary, though, it's become a blanket, the sort a toddler carries. The bear of childhood has never entirely left, and I hope it never will. Sometimes, alone in the woods, I hear it breathing under the bed and simply turn around and walk out.

Now that I live at the edge of suburban Juneau, by far the most peopled place I've called home in over twenty-five years, you'd think I'd have left the world of bears somewhere behind. But at my feet lies our black Lab Gus, an ex–Seeing Eye dog. His previous master, a man named Lee Hagmeier, was mauled and blinded by a brown bear forty-five years ago, just three miles from where I sit. The neighborhood trails where I ride my mountain bike are often posted with bear warnings, and I've lost count of the black bears I've run across, as close as my front yard (a neighbor once called early one morning to let us know one was sleeping under our front porch). As Sherrie and I watched from our living room window the other evening, a four-hundred-pound brown bear strolled down the campground road, just seventy yards away. A few minutes later, I took a break from writing this book and went with our dogs out for a run. Grandfather was in his woods, that was all. I was just passing through.

Grizzly People

Nearby, yet removed from my own tangled wandering through the Maze, others forged forward, seeking their own ursine connections—Timothy Treadwell among them. Grizzly People. What's in a name? In this particular instance, plenty. Whatever they did or didn't do, Timothy and Jewel defined their organization, sentiments, and agenda to perfection. It's doubtful a top-drawer ad agency could have done better. Consider the permutations: People for Grizzlies. Grizzlies and People. Grizzlies *are* People . . . and vice versa. It's all there, encapsulated in two words of two syllables each, reverberating in perfect balance.

While these two grass-roots ecowarriors were among the first to meld the concept to a mass media message, the basic notion was hardly a new or isolated phenomenon. It was preceded in essence by a kinship, spiritual or actual, insisted upon by hunter-gatherer cultures over untold millennia—the trail I'd doubled back upon and followed. In bears, men had long seen the beast most like themselves: intelligent, expressive, and adaptable, able to walk upright, leaving tracks startlingly reminiscent of a naked human foot. Skinned, they resembled men cast in godlike proportions. And they possessed the mystical ability to sleep for months and rise, as if from the dead.

Across Europe and Asia, and almost universally across North America, tribes honored the bear with names such as The Chief's Son, Beloved Uncle, and Elder Brother. Bears, both black and brown/grizzly, were woven through creation myths and elaborate ceremonies of spiritualism and rebirth. Some North American Natives outright refused to hunt grizzlies—a taboo European explorers misinterpreted as fear. *Brother Bear,* the Disney animated feature for which Timothy served as technical advisor, is based on an amalgam of ancient Eskimo and Indian transformation myths—stories in which humans became bears or vice versa. Tales of intermarriage between the two species are prevalent in Native lore as well—Grizzly People in the fullest sense of the word.

In a more immediate sense, Timothy Treadwell might have tipped his hat to a number of individuals, both contemporary and historic, as charter members of his fraternity. It's not as if one passed the ideology, like a torch, to another. These men were or are apparent products of some sort of parallel, spontaneous evolution—and, as such, are evidence of what seems an innate human tendency toward exploring the nature and limits of our relationship with bears.

As far as the American continent is concerned, James Capen Adams, better known as Grizzly Adams, paved the way. He was, in fact, more than a figment of made-for-kiddie TV imagination; a Massachusetts-born ex-shoemaker with some experience as a trainer of exotic animals (as a young man he'd almost been killed by a caged tiger), he emigrated to California in 1849 at age forty-two, all but broke and down on his luck. In short order he became one of the most celebrated mountain men of all time, specializing in capturing live specimens of wild animals for sale or exhibit—wolves, mountain lions, deer, elk . . . and, of course, grizzlies. Though some of his bear-training methods were brutal by contemporary standards (he tamed his cubs by first killing the mother, then "reproving" the infants early on with a cudgel), he nonetheless established an extraordinary lifelong bond with two bears, whom he dubbed Lady Washington and Ben Franklin.

They accompanied him wherever he went, shared his food, defended him against other bears, and even carried backpacks and towed sledges. Of Lady Washington, he said, "she was faithful and devoted. . . . I felt for her an affection which I have seldom granted any human being." Adams, much scarred by his numerous adventures in the wild animal trade, caused quite a stir by walking the streets of San Francisco in the 1850s in the company of the Lady and Ben. He opened a wild animal "museum" in a basement on Clay Street, which was a huge success. When Ben the bear died in 1858, he was enough of a celebrity that the San Francisco *Evening Bulletin* ran an obituary titled "Death of a Distinguished Native Californian"—indicating the level of ambassadorship for the species Adams and his bears had attained.

In 1860 the enterprising and apparently tireless Adams loaded his menagerie of several dozen animals in a clipper and sailed around Cape Horn to New York, where he both exhibited in the city and toured with P. T. Barnum to wide acclaim. In failing health due to an old head injury, he died not, as he'd hoped, in the Sierra Nevada "among the rocks and eternal pines" with his beloved bears at his side, but in a small mill town not far from his Massachusetts birthplace. While his methods and philosophy were certainly not Timothy Treadwell's—Adams apparently killed thousands of animals, including many grizzlies, over a decade of both capturing and hunting—the bond between Grizzly Adams and his ursine companions remains a singular landmark in bear–human relations, far ahead of its time.

Naturalist Enos Mills was the greatest and most peaceable early champion of grizzlies. In the late 1800s and into the early twentieth century—a period where most people considered the bears to be savage vermin—Mills walked the mountains of Colorado unarmed, approaching bears and observing them in thoughtful, loving detail. His slim 1919 volume, *The Grizzly: Our Greatest Wild Animal,* documents decades of close encounters, and is a plea for preservation. Mills, like Timothy, saw brown/grizzlies as gentle, intelligent, and highly misunderstood creatures. "It is a national misfortune," he wrote, "that the overwhelming majority of people be imposed upon with erroneous natural history . . . the grizzly does not look for a fight; he is for peace at almost any price." Mills maintained steadfastly that grizzlies would only attack if threatened first, and that they would refuse human flesh, even if discovered as carrion. Building up to a positively New Age utterance, Mills stated, "It would be a glorious thing if every one appreciated the real character of the grizzly bear. A changed attitude toward him—the great animal of the outdoors—might cause the wilderness to appeal to all as a friendly wonderland."

While a number of scientists, naturalists, and hunters turned conservationist played a strong role in grizzly preservation from the turn of the century through the 1960s (the Craighead brothers of Yellowstone rightfully at the fore; Frank Wright, Theodore Roosevelt, and Harold McCracken among a double handful of honorable mentions), none truly qualify, in the full sense, as Grizzly People—those who wanted not just protection and greater tolerance, but the establishment of diplomatic relations between the species, a breakdown of the adversarial wall that separates them from us. The concerted development of that notion is a phenomenon of the past two or three decades.

One of the first individuals who set out to prove wild bears and people could interact peacefully was Minnesota biologist Lynn Rogers. Architect and executor of a long-range study on black bear behavior in the 1970s, he documented the movement, feeding, sleeping, mating, parenting, and denning habits of a study group of black bears—not the brown/grizzly, but *Ursus americanus,* the bear found across the continent, from Florida to Maine to New Mexico and on up through most of Canada and Alaska.

In the process he came to realize that the bears he met and the bears of common knowledge (even according to the scientific community) were entirely different creatures. "I'm a cautious sort of guy," he says, "and it took me years to overcome my own belief in all the myths about black bears—the special danger of females with cubs, the natural ferocity of any bear, all the rest of the stuff you see on the cover of *Outdoor Life*. I was as fearful and brainwashed as anybody. . . . As I gradually learned their language, I began interpreting apparently aggressive behaviors as manifestations of their own nervousness and fears."

In other words, the bears might huff and blow and swat the ground, but these were ritual displays that didn't lead to attacks at all. They were just as afraid of him as he was of them. Rogers found that he could calm bears through a variety of methods, including lying down (not playing dead, but reducing his apparent threat level) and by responding to their cues. He also discovered that he could, in the line of his work, go so far as to catch bawling cubs in front of their mothers or enter dens without being attacked—even when dealing with totally wild, unhabituated animals. Meanwhile, he gained the tolerance of certain individual bears through repeated, careful, nonthreatening contact. Under proper circumstances, he could follow, approach, touch, and even hand-feed wild bears without danger.*

By the mid-eighties Rogers was focused on not only understanding black bears, but spreading the message that the common perceptions of them were false and misleading. At the nonprofit Wildlife Research Institute, in Ely, Minnesota, he began conducting tours where small groups of people could observe and interact with wild, free-ranging bears—and, in the process, gain understanding and lose irrational fear. These "bear tours" remain a main-

---

*Rogers acknowledges the extremely rare but serious possibility of predatory black bear attacks, but in all his thousands of hours of contact, he's never encountered such behavior.

stay of the Institute's funding; touching the animals is one of the advertised attractions, and photos of Rogers literally side by side with bears (in one case, taking a pulse) are featured on the Institute Web site. He's been featured on Animal Planet as "The Man Who Walks with Bears." "I've reached tens of millions of people, and the truth about black bears is finally getting out," Rogers says. He's also worked the past few years as a tour naturalist/guide along the same Katmai Coast that Timothy Treadwell walked and freely admits that black bears aren't the same critters as their larger, generally more volatile cousins. However, he also believes that many of the same basic truths and principles apply to both species; *Ursus arctos* is hardly the savage killer of legend. "There's a lot we have to learn about grizzlies," Rogers says (unlike most Alaska biologists, he doesn't make the distinction between coastal browns and interior grizzlies). He observed Timothy interacting with bears at Hallo Bay and was impressed both by the level of trust between man and bears, and by the understanding of bear body language and vocalizations that Treadwell demonstrated.

"Over twelve years, Timothy . . . conducted important work that shows we can get closer safely than anyone thought," he says. When I point out the obvious, that Timothy's end belies that conclusion, Rogers admits, "I don't think I'd push it as far with grizzlies as I would with black bears . . . and certainly not as far as he did."

And in the next breath, he points out that Timothy was indeed successful for all those seasons until this one incident. Asked if he believes a person can truly establish a friendship with a wild bear, he's cautious. "With the exception of one black bear, a very special case, I don't think I ever reached that level. I believe it's more tolerance than friendship. I'm not a friend, but I'm not a foe." He adds, "Even after thirty-eight years, I'm still a very careful guy around bears. I'm always on guard, judging each individual from moment to moment."

Rogers enumerates other members of the fraternity dedicated to providing evidence that bears—specifically brown/grizzlies—and people can coexist peacefully. There's Charlie Russell, the Alberta rancher turned naturalist, who's spent the past fifteen years attempting to demonstrate the point, as well as protect bears from very real poachers, on Russia's Kamchatka Peninsula; independent biologist and author Stephen Stringham, who regularly conducts close-range bear research on the Katmai Coast and counted Timothy as a friend; and Vitaly Nikolayenko, who for thirty-three years moved among Russia's Kamchatka bears and arguably outdid everyone else, following bears at close range and documenting the lives of individual animals. Pioneering the sort of technique later adopted by Timothy, Vitaly gave bears names and followed them closely, filming and jotting notes as he went. Each autumn he accompanied his favorite, an enormous old male he named Dobrynya ("Kind Bear") to his den, lay down at the entrance, and drank a toast to the animal's upcoming winter sleep. When Dobrynya died, apparently of natural causes, Vitaly was as unconsolable as if the bear had been his son.

If the cumulative record of all these behavioral experiments is meant to demonstrate the capacity of people and bears to get along, Lynn Rogers has secured his point about black bears. In addition to his personal research, the wide-flung presence of *Ursus americanus* in the lower forty-eight seems irrefutable evidence that the black bear can indeed manage to live around people—quite peaceably and unobtrusively, in fact—on the edges of housing developments from Pennsylvania to northern California. But when it comes to the big ticket item—brown/grizzlies—the overall result amounts to a negative landslide. While Charlie Russell certainly has demonstrated that he can both move safely among wild bears and serve as a surrogate parent for a succession of semiwild orphan cubs, his peaceable kingdom in the Russian Far East came to an abrupt end in spring of 2003 when he returned to his research site at remote Kambalnoye Lake to find all the bears he'd taught to trust human presence, as many as twenty animals, gone, slaughtered by poachers. A young bear's gall bladder was nailed to his cabin wall, as if in rebuttal. Apparently Russell's habituating the bears made it all the easier to approach and shoot them. Vitaly Nikolayenko fared even worse; he was killed two months after Timothy and Amie by a dominant male he followed through deep snow into a dense thicket, ignoring pointed and repeated signals from the bear (recorded in his journal) that it was intolerant of humans—intent stares, growls, jaw popping, and bluff charges. That Vitaly knew the bear was on edge was evident by the fact that he entered the brush with pepper spray in one hand, camera in the other. Still he went, somehow believing that all would be well. The bear exploded from the alders at a distance of four paces, and Vitaly was dead. The snow was spattered with a dense cone of orange bear spray, as if he were hit before he got a chance to aim. The incident seems to have been a purely defensive-aggressive charge, culminating in a massive, killing blow to the skull. The bear ran into the hills and disappeared, apparently into his winter den.

All in all, 2003 was a lousy year for the collective experiment in brown/grizzly-human *amistad*: three humans dead (Timothy, Amie, Vitaly) and a pile of habituated bears poached. Not to mention the two bears killed at Kaflia by the rangers. There's no doubt that the rate of carnage over this period is unprecedented and anomalous; and one can point to the cumulative decades these men managed to move safely among the big bears—and the bears among them. Nonetheless, the final tally stands.

The most salient question in the Grizzly People experiment is less obvious than the raw outcome. What's the point? More specifically, what's the benefit of trying to prove grizzlies and people can get along in close quarters? If the bears' own well-being rules all other considerations, the conclusion seems a no-brainer: The only certain way to keep brown/grizzlies safe from humans, and vice versa, is to give the bears large chunks of protected habitat and step back. Repeated and prolonged contact at arm's length, even by well-meaning experts in bear behavior, has just been proven, QED, to be, sooner or later, a recipe for disaster, and the bears are the ultimate losers. Over and over, biologists, viewing guides, and others who know the Katmai Coast and its bears make the same point—it's not a question of *if* we can habituate free-ranging brown/grizzlies to point-blank human presence, but if we *should*.

In the largest sense, we already knew the answer to the question of grizzly–human interaction. As a glance at a map of remaining brown/grizzly habitat will confirm, these bears thrive in suitable habitat wherever people are few enough. More humans means a diametrical decrease in bears; in the cold math of logic, alternates exclude. Consider the examples of San Francisco and Denver— once prime grizzly areas now devoid of bears—and the issue becomes crystal clear. Build enough condos and strip malls on the Katmai Coast or in Yellowstone, and kiss the bears good-bye. Preserve habitat and give them enough room, and they'll be fine. There will be no grizzly in the backyard, fence-hopping like some mutant squirrel, nibbling a few nuts here and there. White-tail deer and raccoons, coyotes, and even black bears can make the suburban transition; *Ursus arctos* has demonstrated by its simple absence in such environs that as a species, it can't. It might be pretty to think otherwise, but the evidence offers scant room for debate. They're creatures that demand landscapes as big and wild as themselves.

Of course, there are rural areas where human and brown/grizzly habitat overlap—my backyard in Juneau, Alaska, for example, or the rangelands adjacent to Yellowstone and Glacier National Parks (the latter, in the general area of Charlie Russell's family ranch). In comparatively rare locales like these, our tolerance of these animals as neighbors is indeed an issue. But by and large, local residents in places like this already accept bears as part of the landscape. My neighbors, for example, know there are brown bears around (occasionally someone gets shaken up by a close encounter or even a bluff charge) and still they walk their dogs and kids without worrying too much or carrying guns. People who live around bears who would shoot first and ask questions later are hardly the sort to be transformed by a message of peaceful coexistence—especially one borne by Timothy Treadwell's ghost. One might argue that the Grizzly People message à la Charlie Russell is largely an exercise in preaching to the choir.

At any rate, the keystone to the survival of *Ursus arctos* in a strategic, worldwide sense doesn't hinge on close-quarters tolerance in these fringe habitat areas, but upon continued or expanded protection of habitat already encompassed by national parks, preserves, and similar areas. Certainly work of the sort accomplished by Russell in Kamchatka (he has been instrumental in securing a designation of World Heritage Site to a large chunk of prime Russian bear habitat, and gaining funding for rangers) is of enormous, undeniable value. On the other hand, most bear biologists agree that attempting to prove that grizzlies and humans can make nicey-nice is less about species survival than ideology and personal agenda. The point is moot to the bears, who couldn't care less about human trust or physical affection. They're too busy being themselves, and are at best indifferent to our existence unless we insinuate ourselves into their lives.

Nonetheless, one can understand where the Grizzly People impulse comes from, and empathize with its adherents. Beyond that ancient-rooted profession of kinship—a bond so pervasive it verges on archetype—recall that at the time of Lewis and Clark fifty thousand or more grizzlies roamed the American West. Their 1804 expedition reduced that number by forty-seven individuals and the downward spiral proceeded from there. In the 1860s a former army major named Bell reported in his memoirs that in the canyons of Malibu, where Timothy Treadwell would one day make his home, grizzlies were "more abundant than pigs," and that "the rearing of cattle [was] impossible" due to the sheer volume of predatory bears. By the early 1920s, thanks in no small part to a ten-dollar state bounty for each grizzly scalp (a considerable sum at the time, which created for some hunters a full-time job), the only big bear left in California was on the state flag.

Across the West, no one considered conserving the species for any reason—sport, a stable ecosystem, spiritual concerns, or aesthetics. The objective was pure and direct: complete and utter extermination, in the name of the common good. The I-Thou relationship between humans and *Ursus arctos* that had existed for millennia was, in a matter of a century, replaced by a blunt I-It equation. By 1950 only a few hundred animals remained in the lower forty-eight, pushed back into tiny fragments of their former range, mostly in Montana and Wyoming, in the vicinity of Yellowstone and Glacier National Parks. Their future hung by a thread. Not until the general greening trend that asserted itself in the latter half of the twentieth century (a notable example being the Endangered Species Act of 1973) did the great bears begin to recover. Once the westering was done, it seems that we began to rediscover in ourselves the deeply rooted, mystical bond between the great bears and ourselves—a trend that continues to this day.

And from here, the trail leads back to Timothy Treadwell. He emerged out of this backdrop, shaped by it, part and parcel of it. After Malibu, cluttered with beach houses and BMWs, the wild expanse of the Katmai Coast must have seemed a place out of time. Whether he knew all the details of history or not, he sensed them—this is what California once was. All these great bears going about their lives, ignoring human presence. And out of this realization sprang that epiphany: *These bears must be saved. I will save them.* His fervent animal-rights stance was an offshoot of that aforementioned greening trend, which itself seems a reaction to the excesses of the preceding two centuries. The fact that Katmai wasn't California, and Alaska's thirty-some thousand brown/grizzlies were as numerous as ever, was easy enough for Timothy, a product of his environment, to overlook.

In one real sense, though, Treadwell was correct. These bears are endangered—not in an immediate sense, but a dispassionate observer would concede the Katmai Coast is one of the last places in the world where concentrations of brown/grizzlies so great in both size and numbers exist. Timothy, who'd never been hunting in his life, must have been overwhelmed by Alaskan culture—which is as unapologetically predatory as it comes. It was all too easy to morph rumors and old stories of poachers in Katmai National Park into a deadly, moment-by-moment threat under which the bears lived. To his lower-forty-eight audiences, most of whom live in a landscape long shorn of large predators, Timothy's assertions made perfect sense. Among supporters, he was—and still is—hailed as a warrior manning the walls of a distant, embattled outpost. And it's all a reaction to the legacy set in motion by Lewis and Clark.

Aside from those dedicated to seeking a spiritual bond between humans and the great bears, uncounted millions of people appear to be magnetically drawn into the maze. In fact, the prominent place bears occupy in modern culture seems an extension of the ancient professions of kinship. We don't have to look very far to butt against dozens of representations in popular culture—some complimentary, some negative, others contradictory, and all somehow true to us. Consider Yogi, the comical, happy-go-lucky thief; the fearsome beast on seemingly every other outdoor magazine cover; cute and cuddly Teddy; solemn and wise Smokey; the cloyingly kind Berenstain Bears; the lurking, man-eating monster in dozens of films. To be sure, we're fond of lions, wolves, elephants, apes, and whales, but no single wild creature takes up as much space in our bestial cosmology. An anthropologist from another planet would no doubt be intrigued by our preoccupation, and how we garnish our lives with bears—Care Bears, Gummi Bears, and the Chicago Bears; Gentle Ben and Goldilocks's famous trio; the skin rug before the fireplace. Our visitor might scratch his head and wonder what sort of god we've chosen, and why we cast him in such strange and varying light.

The tale stretches from the uncertain reaches of prehistory, through our species's headlong expansion across the northern hemisphere, into the dawn of the twenty-first century—a tracing of the mingled destinies of bears and humans, and of our ambiguous, at times schizophrenic relationship. Over the centuries, we've swung from worshiping them as gods to exterminating them as pests to striving for their preservation. Bears are the demonic beasts in the night; yet generations of children have cuddled and gained comfort with their stuffed likeness and giggled at the antics of Winnie the Pooh. We see ourselves in them, turn them into sports logos, cast them up into the sky as constellations, cherish them as living treasures, and kill them for sport. Whatever its source or impetus, our obsession with bears shows no sign of fading. Timothy Treadwell's media success was propelled by it; Charlie Russell, Lynn Rogers, Canadian Jeff Turner, and German adventurer Andreas Kieling each have starred in well-received and frequently rerun television specials in the last few years, all of which present, in one version or another, the Grizzly People message: peaceful bears and humans, hand in paw.

On the silver screen, let's not forget Disney's *Brother Bear*, the French film titled simply *The Bear*, and, as antidote, the recent retro killer-griz flick, the 1996 Anthony Hopkins/Alec Baldwin vehicle, *The Edge*. The latter two also featured Doug Seuss's enormous Kodiak bear, Bart (now deceased)—one of the few trained animals ever to gain star recognition in their own right. And over his career he kept more than busy, working everything from commercials to bit parts (remember that cave bear in *Quest for Fire?*) to stock photography shoots. His popularity was no coincidence; it was species specific, driven by our lust for bears. We have, for example, no Lobo the Wolf or Elmer the Elephant, known and loved by millions.

On the darker side, a smattering of inane bear programming has emerged on television, all but exhorting bad behavior; one such example from the bottom rung is on the November 2003 episode of the MTV series *The Wildboyz*. It features a trio of leering grunge heads performing a variety of irreverent acts with wildlife—among them, approaching brown bears while wearing a bear suit and snorkeling within ten feet of foraging bears at well-known Wolverine Creek, all with broad winks to the audience and reminders to not try this at home and that this is all "in the name of science." And the way they say it, it's clear they mean the opposite. Then there's Crocodile Hunter clone Jeff Corwin on Disney Educational Productions' *Going Wild!*, traipsing around in the black of night with a headlamp in heavy brush, approaching what's represented as a wild grizzly in Montana's Glacier National Park. One problem—of many—is that the footage is actually filmed down the road at the Triple D Game Farm, with a rented bear named BJ, and that attempting to duplicate the same feat in wild habitat in Glacier (which is the clear invitation) is liable to get someone's scalp ripped off. And the target audience—this is an educational film aimed at elementary classrooms—is instructed to sneak around quietly in bear country and to maintain a distance of only thirty meters—both directives, according to bear safety literature, thoroughly bad ideas.

One last, far milder example of bear television gone awry is a BBC wildlife special, "Grizzly: Face to Face," featuring Canadian filmmaker Jeff Turner. Turner, a Grizzly Person if ever there was one (as well as a talented cameraman) at one point gives the viewer careful, step-by-step general instructions on how to closely approach bears, including a female "grizzly" with cubs—while the video in question is of a certain highly habituated, tolerant coastal brown bear that knows Turner well. At one point, a cub nuzzles the camera lens. An experienced bear hand might know the difference between this encounter and a cranky interior Alaska griz; but the audience is far broader than that. The message is there for Joe Blow from Yonkers: *Yo, you, too, can do this.*

One might expect that this sort of exposure in the media has led to increased interest in getting personal with the real thing in his woods, and indeed it has. In the only places in the lower forty-eight where folks might realistically hope to see grizzlies—Yellowstone and Glacier National Parks—any sighting by park roads results in what rangers call a "bear jam," a knot of people, cameras in hand, crowding to glimpse a grizzly. They often ignore official warnings to keep back, sometimes elbowing to within mere feet of females with cubs, or bears feeding on carrion, without having a clue of the potential danger. Chuck Bartlebaugh, director of the Center for Wildlife Information in Missoula, says, "It's my belief that the media is creating an enthusiasm for wildlife without instilling proper respect or responsibility. . . . They see Jeff Corwin faking a grizzly experience and think it's safe if they do the same thing in the wild." As a Yellowstone bus driver years ago, Bartlebaugh was arrested once (he's proud to say) for trying to keep an excited, unrestrained group of viewers from crowding a grizzly.

Meanwhile, in Alaska, that incredible surge continues in the bear-viewing industry, focused on the Katmai Coast (due to its superior opportunities) but overflowing across Alaska from Anan and Pack Creeks in the far southeast to Denali National Park in the state's center, and north to the Arctic Wildlife Refuge. Visitors want, more than anything else, to see bears, specifically "grizzlies," and are disappointed if they don't. And the fact is, most of them won't, unless they're lucky—though if they head for Katmai or a handful of similar places, they can marvel at the same coastal brownies (in some cases, the very same bears) that enthralled Timothy. Even there, however, folks might see them near enough to count their claws, or they might not. Wild bears don't often pose and wave, and really don't care if we get a good look. People don't get it—and they want their bears up close. Like those people down south, they saw it on TV and paid their money to get here, often many thousands of dollars, which ups the ante and puts more pressure on the guide to slip just a bit closer. Most do resist the pressure, but a few inevitably give in. There's enough competition in the industry now that some carriers are having difficulty filling up their planes above the break-even mark, and the word of who gives a good "view" gets out. Delivering is a matter of livelihood. The fact that there hasn't been one incident of a bear-caused human fatality (or vice versa) among guided bear viewers on the Katmai Coast might be interpreted as a sign that everyone's operating safely, but it's also a tribute to the still-astounding tolerance of the bears. That fact also breeds complacency, and the temptation, among a few, to edge in just a bit closer.

The ultimate irony is that the crowds' jacked-up expectations and sometimes churlish actions are at least in part the product of a few men who loved bears above all else and dedicated their lives to creating greater understanding and protection. Timothy Treadwell could lament the increasing pressure brought on his bears by the viewing industry, but it was, in fact, a beast he helped to create. All his media spots, the specials, and the footage he shot might as well have been infomercials for Hallo Bay. His attempts to disguise his locations were at best naïve, considering anyone who plugs "Bear Viewing Alaska" into a Google search will un-earth dozens of well-tooled operators clamoring to take you to the Katmai Coast. This might have been Timothy's greatest act of hubris: Somehow he thought he could present such images with-out fueling both the awareness that such places existed and the desire to go there. He helped build it, and sure enough, they came.

Treadwell's Bears

I sit at my window, staring out at a rain-spattered autumn landscape, the willows flickering yellow beneath a lowering sky. October 5, 2004—exactly one year since Timothy Treadwell and Amie Huguenard died. I've just returned home to Juneau from a week at Kukak Bay, on the Katmai Coast, watching and photographing bears—no doubt some of the same ones Timothy knew and named. This was the place he'd called the Forbidden Zone, where he'd once called for an emergency pickup. He sometimes camped on the grassy point we skirted each afternoon, on our way to the creek and tidal flats where bears wandered in and out of sight as they foraged for the season's last salmon. Most moved past us with scarcely a glance; but one enormous old male bounded off after catching our scent at a quarter mile. Another dark, chunky bear served us notice by suddenly detouring across the creek, swaggering with elbows out and head low, to within ten feet of us, before breaking off his stare and going back to pretending we didn't exist. Each bear was an individual, responding to cues we could guess at but never know. There was no hint of kinship or interest; only that one brief flicker of animosity. They seemed to tolerate us in remarkable fashion, even as our presence sometimes seemed to deflect their chosen paths. The envelope between us and that one bear, the difference between his walking away or making contact, was thin but intact nevertheless; in physical terms, not much more than the span of my arms.

Across the bay and over a low rise lay Kaflia, and Timothy's Grizzly Maze—no more than five miles, an afternoon's walk for a bear. I could picture that knoll above the west end of the lake; how the summer's grass, now dying, had overgrown the campsite; the bear bones and clumps of hair scattered in the alders, bleached by sun and rain, nibbled by voles. And the bears themselves, drifting like ghosts along the tunneled trails through the thickets, as they had for centuries. If the land ever knew that Timothy Treadwell existed, it had already forgotten.

The human world is another matter. Along the Katmai Coast and in Kodiak people still trade Timothy anecdotes as if they just saw him yesterday; of course, you'd expect it there. But from Hollywood to New York and across continents, the Timothy Treadwell story—on its way to becoming the single most publicized bear attack in history—continues to reverberate. Now the third wave of Treadwellia is massing: books, films, and a smattering of televised treatments. While none has been released at the time of this writing, no doubt these efforts will, like the second wave, continue to run the gamut, from breathless ambulance-chasing to scathing critique to heroic apologia. If bears were the prism in which Timothy saw himself, he has become in death the same for us; the battle over his legacy and soul continues apace. While friends and family, as well as those who oppose what he stood for, may find the level of attention discomfiting, we can guess at one exception.

"If Timothy is looking down from somewhere and watching," says Joel Bennett, "he's rubbing his hands together, loving every minute." At five minutes past midnight, he's famous at last.

So far, the most notable and clear-cut media face-off over

Timothy is represented by two films, both of which will have aired by the time this is published: first, *The Grizzly Man,* A Lion's Gate documentary directed by German Werner Herzog, slated for theatrical release and subsequent airtime on the Discovery Channel. With Jewel Palovak of Grizzly People named as executive producer, it's likely there will be a few poachers lurking in the shrubbery and a heroic slant on events.* In the opposite corner is a far more modest thirty-minute effort by Kodiak filmmakers Stefan Quinth and ex–state biologist David Kaplan—*Deadly Passion,* a documentary tracing, its makers say, the simple, unvarnished facts of the tragedy. Says Kaplan, "This isn't a personal attack on Timothy Treadwell. However, this is an Alaskan story and we need to take ownership of it. This isn't about magic, it's about basic mistakes that Timothy made, mistakes that ultimately resulted in the deaths of two people and two bears. We need to get the word out to prevent this tragedy from repeating itself. What business do outsiders have, people who have never seen a wild bear before, coming in and creating a legend where none exists?" Though Kaplan has an edge on his voice, his logic seems straightforward. Regardless, when show biz and Kodiak square off on the silver screen, the outcome, in terms of audience reached, seems a foregone conclusion. Consider that one is slated to premiere at the 2005 Sundance Film Festival; the other at a decidedly less prestigious event in Anchorage, Alaska.

Before our eyes, the story of Timothy Treadwell is shifting with each retelling, with each rotation of spin applied by those who feel compelled either to defend or condemn him. Either way, the process is insidious, and if we don't watch carefully, we'll miss the morphing of half-truths or conjecture into fact.

For example, a few weeks ago I ran across a syndicated *Washington Post* story regarding the Bush administration's proposed

---

*Another project, a scripted drama starring Leonardo DiCaprio as Timothy, is apparently on hold.

delisting of the grizzly as an endangered species in the lower forty-eight. In a section about the potential danger the bears posed, it referred to the death of Timothy, and positively named the bear that killed him: The Big Red Machine. The source? A chatty *Vanity Fair* article with significant fact-checking lapses. The writer, Ned Zeman, had posited the identity of the killer bear as The Big Red Machine. He allowed his conclusion wasn't watertight but was strongly supported by circumstantial evidence—a point with which I concur. But now, by being printed in the hallowed pages of *The Washington Post*, the killer bear's identity is fixed. Clearly the past (as any honest historian will admit) may be subject not only to interpretation, but revision.

The battle continues on personal levels as well, below the glare of media lights. There are still bear biologists, bear-viewing guides, and wildlife rights advocates out there, grinding their teeth over what they see as an impending beatification of Timothy and an inevitable wave of wannabes blundering out into the brush to find their own bears to befriend. Some of these opponents, separately or in concert, refuse to let the matter fade. One obvious such attempt showed up in my e-mail in-box six months after the tragedy—as well as those of many other writers and bear scientists—with a note at the end to pass it forward. The document, a full ten single-spaced pages titled "Bear Activist and Companion Mauled to Death in Alaska," follows a point-by-point question-and-answer format, comparing "Hollywood Hype" in each case with "The Reality." Artful and concise, it's obviously written by a trained professional who has both done his homework and invested many hours in craft; I'd argue, due to language choices, points of argument, and logic-tight, rat-trap construction, a professional scientist with more than a few papers under his belt. The document is a wire-to-wire body slam clearly meant to counter any attempt to cast Timothy in the least flicker of positive light. The identity of the author is shielded by an anonymous e-mail account. What separates this document from knee-jerk reactions immediately following the tragedy is the clear intent to sustain a negative campaign. Obviously, Timothy Treadwell is still alive and well, and a threat to someone, somewhere.

Unabashed Treadwell apologists, many self-styled ecowarriors themselves, continue to counterattack, loath to admit the least hint of negative press concerning Timothy. He remains in death what he was in life: their Bear Whisperer, a selfless martyr in the battle for bear preservation and a guiding light. Their faith refuses any complications in this vision; any shred of evidence to the contrary is dismissed as right-wing propaganda or the product of beetle-browed evolution. Some of these supporters, including Jewel, point to the senseless killing of several bears in summer 2004 at Funnel Creek, near the southern shores of Lake Iliamna, as vindication of Timothy's claims of poaching—and of his effectiveness in preventing such horrors. As an article by Sean Neilson in the fall 2004 issue of *California Wild* (a magazine published under the auspices of the California Academy of Sciences) states, "Since his death there has been an increase in bear poaching in Katmai National Park. To keep bears safe, Treadwell must have known that he had to keep himself safe." Regardless of the writer's intentions—in this case, altered by an editor—the implication is clear: Because Timothy is dead, this happened. Timothy, however, never ventured anywhere near Funnel Creek; to suggest that his presence a hundred miles to the southwest in Hallo or Kaflia Bays would have prevented the shooting is dubious spin at best. And the shooters have been traced to a nearby Native village; the carcasses showed no signs of sport or market poaching—skins, gall bladders, and all but a few of the claws were untouched. Investigators posit an unplanned, isolated thrill kill by local young men.

Others suggest the killings were committed in fact *because* of Treadwell—a reaction by someone made overly fearful and edgy by his and Amie's deaths. Without a doubt, the ideological saw cuts both ways, and the players on each end are impelled by un-shakable conviction.

Almost drowned in the continuing wrangles are the voices of those who simply knew Timothy, the Katmai Coast, and its bears, and counted all three as friends—people like Joel Bennett, Kathleen Parker, and Willy Fulton. None of them denies or apologizes for Timothy's foibles and contradictions, and don't share his starry-eyed vision of the natural world. Neither do they have an agenda to shove forward. They merely saw his essential goodness and humanity, his commitment to his cause, and a personal warmth that transcended all differences.

Fulton, a year later, stands by Timothy. "He was a fine guy with a lot of character. Even though we came from different spaces and I'm a hunter, he could see past all that and be my friend."

Parker says, "He was just a great, great person. So intelligent and full of energy and life." In practically the next breath, she laughs over his mechanical incompetence, his junk-food diet of Coke and candy corn, his inability to pitch a tent that wouldn't blow away. And then she reflects how the world seems emptier without him. His tents and gear still lie in her basement. She still weeps now and then, though she admits she knew he couldn't last forever.

What do I think of Timothy Treadwell, this familiar stranger, after a year of being immersed in the details of his life and death? Some days I catch myself mourning him too; at other times, anger wells up as I mull over the dozens of gaps between mission and deed, and where it all led; but always I return to the question posed by Joel, which has become some sort of dangling mantra: *What sort of man would do that?* Not much different from what my old Eskimo neighbor Ned Howarth asked me: *How come you try to do that?* And depending on the day or moment, I arrive at any of several answers—saint, sinner, wise man, fool. Conflicting, contradictory, yet occupying the same space, the same truth. I expect that even if Timothy and I had known each other for years I'd feel the same. And the details of the case, after all this time, are no less enigmatic—though the broader vision of what happened and why seems to have jelled somewhat. Still, compelling theories continue to eddy around the case; impossible to either prove or refute, they nonetheless offer flickers of insight. For example, an interpretation offered by bear-viewing guide Gary Porter:

"I think Timmy made a fundamental anthropomorphic error," he says. "Naming them and hanging around with them as long as he did, he probably forgot they were bears. And maybe they forgot, some of the time, he was human." Trying to make further sense of the tragedy, Porter points out that old, dominant males generally avoid people and are intolerant of other bears. A subordinate bear that refuses to move is attacked and, if it doesn't retreat, is often killed and eaten. Larry Van Daele calls such an event "apparently more of a disciplinary action than predatory." And he, too, agrees there may be something to the theory, especially given "the strange, ambiguous signals Timothy sent to bears." Porter shrugs. "Maybe that big guy figured Timmy was just another bear." If so, it was a final, ironic compliment to a man who strove, among bears, to become as much like them as possible. And it's a conclusion some of Timothy's staunchest supporters hold as evidence that their hero did indeed gain the ultimate badge of acceptance in ursine society.

The musing over what and why seems destined to wander off toward a vanishing point in the brush; but in the end, I think the answer to the salient question is simple. What killed Timothy Treadwell wasn't a choice of campsite, lack of pepper spray, or even a bear. It was love, the intense, all-consuming passion of a tragic hero—a protagonist motivated by noble intentions, yet somehow doomed to destroy not only himself but the things he cherished most. Othello, Romeo, and Captain Ahab would be right there at his elbow, nudging him forward, with audiences of millions leaning in. And as we watch in horrified fascination, no suspense beyond the inevitable tug downward, we're powerless to help. We want to shout, *Don't do it, look out,* but it's no use. As Timothy unzips his tent one last time and steps out into the rain, he forges the last link in a chain of events shaped by his essential nature. We can only watch him go. Somehow, at the end, what dies is a little of ourselves, a death that curiously lifts us up, allows us to see in a flashing instant our intertwined capacity for greatness and folly. In the process of telling Timothy Treadwell's story, we end up telling our own.

And though we've left our stone-tooled, hand-to-mouth lifestyle far behind, the impulse clearly remains, evidenced by our continuing preoccupation with bears. Timothy Treadwell's life and death, and our collective reaction to his tale, serve to remind us of this bond that seems implanted in genetic memory, so deep that we're almost compelled to listen. Grandfather. Elder Brother. Beloved Uncle. Maybe our ancestors, actual or metaphorical, were onto something—and we keep snapping our fingers, trying to remember how the story goes. What was Timothy Treadwell but a reflection of that age-old longing—quite different in action from the contemporary Eskimo, the bear biologist, or the well-heeled trophy hunter, yet so much in essence the same? A shaman from another century, watching Timothy wander or sit among his bears, mimicking their movements and postures, might have understood his actions perfectly: He was, as he so often insisted, trying to become a bear—perhaps had even succeeded.

New Age gobbledygook? Fits of over-the-top, faux transcendentalism? Grounded as we are in a culture dominated by rational thought, ruled by the scientific method, it's easy to write off Timothy Treadwell, practically as a conditioned reflex. But you only have to drop back a few paltry years to find millions of people, entire cultures, that would not have found his perspective strange at all. It would be our world view, insisting on the impoverished domain of mere facts, denying the inexplicable forces of the spirit, the magic of the bear, that would seem foreign. Who are we to say what form that magic should take? Even Park Service official Deb Liggett allows, "I'm sure, in the end, Timothy found his whole reason for being with those bears. It was a spiritual thing."

As we wander in the tunnels of the Grizzly Maze, each question, like a worn path, doubles back on another. What of the bears—not only those of Katmai, but the thirty-odd thousand brown/grizzlies that are scattered across the rest of Alaska, the thousand more in encircled enclaves in the American West, and the additional hundred thousand worldwide? The fortunes of local populations continue to wax and wane; the main factors in their survival remain sufficient habitat, sound management practices, and reasonable protection (especially in the Russian Far East) from indiscriminate slaughter. Given that chance, bears—the ultimate survivalists—will do the rest on their own. When the evidence is weighed, it's hard to argue that Timothy Treadwell, ensconced as he was among some of the best managed and protected bears on the planet, had any direct, positive impact on their survival. In fact, there are some that would argue convincingly for a score of minus two.

However, not all successes are measured in such simple terms. Even the negative shadow cast by his and Amie's deaths doesn't negate the thousands of schoolchildren he reached, who shouted bear facts back to him in unison, wrote piles of letters, and went home excited to learn more. Maybe his death is a shock to some; but maybe it's an object lesson to others about commitment to a cause. Conservation doesn't occur in a vacuum, and our collective and benign tolerance of bears is far more critical and real an issue than their tolerance of us. If bears are still walking the beaches at Hallo Bay, the sedge fields of far eastern Russia, and the pine forests of Montana a hundred years from now, it will be because enough people—including the children Timothy touched, and their children—cared enough to make it happen. This is finally not a story about death and failure, but of light and hope. And it's not really about Timothy Treadwell, but the bears he loved.

Bears. As if to remind me, just a few weeks ago, in late July of 2004, my old friend Lynn Norstadt was taken down by a female grizzly in Wrangell–St. Elias National Park, where, thirteen years before, Timothy had met his first and only real grizzly. Lynn was lucky. Considering the circumstances—surprising a female with two cubs—the bear was polite, as they nearly always are. Lynn got off with a massive, paw-shaped bruise on his chest and two deep but clean puncture wounds in one thigh. The bears ran off, Lynn walked out, and that was that. And yesterday, I left the house with the dogs for our usual twilight run, got an odd feeling, and went back to the house for my bear spray. A mile down the trail, I caught the musty, unmistakable scent of a bear in the October woods—fresh, minutes or seconds old. Probably the brown bear female and grown cub that had been wandering the area. The dogs stood stiff legged and silent in the dusk, noses quivering. *Hey, bear!* I said in a low voice, and we trotted on.

Despite the fact that attacks remain as rare as ever, all of us who spend time around bears can't help but see them in a different light. As Larry Aumiller, the manager for the famed McNeil River State Game Sanctuary, a man with three decades of intimate experience with coastal brown bears, says, "Frankly, Timothy's incident and what happened to Vitaly have reminded me that I don't control events." Overall, he's become more cautious as the years have gone on, even given the McNeil Sanctuary's flawless record for bear and human safety. "It's critical," he says, "that we remain incident free." At McNeil, well managed and unique as it is, that may be possible. But elsewhere is another story. If we're realistic, we must accept that the next incident, the next tragedy for humans and bears, is only a matter of time. It's up to us to make ourselves as safe as possible, since the bears can only continue to be themselves. Grandfather is in his woods; what we do with that knowledge is another open question.

From my trip to Kaflia and Timothy's Grizzly Maze a year ago, I remember many things—the furrowed web of bear trails, the flutter of signs in the wind, the way the water tinted green in the shallows, then fell away to darkness. But most of all I remember the huge old male bear we passed as we taxied up the lake for takeoff—quite possibly the same one that had almost strolled through the rescue team. He'd been wading lazily along the shore, picking off the last few dying salmon. At our approach he climbed laboriously up the bank, huffing, and tried to hide his enormous, almost ridiculously fat bulk behind a half-bare alder. In another few days he'd clamber up the mountain, burrow into his den, and go to sleep for the winter. He didn't need anything from us. He wasn't our friend. He had no name. All he wanted was to be left alone.

Afterword: The Beast of Nightmare

This entire story leads toward a couple of overwhelming questions: First, how dangerous are bears, anyway? Second, short of staying out of the woods or shooting bears right and left, what can be done to make both bears and people more safe? The answer to number one seems self-evident. Aren't we talking about a thousand-pound predator here, an animal combining the speed and agility of a quarter horse with the raw power of an ox and an intelligence that at times seems to rival our own—with a proven record of killing and eating humans? And doesn't the case of Timothy Treadwell just add one more scrap of grisly evidence to an already sizable pile? But, like almost everything having to do with *Ursus arctos*, there seems to be no single answer. It all depends on perspective and whom you talked to last.

Let's focus on the middle ground, sidestepping the slippery slope of personal belief and ideology. What do the numbers tell us? Oddly enough, there is no definitive, one-stop-shopping database on bear attacks for either the world or North America—this despite our endless fascination with such incidents. Attacks without injuries, which are quite common, generally go unreported, especially outside of national parks. And injury accounts might make the local headlines but not the national news. It's not like there's been some national bear-attack statistics clearinghouse in operation, now or ever. Even for just the United States over the past century, the exact tally of bear attacks resulting in human death is uncertain. The numbers available may well exclude a few. This caveat aside, we do have enough statistics available to give us a decent handle on the issue. Dr. Stephen Herrero, widely regarded as a, if not the, leading scientific authority in the study of bear attacks, offers a database covering bears attacks in Canada and the United States (including Alaska) from 1900 to 1980, built largely from National Park Service statistics plus a few other documented cases. According to his figures, over this eight-decade period, brown/grizzlies were responsible for 165 injuries in a total of 143 attacks, including 41 deaths. Herrero allows that the number of injuries (excluding fatalities) is probably underreported by half. So let's say, over eighty years, 330 injuries, including 41 deaths, in all of North America. Meanwhile, black bears (not counting captive animals) were responsible for 23 human fatalities, which works out to a grand total of 64 bear-caused deaths. No total for black-bear-caused injury is reported for the entire period, though Herrero does state that from 1960 to 1980, just two decades, over 500 injuries were attributed to black bears. More on that last, curiously high figure later.

There's a more recent database, created by Dr. Tom Smith of the USGS and Dr. Herrero again. This one focuses just on Alaska over a 102-year stretch, 1900 to 2002. Considering that ninety-odd percent of the state is brown/grizzly habitat, and we're talking about 30 to 40 thousand animals in all plus roughly 640,000 human residents (not to mention 2 million visitors per year), this seems a more relevant set of numbers. After all, Herrero's first database includes brown/grizzly-caused deaths in areas where the bears have been extinct for three quarters of a century. And from

1940 on, we're talking about a total lower-forty-eight *Ursus arctos* population of around 1,000 bears, wedged into a mere postage stamp of their historic range. Meanwhile, Alaska bear numbers have remained basically stable over the last century, while the human population continues to expand. Our largest state is thus a far more stringent litmus test of ursine–human relations. (Alaska's black bear population, by the way, is estimated at 110,000 or more additional animals, and polar bears, roughly 7,500; this brings the total ratio of resident humans to bears in Alaska to roughly four to one).

Anyway, Smith and Herrero came up with 500 Alaskan incidents over a century involving three species of bear (brown/grizzly, black, and polar). There were a total of 56 bear-caused human fatalities over the period (this figure doesn't include Timothy and Amie, who died in 2003). Overall, the numbers break down to just over one bear-caused fatality every two years for all three species. Even many folks who know bears well are surprised when they hear how low the overall fatality figure is. Still, the death rate is much higher proportionately than that indicated by Herrero's earlier study, which, including as it did the entire population of North America, reflected an exponentially higher human–bear ratio, at least a few hundred thousand people per bear. The truth is, for the average reasonably active outdoors person today, the statistical probability of being killed by a bear ranks up there with choking to death on a baseball bat or being whacked by a flying piano. Of course, the more you work or play around bears, especially alone and moving quietly, without defensive backup, the more the risk increases; the cases of Tim Treadwell and Michio Hoshino seem to confirm that generalization, but they hardly represent the norm.

Why, then, do we have the impression that bear attacks—especially brown/grizzly—constitute a significant menace to life and limb? Part of it has to do with the high-profile nature of the more spectacular and gruesome maulings, and our horrified fascination with the details. What if Tim and Amie had died in a motorcycle crash instead, or of galloping staph infections? Even in their hometown papers, they'd have rated a quick obituary at best. Instead, they've launched an international media tsunami that's still rolling inland. It's not just Tim and Amie either—though the circumstances of the case and Tim's relative celebrity are certainly factors. Bear mauling stories get told again and again until each seems to clone and multiply, like those bucket-lugging brooms in *Fantasia.*

Despite the relatively small number of cases, bear attack books have practically become a genre by themselves. There's a pile of them out there, with titles like *Bear Attacks: The Deadly Truth,* *Some Bears Kill,* and *Killer Bears.* Some authors, like Canadian James Gary Shelton and Alaska's Larry Kaniut, have made a career of writing damn near exclusively of bear attacks, producing several volumes each. Overall, these books range from well done and thoughtful to superficial and sensationalistic. Either way, they sell. And one needs only to log on to the Internet and run a Google search on "World Record Grizzly" to run across a bear-attack story of epic proportions—the story of a man-eating brute gunned down by a heroic U.S. Forest Service employee, complete with photos of the monster bear and a ghastly image of a mangled human leg and lower torso. There's only one problem: The whole thing's a bald-faced hoax. The bear in the photo was a big one, but not even in the top twenty, let alone close to the world record; it was killed by an ordinary sport hunter; and the snapshot of the human remains, while real enough, records a tiger mauling in India (if you look close, you can see the out-of-focus palm fronds). Nonetheless, the Web site has registered uncounted thousands of hits, and the story has reached mythic status, repeated by credulous folks until it's become almost true. People want to believe it. We do indeed love our monsters—especially if they're bears.

But let's get back on track, focused on those numbers compiled by Smith and Hererro—research so current the scientific paper, as of summer 2004, hasn't been written yet. These guys not only compiled Alaska bear-attack statistics covering a century; they cooked them down, sifting through an impressive array of variables and categories (eighty-five in all) to create a series of graphs and tables—delineating everything from what people were doing when attacked, to where in the state the attacks occurred, to species and sex of attacking bear, to general trends. Like any good scientists, they didn't try to force numbers where they didn't fit; if something wasn't clear, they made categories to reflect the reality as best they could. And their conclusions, whether they refute or confirm long-held beliefs, are illuminating.

Point one: Bear attacks in Alaska, viewed in a bar graph of five-year intervals, are no doubt on the rise. In 1900–05 there were fewer than 5 encounters registered; between 1975–80, over 50; from 1995–2000, over 115. This sounds ominous, but a line graph charting the increase of encounters overlaid with another tracing the increase in Alaska's population works out to a statistical wash; in other words, the number of bear problems is increasing in almost direct proportion to the number of people. So much for a new generation of aggressive bears that have lost their fear of humans—an alarm raised by, among others, Canadian author and bear-attack consultant James G. Shelton. And the data also tends to refute the idea that Alaska bears, through being hunted or otherwise killed by humans, are "learning" to avoid trouble— or that people are becoming more bear wise themselves. Not all good news, but not bad either.

The next conclusion: Grizzlies are, in the words of Smith and Herrero, "incredibly more dangerous than the other two species."

Over the 102 years spanned by the data, brown/grizzlies accounted for 45 of the 56 bear fatalities in Alaska (and probably 4 others, where the bear species was undetermined). Add on Timothy and Amie to make 47. Meanwhile, polar bears killed just one. This flies in the face of the oft-held belief that polar bears are the most dangerous bear of all—a pure carnivore that will actively stalk and kill a human as prey. One could argue that their relatively low population numbers and the fact that they tend to live out on sea ice, away from humans, might account for the almost nonexistent statistical threat they pose. But Smith, who's studied the animals in depth, dismisses that notion. "Look," he says, "there's been plenty of contact and opportunity over a hundred years. Polar bears come right into coastal villages every fall to scrounge whale carcasses and don't maul anyone. Then all those Eskimo hunters out on the ice, not to mention researchers. Yes, they can be curious and they certainly are capable of killing. But the numbers just don't reflect a high level of aggression." As his data points out, polar bears constitute five percent of Alaska's total bear population, yet account for just one and a half percent of the conflicts (this includes two recorded injuries, plus that single death). By comparison, brown/grizzlies make up twenty-three percent of Alaska's bears, yet are involved in just over eighty-six percent of conflicts. By Smith and Herrero's calculations, the average brown/grizzly is thirteen times more dangerous than the average polar bear.

But if that's a surprise, the real eye-opener is the statistically slight, almost nonexistent danger posed by black bears. Despite a spate of recent popular articles and book treatments that trumpet the danger to humans posed by *Ursus americanus*, black bears have killed just 6 people in Alaska over that 102-year period—in other words, roughly one every 17 years—and were responsible for just 24 reported injuries. This with more than 100,000 of them out there, prowling the same trails where people hike,

camp, fish, and hunt, and wandering through suburban neighbor-
hoods like mine. If you want to play Vegas odds, the average
brown/grizzly is twenty-two times more dangerous than its more
common cousin. Black bears, while certainly capable of wreaking mayhem—even a suitcase-sized adolescent is stronger and faster
than an NFL linebacker—are hardly a statistical danger to humans.

But wait a minute. What about that figure of 500 black bear
injuries over just 20 years, from Herrero's earlier study, which included all of North America? As Herrero himself is quick to point
out, black bears, especially in the lower forty-eight, are far more
common and widespread than brown/grizzlies. Besides, ninety percent of those black-bear-related injuries were caused by bears habituated to human food or garbage, and in many cases resulted
from people attempting to crowd, hand-feed, and even pet wild
bears (this in the days when such antics were common practice in
national parks like Yosemite and Yellowstone). And of these 500
injuries, ninety percent were rated as "slight"—mostly nips and
scratches not requiring hospitalization, not even love taps as far
as the bears were concerned. Black bears in most situations seem
to go out of their collective way to take it easy on us—gently
brushing away our unwanted advances, while plucking Oreos from
our outstretched fingers. Meanwhile, Herrero notes, more than
half of all injuries caused by brown/grizzlies were counted as
"major." (Think faces chewed off, muscles shredded, and stitches
like railroad tracks—not to mention some very dead people.)

What's more, both studies belie the risk posed by a female
black bear with cubs. In the Alaska data, those 500 incidents for
all species included just one injury and *zero* fatalities attributed
to a cub-accompanied female. Neither are sudden brushes with
black bears of any sex likely to lead to an attack. Herrero's earlier data tells the same story. In his well-regarded book, *Bear
Attacks: Their Causes and Avoidance,* the biologist flatly states,

"Sudden encounters with black bears, even mothers with cubs, almost never lead to injury." He does warn that the bear may make a fearsome display that looks like the real thing—swatting the ground, snorting, and making short, huffing rushes. But even given inappropriate human responses, these bluffs seldom are followed by an actual attack. For what it's worth, my own experience with unhabituated black bears—a few dozen chance encounters, sometimes as close as ten feet—supports Hererro in full. Matter of fact, I've only had two bears, both females with young cubs, even get to the bluffing stage, and neither seemed serious. Most black bears, even large males, hightailed in the opposite direction when surprised, apparently more scared than I was. Others moved off at a more leisurely pace, though clearly nervous about my presence. Only two or three fully wild black bears ever seemed to shrug and figure my presence was no big deal. Roadside, campground, and other human-acclimated black bears were, as Herrero indicates, another story—largely unafraid and sometimes downright bold, but still generally interested in food, not carnage.

To refresh ourselves as to why black bears are so comparatively mellow, think back to their evolution—creatures of the forest and shadow, who developed retreat as a response to threat. This is in sharp contrast to the brown/grizzly, molded by the fierce, open environment of the Pleistocene steppe, where safeguarding food, young, and personal space from a host of predators required the mentality of a cornered pit bull. Even the polar bear, we might surmise, is less aggressive for a similar reason. Though descended from *Ursus arctos*, it moved into a world of ice and cold, away from those mean streets, out onto the pack ice where it became the undisputed king of its domain. Being overly aggressive wasn't evolutionarily rewarded, and so the trait was relegated to a back shelf.

So we don't have to worry about black bears, right? Well, not exactly. It would be reassuring to write off *Ursus americanus* as a timid, essentially harmless creature, since it's the bear most North Americans are likely to encounter—due both to distribution and sheer numbers, from Florida to Maine, Mexico to Ontario to Ohio and on to California and north to Alaska. But the facts aren't that simple. As usual with bears, we're confronted with paradoxical behavior. Here's the conundrum: Black bears hardly ever make all-out attacks on people. However, when they do, it's seldom to protect personal space, young, or food. It's with the most basic motive of all: to kill and eat us. Herrero's earlier data suggests that up to ninety percent of all black-bear-inflicted deaths are motivated by bald-faced predatory drive. *Ninety percent*—whereas predatory behavior by brown/grizzlies on humans is rare at best; no more than a half dozen of those 45 deaths attributed to Alaskan brown/grizzlies over a century included the bear feeding on human flesh.

The facts inspire a completely different headspace from conventional wisdom, and one that takes some getting used to. Brown/grizzlies are, far and away, the bears most likely to attack; black bears are almost always safe. Yet if a black bear does commit to an all-out assault, it's the ravening beast of nightmare. What gives?

All the more odd, considering the diet of most black bears is made up of ninety percent or more vegetable matter. Insects and carrion provide the bulk of available protein; few, if any, bears have access to a steady, available source of live, catchable animals of any size (an obvious exception is the relatively few bears with access to salmon spawning areas). It's a lucky bear that manages to snag an occasional newborn moose calf or deer fawn; rodents like voles and mice are the most commonly available tidbits. But all that doesn't mean a black bear doesn't *want* to eat more meat.

Their evolutionary roots are carnivorous, and they merely adapted to plant foods because they were more available. Any bear is food driven, and animal protein or fat represents, in McDonald's terms, a value meal, not to mention a fond stroll down memory lane to some distant time when all food was as rich and fatty as this. And black bears are, like their larger and more touchy brown/grizzly cousins, opportunists. If some critter looks vulnerable and helpless, it may be tough to pass up. This would explain Herrero's finding from his first, pan–North American set of data that indicates half of twenty black-bear victims in that study were under the age of eighteen; and five were younger than ten years old.* This suggests that black bears are greatly encouraged by what appears to be a smaller, more vulnerable target. But several full-grown and able-bodied men are also included in the tally, indicating that a determined black bear is certainly capable of killing larger prey.

A fair amount of evidence exists, much of it anecdotal, but widespread enough to gain credence, that unusual hunger lights the fuse in many of these cases. Many folks living in black bear areas note an increase in bear incidents in lean years, when, say, a berry crop fails. The recent ongoing droughts in Arizona, New Mexico, and Colorado dovetailed with record numbers of black bear–human encounters, most of them involving food-seeking behavior, including dozens of break-ins into cabins and private homes, and at least one fatality (an elderly woman who was literally eaten inside her house). James Shelton, focusing on British Columbia, posits the same. And the hungry-bear rationale makes good sense.

Exceptions, though, define the rule. A sizable percentage of human-killing black bears that were killed and examined after

---

*The three additional black-bear-caused fatalities were in Alaska, with only cursory records, and so not included in this total.

the fact, seemed perfectly healthy, even robust. In sum, a number of factors contribute. No one can say exactly what sets off this exceedingly rare predatory behavior, but think of it in these terms— a trigger, rusty and hard to pull, but operational nonetheless. In the light of the facts, Shelton's admonishment not to be careless with black bears makes perfect, crystal-clear sense.

Herrero has another useful tidbit of information: Most black-bear-caused fatalities occur not in campgrounds at night, as one might expect, but in broad daylight—and except in one instance in his lower-forty-eight and Canadian cases, outside of national parks, and rarely around campsites. So it's not the food-seeking, highly habituated bears we might expect that are to blame, and you're not likely to get snatched from your tent by a marauding black bear (a brown/grizzly is another story). And, as we've seen, surprise encounters or cubs aren't a real factor in black bear attacks of any kind. Generally, though, predatory black bear attacks are most common in rural or remote areas, and often seem to involve bears with little human experience. More recent analysis has suggested that the predatory attackers are often young animals, sometimes as small as 125 pounds, and much more often male than female (when such identifications were possible).

A typical predatory black bear incident follows this basic script, gleaned both from investigations and from encounters where the person lived to describe it. A food-seeking bear, in the course of its normal wanderings, senses a human—generally alone, quite possibly appearing to be small or otherwise vulnerable. The animal may immediately make a strong, decisive attack; or it may follow and stalk its potential prey, as if sizing it up. It may even seem timid and uncertain. The person may very well be aware of the bear following him or her, or lurking about. But when the bear attacks, it does so suddenly and with full force, in a single charge; (meaning that if the bear charges and retreats, then charges again, chances are excellent you're *not* facing a predatory bear, but a bluff.) Often, when knocked down or bitten by a black bear, a person follows the old basic rule and "plays dead" or otherwise is passive. The predatory bear, finding no resistance and tasting blood, presses home the attack, and the mauling intensifies. At this point, unless the bear is driven off or startled by determined, desperate resistance, the victim is doomed.

Faced with a predatory black bear, every expert agrees there's only one recourse: Fight back with everything you have, as if your life depends on it—because it does. There are a number of cases of people, even children, driving off or killing predatory bears with tree limbs, fists, hatchets, knives, rocks, pistols, and (in one case) a pan of scalding water. Even better, says Shelton, is to immediately and aggressively drive away any black bear that seems to be exhibiting lurking, prepredatory behavior, before it gets started. Yelling, throwing objects, and even running at a bear (especially in a group) is quite effective at derailing the bear before it gets started.

This information about black bear predatory behavior isn't all that new. Herrero and others have been espousing it since the mid-1980s. It just seems that cutting-edge science takes a decade or two to filter out and become common knowledge; meanwhile, old notions die slowly—especially, it seems, when it comes to bears.

Brown/grizzlies are quite a different story. But before we get scary and gruesome here, we need to dial in to the axiom presented by Alaska state biologist Derek Stenerov: *Ursus arctos* is "always on the ragged edge of leaving." In other words, the bear's first inclination, despite its fierce rep, is to flee—not only from us, but from any perceived threat. And this is far and away the bear's most common response. It's worth keeping in mind that bears of any kind have just three choices when dealing with humans: run, fight, or ignore. Only a bear fully habituated to low-stress contact with people is likely to do the latter. We want to do everything we can to encourage it to do the first.

A brown/grizzly doesn't defend a staked-out territory in any systematic way, though most bears demonstrate a fairly predictable home range, which usually overlaps that of other bears. What they do defend is a bubble of personal space, which expands or contracts according to situation and the bear's individual temperament or mood. In some extreme situations, a quarter mile is too close; in others, touching distance might be the trigger point. If a bear is already stressed—by, say, a conflict with another bear, the presence of cubs, or hunger—it stands to reason that the trip wire is farther out. The same animal, calm and well fed, may scarcely give a hoot if you tromp right by. There's no doubt that an extraordinarily concentrated food source, such as a salmon stream or a huge meadow of newly emerged rye grass, reduces tension and encourages bears, normally loners, to tolerate the presence of other animals—including bears and people—at closer ranges than normal. Where food is scarce, as it often is in the Arctic interior, bears generally are much more intolerant of company; the brown/grizzlies I knew up north were much more skittish (both more likely to run away and more likely to attack) than the well-fed, socially acclimated bears of Treadwell's Katmai Coast.

So, when a brown/grizzly charges, almost all of the time, it's not as a predator, but in defense of this personal space. Herrero and other biologists label such attacks "defensive-aggressive." You spot a grizzly as it swings toward you and say to yourself, *Oh, shit.* Meanwhile, the bear, at some genetic level, sees you as a saber-toothed cat or short-faced bear and says the same thing. It launches an attack as a preemptive strike. If we subscribe to statistical probability, the attack that killed Tim and Amie was triggered by this mind-set—and the fact that the bear on the tape initially retreated before returning is strong support. In defensive-aggressive mode, bears simply do enough damage to neutralize the threat and run off as if terrorized. Unfortunately, the ursine definition of "enough damage" seems to vary from bear to bear and case to case, and bears sometimes back off and then renew the attack if the person moves or cries out. Some victims get off with a few minor scratches; some end up dead several times over.

Subadult brown/grizzlies and females with cubs seem to be responsible for most of these defensive-aggressive attacks; big, dominant males are generally more reticent (though when they do attack, the results are often horrific, if not fatal, due to the larger bear's incredible power). Interestingly enough, female grizzlies with cubs, though responsible for a large proportion of attacks, were statistically far less likely to actually kill people (just three fatalities) or to inflict serious damage. Remember the case of my student, Cody Mills. It seems mothers tend to focus on getting their children out of harm's way, and so break off the mauling quickly. Of course, there are enough exceptions to any of these general rules to trigger a discussion, if not an all-out argument.

Another leading cause of brown/grizzly attacks is a variation on the defensive-aggressive category labeled "carcass defense." In this case, the bear is protecting a highly valuable food source—say, a winter-killed caribou or moose—from those genetically imprinted Pleistocene hordes. A luckless hiker or hunter stumbles too close, precipitating anything from a bluff charge to a fatal mauling. While, bluffs aside, black bears seldom engage in such behavior, their larger cousin often takes strong exception to any intrusions near its stash. Some experts consider carcass defense to be the most dangerous type of attack; and this could well be what Bear 141 was probably up to when he chased Willie Fulton down the hill at Kaflia, and later confronted the rangers (though the witnesses' claim of predatory bahavior is equally plausible). Typically, a bear claiming a carcass, whether killed by itself or scavenged, will cover it with whatever is handy—dirt, willows, even logs—forming a mound known as a food cache (as 141 did at Kaflia with Huguenard's remains, and later on, other bears did with the two dead bears). If you're traveling in brown/grizzly country and you run across such a disturbed area or catch a whiff of carrion, it's time to pull out the bear spray or firearm, back off quietly, and give the area a wide berth. A bear seldom abandons a claimed kill, and may well be scant yards away, gearing up for a charge.

In areas where human hunting activity for deer, moose, or elk is heavy (places in Montana and Alaska's Kodiak and Chichagof Islands come to mind), brown/grizzlies add a further wrinkle to the carcass defense issue. Some bears have clearly learned that a gunshot is a dinner bell—and they come running. Often they wait for the hunter to butcher his kill and leave before they move in on the gut pile; sometimes they don't. Smith and Herrero's research, which includes an Alaska map pinpointing where attacks took place, shows heavy clusters of bear–human conflicts in just such popular hunting areas. And there's no doubt that a number of fatal attacks have been tied to hunters with downed game. (Keep in mind that black bears tend to be far less likely to actually attack over food—though a healthy dose of respect is in order for them as well).

In incredibly rare instances, a brown/grizzly makes an all-out predatory attack. In the lower forty-eight, as we've seen, a preponderance of these involve animals who've come to associate people with food, and a number of Alaskan attacks demonstrate the same link. And a high percentage of predatory brown/grizzly attacks take place at night, and involve a bear attacking a person in a sleeping bag or tent. But there have been a number of cases where a predatory bear, in broad daylight, deliberately stalks or otherwise attacks a human as food. Considering that bears routinely do the same with moose calves and fawns, and will take down a bull caribou or elk if the situation presents itself, the only real surprise is that brown/grizzlies don't attempt to eat people more often. They certainly have both motive and opportunity. Clearly, a certain reticence is there—maybe an expression of instinctive avoidance, due to the centuries of humans' killing bears. Shelton posits the compelling idea that bears recognize us as top-of-the-heap predators by our confident mannerisms, pack mentality, and our forward-facing eyes. However, that doesn't explain why attacking black bears see humans as prey far more often than brown/grizzlies do. But, whatever the reason, bears of any species rarely eat humans.

Predation by a brown/grizzly after a defensive-aggressive attack certainly does occur—a switchover from one mode to another, apparently what happened in the case of Timothy Treadwell—but again, it's tough to tell what's on a bear's mind and confirm the original motive. And there are finally so few cases of brown/grizzly predatory attacks that it's hard to make any valid generalizations at all. They happen just often enough to capture our horrified attention, and to offer the illusion of likelihood.

Though Herrero and other biologists might look askance, I believe there are at least two more categories of brown/grizzly attacks on humans. As a nonscientist, I'm able to indulge in free-ranging speculation, and dabble in things that can't be measured or proven. Neither of my notions is that radical; I certainly didn't invent them, and many folks who have spent much time around brown/grizzlies are likely to concur. My first suggestion: I think these bears sometimes attack out of sheer irritation. Brown/grizzlies, intelligent, complex, and physically dominant as they are, with an already genetically programmed tendency toward aggression, have a definite capacity for losing their tempers in a manner that would make any spoiled three-year-old kid proud. A bear who's frustrated may thrash a patch of brush apart just to vent his anger, or take it out on any other nearby thing—

including another bear. Or maybe a person. You could lump this sort of response into the defensive-aggressive category with perfect justification, but I think it's more basic than that. The bear isn't defending its personal space, or anything else. It's just plain pissed, and anyone or anything unlucky enough to be in the way becomes a whipping boy. It's entirely possible that Timothy and Amie ran afoul of a bear that had already had it up to here, for reasons we'll never know, and, encountering the camp, went into meltdown. The predation that followed could be explained by a crossover from one mode to another—or, as Tom Smith and others suggest, the killer and the eater were two different bears, each acting alone.

My second posited category of bear attacks is far more broad and vague, and echoes bear-defense expert James G. Shelton. It's titled simply "unknown." Even Ph.D.'s who've dedicated their lives to bear behavior will admit they can't claim to understand all the complex wrinkles of bear psychology. Despite the fact that bears are, in the broadest sense, quite predictable on both a species and individual level, they sometimes do things that leave the experts puzzled. And in many cases, no one can say for sure why a given bear attacked. Was the prime motive curiosity—bears are, after all, fond of chewing up things in order to explore them? Or was a mauling simply a misunderstood desire to play? Perhaps a manifestation of brain damage or mental illness (certainly diagnosed in pet dogs, so why not bears)? Or maybe a bear was responding to a sensory cue too subtle for us to pinpoint, or acting on individual memory or experience— a wounding by a hunter, or deep-seated insecurity from being an only cub, perhaps? Maybe that last one is going a bit far, but the point stands: Exceptions and unanswerable questions are bound to creep in. The exact causes, on the bear side of things, anyway, are often destined to pass into mystery; and the tragedy of Timothy Treadwell and Amie Huguenard seems to be one of these.

At this point, this jumble of information probably seems clear as a mud puddle. Rendered to essences, here's what we have.

1) Statisically speaking, none of North America's three bear species poses a significant risk to people traveling in their habitat—unless, of course, you happen to belong to that fraction of a percent that's exposed on a regular, high-risk basis.

2) Brown/grizzlies are by far and away more dangerous than black bears, and their attacks are often triggered by surprise encounters. An aggressive brown/grizzly is most likely acting in defense of a highly elastic personal space or, in the case of a female, its young.

3) When it comes to food, brown/grizzlies are much more liable to attack in defense of food, especially a carcass, and can become predatory if habituated to human food sources such as garbage or campers' leftovers. Black bears seek out such foods, but aren't nearly so likely to violently attack a person over them, or to switch from eating your picnic basket into predatory mode.

4) If a black bear commits to an all-out attack, it probably means to eat you; a brown/grizzly generally is going to slap you around—perhaps violently—and then retreat. Furthermore, predatory black bear attacks tend to occur in broad daylight, and seldom in a camp situation. In contrast, predatory brown/grizzly attacks often take place at night and involve campers.

5) Contrary to popular opinion, female black bears with cubs aren't likely to attack and maul in defense of their offspring; but mother brown/grizzlies are a direct opposite.

Okay, so now we're down to the fifty-cent, two-part question: What can the average outdoors person do to reduce the risk of a bear attack, and what to do if the unthinkable occurs? All considered, the first part is remarkably straightforward. Smith and Herrero's analysis of their century's worth of Alaska data indicates two clear points: 1) Bears can count; 2) they don't like surprises. Consider the following graph:

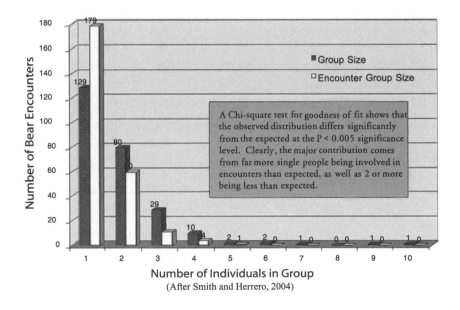

Number of Individuals in Group
(After Smith and Herrero, 2004)

Your chances of being attacked go up steeply if you're alone, and diminish with each person you add to your group. Matter of fact, hiking groups of four—provided they're reasonably close to each other—are just about never assaulted. Five, six, or more people camping or walking together in bear country reduce the odds of attack to virtually zero. As Smith and Herrero put it, "It seems bears size up the odds before engaging and if it is one-on-one they appear much more likely to mix it up with a person than otherwise."

Now graph 2:

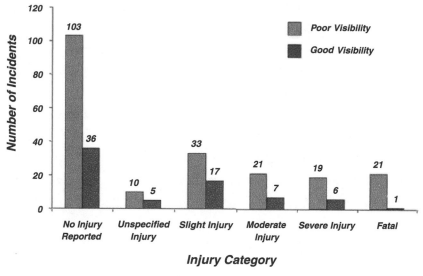

(after Smith and Herrero, 2004)

The evidence is lopsided. Most bear attacks clearly take place in thick brush or woods and obviously involve a surprise, close-quarters encounter (we can extrapolate, from what we already know, that brown/grizzlies, with their penchant to aggressively defend space, must be the culprits inflating this statistic, since black bears typically run in such situations).

So, there you have it: Hike and camp in small herds and, in brown/grizzly country, avoid brushy, low-visibility situations whenever possible. And when bushwhacking or walking alone is unavoidable, hoot it up; loud conversation (even with yourself), regular shouts, and handclaps or rocks pounded together (which carry well, and theoretically mimic the sound of an agitated bruin popping its jaws) alert bears, giving them the chance to fade back and dodge trouble—far and away their first choice.* Just sticking

---

*Other popular noise-making options: "Bear bells," especially those of low pitch, hung from a belt or backpack seem to help, and if the woods are noisy, an occasional blast from a hand-held air horn is a good option.

to these two tenets lowers the already minuscule odds a few dozen notches to just above nada.

Common sense about distance and food comes next. There's no sense in deliberately elbowing in on bears of any species, regardless of your intentions. Staring at or closing in on any wild thing is a clear threat message—indicating a desire to eat it, chase it off, or engage in some kinky, out-of-season mating behavior. A hundred yards, minimum, is a good reasonable viewing or passing distance, though in some situations, it may not be enough. A bear that seems to be pointedly ignoring you is not necessarily safe either; it may be just trying to avoid conflict by not making eye contact and hoping you'll go away. Charges can come with jack-in-the-box suddenness, with little or no warning.

Keeping human food away from bears is a basic, considering that food-related conflicts probably result in more dead bears than any single factor short of sport hunting. Just because you get away with feeding a bear doesn't mean the next person is going to be so lucky—or that the bear will be. Food habituation generally leads to increasingly bold behavior, and to trouble. The adage that a fed bear is a dead bear is as true as it ever was; it's finally our deep-rooted fear and misunderstanding that leads to conflict, and bears, statistically, hardly stand a chance when push comes to shove.

Of course, feeding isn't necessarily deliberate. The problem is that food is one hell of a motivator to your average bear, who's totally capable of peeling the door off an SUV like a hunk of foil off a candy bar if something inside smells tasty enough. A tent wall might as well be tissue paper. Needless to say, if you're worried about an uninvited, hairy roommate with bad breath, cooking or keeping food in a tent in bear country is crazy. Don't be the guy (true story) who put a chunk of bacon under his pillow to keep a bear from getting it. Stored food belongs in a special bear-resistant food container (BRFC) well out of camp, the trunk of a car (not the backseat, or any window-accessed area that a bear can break through), or up a tree, suspended from a limb at least twelve feet off the ground.

Aside from food, if there was a surefire way to keep bears out of any camp, you'd think people setting up in thick bear concentrations, or those who suffer from acute bearanoia, would deploy it as a matter of course. Fact is, the magic bullet has been around for years: lightweight electric perimeter fencing that administers a harmless but startling shock—for safety's sake, heavy in voltage but low in amperage. The idea's been adapted from livestock and pet fencing, rendered light and inexpensive enough to be practical for just about everyone under real field conditions. The ubiquitous Dr. Smith, in conjunction with the Alaska Science Center, has field-tested a number of alternatives, some of them weighing just several pounds and costing under a hundred dollars. Some models use just two "D"-size batteries, and consist, at a very functional no-frills minimum, of a charger, lightweight wire, and a couple of aluminum grounding stakes. You can carry fiberglass wands for posts or attach to existing bushes; the effectiveness of the fence doesn't lie in its strength. Even the more diaphanous versions have been field-proven to work—get this—one hundred percent of the time. This includes at Hallo Bay with its incredible early-summer assemblage of bears, where Smith and Timothy Treadwell both camped. According to Smith, who uses these fences as a matter of course in his field work (not due to fear, but to protect thousands of dollars of valuable equipment from bears' often destructive curiosity, and to protect the bears from associating people with ill-gained food rewards), "Over the past decade I have tested many fences in many settings—all of them thick with bears—and have never had an electric fence fail to keep bears out." And despite the fact that the high-voltage charge is more startling than painful (both to bears and humans), a single momentary contact with the wire is all it takes. Says Smith, "Most bears I've witnessed getting shocked cannot put enough distance between themselves and the fence fast enough."

One more point to consider for those who want a bear-free camp: brown/grizzlies are attracted to the bright nylon colors typical of most tents. Researchers in Katmai led by Smith found, quite by accident, that bear investigations and incursions on their camps dropped dramatically when they switched to the dull camouflage versions featured in hunting catalogs. All the scientists were trying to do was to cut down the visual pollution of their presence for the sake of visitors, and they stumbled onto something. In the process, they shot additional holes in the theory that bears are colorblind or don't see well.

So—can you get away with violating common sense and turning your nose up at bear precautions and still breathe right? Plenty of people will snort that such measures verge on phobia, and the statistics *do* speak for themselves. A person can pull off all manner of foolhardy or brave bear stunts in serial fashion for decades in bear country and still never have so much as a close call. You have to remember, too, that this isn't just about your own safety and life; it's about the bear's, and maybe someone else's down the line. Preventative safety with bears is all about fundamental, abiding respect—a large enough topic to warrant its own space later on. As Smith and Herrero note, "Importantly, we see that a large number of bear–human encounters could have been avoided had people done the right things." Their graphed data analysis of "Fault Assessment" (admittedly subjective) suggests humans are "likely" or certainly to blame in more than a third of all bear encounters.

One final, interesting point from Smith and Herrero's database: Bear encounters in Alaska can and do occur in every month—including December through February, when you'd expect any self-respecting bear to be hibernating. But bears occasionally do

wake up and walk around, and people stumble onto dens, sometimes with fatal results.

Now we're down to the nitty-gritty. Let's say, despite all your
precautions, or maybe due to lack of them, you've got a highly agitated bear up close and personal. What to do? The answer takes
the form of a short flow chart, with diverging arrows at several
points.

Pretty much everybody who knows bears agrees on step one: If
a bear of any species makes an aggressive display or even charges,
don't run—repeat, don't run—no matter how much your instincts
inform your heels.* As with a barking dog, hauling butt invites a
chase, and may well trigger a mauling. Keep in mind that most
threat displays are just that, even with brown/grizzlies and almost
always with black bears. All those signals—laying back ears, jaw
snapping, foot stomping, and paw cocking, stylized pacing, holding the head low and staring—are designed to avoid, not precipi-
tate, a fight. (Standing on hind legs isn't an aggressive move, by
the way; the bear is just trying to get a better look at you. A high,
bouncing charge is a threat; the most serious charges are generally
straight in, elbows out, low and hard, and often eerily silent.) But
most rushes amount to fist shaking and stop short of contact,
sometimes unnervingly so—sometimes ten feet or less. Consider
the encounter as a rather tense and urgent interspecies conversation, one you can't afford to botch. You want to send the message
that you don't want trouble, either, but you aren't an easy mark.
Stand your ground, face the bear, and shout—the most firm, low
voice you can muster (don't worry about what to say—it'll come
to you; a forceful *HEY* is as good as anything). If you're in a

*There are exceptions to this rule. For example, if you have a desperate situation and a
nearby refuge—a tree to climb, a car, a boat, a cabin—and you're sure you can get there
first, it might make dang good sense to run.

group, bunch up without hurrying and stand together, making as large a profile as possible; a bear turning sideways is trying to show you how big *it* is—an invitation to stand down—so it makes sense to do the same. Then back off, a step at a time. Some favor lowering their gaze to avoid a threat signal; Herrero suggests keeping your eyes on the bear so you can react, and points to data indicating that eye contact doesn't seem to make much difference. If the bear steps forward when you step back, keep going. And the low, forceful vocalizations seem to help; if nothing else, they make you feel better. Stumbling or falling down, or any other sudden motion, while understandable under the circumstances, is a crummy idea. Most of the time, a bluff-charging or otherwise aggressive bear, met properly, will retreat, often in rapid fashion.

A word on tree climbing: Black bears can climb like cats, so they may well follow you up and attempt to drag you down. Then you end up fighting the bear in the tree. Some brown/grizzlies, contrary to popular belief, can climb at least as well as humans if there are limbs to hook with paws. But still, many people have avoided bears, especially brown/grizzlies, by climbing a nearby spruce or birch. How high should you go? Don't worry. That detail will work itself out, and probably will precisely coincide with the height of your chosen tree.

Let's go to that next level, rare as it is: The bear, instead of backing off, bites or claws you, even knocks you off your feet. Here's where some variance of opinion sets in. Herrero once preached playing dead for a brown/grizzly, fighting back against a black bear. Considering the first species's penchant for defensive-aggressive responses, and the latter's for predatory attacks, that makes perfect sense. You roll up in a ball or lie belly-down, fingers locked over your neck, doing your best to protect your head and internal organs. You do your best not to move or cry out. The brown/grizzly, seeing you pose no threat, leaves. The black bear, seeing you offer no resistance, is enouraged—so you need to fight back with everything you've got.

But there's a problem here: Sometimes—at night, for example, in thick brush, or if you're hit from behind—even an expert has trouble figuring the identity of the attacking bear. In most of North America, that's not an issue, since only black bears are present. But in most of Alaska and a good deal of western Canada, not to mention any of the brown/grizzly's lower-forty-eight habitat, it could be either species. Identification is complicated by the fact that some brown/grizzlies are nearly black, and a black bear's hide might be any shade of brown, even blue-gray or cream colored.* There's at least one more complicating issue. Sometimes brown/grizzlies do make predatory attacks, or switch over from defensive-aggressive to kill-and-eat mode, and playing dead won't help then.

Herrero has since simplified his advice: If you think you're facing defensive-aggressive attack, play dead; if you decide the bear's doing too much damage or trying to eat you, fight back. It still may be hard to decide which sort of attack is which, but if you're getting chewed to pieces anyway, you don't have a whole lot to lose. In general, a bear of any species that bluffs and stops and makes a big show is probably being defensive, as in the case of a mother with cubs; one that stalks you or grabs you in camp at night probably isn't. But how are you supposed to keep all this stuff straight? It's a lot of information for anyone to juggle, especially in the middle of being slammed around.

When it comes to what to do in a bear attack, James Gary Shelton has a decidedly different point of emphasis, and a more

---

*If you do get a good look at the bear, a brown/grizzly has a more "dished" facial profile and a prominent shoulder hump, plus front claws as long as three inches; a black bear's profile is more of a Roman-nosed look, and, head raised, it lacks the shoulder hump. Front claws are an inch or shorter.

direct approach. A lifelong resident of British Columbia, Shelton isn't a biologist but has his own credentials to offer. Besides being an ex–hunting guide who's lived in bear country most of his life and faced dozens of aggressive bears, several in life-or-death situations, he makes part of his living teaching what he calls "bear hazard safety courses." These include live-fire shotgun practice at pulley-drawn targets simulating the size and speed of a charging bear. Among his clients are Canadian government agencies and private companies whose employees work in bear country—wardens, biologists, surveyors, lumbermen, and so on. As you might expect from his course description, Shelton isn't about to play dead for any bear, and doesn't think anyone else should either. He also recognizes the difficulties the average person might face figuring what to do in a given attack situation. Instead, Shelton preaches a simple message: Carry a big stick at all times in what he calls "bear hazard situations"—preferably a large-caliber rifle or shotgun, or at the very least pepper spray—and be ready to use it. In his rather bluntly titled first book, *Bear Encounter Survival Guide,* he writes:

> If you are foolish enough to believe that it's not necessary to defend yourself against bears, you have no choice but to play dead in a defensive-aggressive attack, and fight back in a predatory attack—that is, if you are lucky enough to experience an attack that clearly falls into one of these categories. (p. 125)

Shelton has a point in not leaving the "fighting back" part to chance. Raise your hand if you think you're up to driving off a bear with a stick or a pocket knife, and then consider what you might look like when you're done. Shelton's favored weapon is a slug-loaded Remington model 870 12-gauge pump shotgun with rifle sights, and he recommends regular practice. The "safety" part of his course title clearly applies to people first and bears second; still, it's hardly a shoot-first-ask-questions-later philosophy. Shelton points out that most bear encounters don't end in a mauling, and that you need to give the bear a chance to defuse the situation. His guidelines call for shooting only inside twenty-five yards, and only at a bear that's exhibiting predatory stalking behavior or coming hard in an all-out charge. But if you shoot, it's to kill—at a vital zone roughly a foot square, bounding toward you at twenty-five-plus miles an hour. He figures you have less than two seconds, tops. When you think of it that way, a little shooting practice sounds like a damn good idea.

Then again, Timothy Treadwell definitely wouldn't have thought so. The idea of even carrying a firearm was out of the question. So one might suppose he would have embraced a nonlethal form of deterrent, something that was nearly as effective as a shotgun at stopping a charge, with no lasting ill effects. Of course, we're talking about bear spray—an aerosol can roughly a pound in weight, hurling a cloud of choking, blinding, but ultimately harmless mist into the face of an oncoming bear. The active ingredient is oleoresin capsicum—an oily concentrate of cayenne pepper. Cops carry palm-sized cans of the stuff, a spritz of which is enough to knock a PCP-crazed gangster flat. In the seventies Montana bear biologist Charles Jonkel and businessman Bill Pounds developed a Costco-sized version of the same nasty gumbo for use against bears, which they dubbed Counter Assault. In repeated tests, both staged and in the field, it proved capable of poleaxing bears in full charge, again and again—acute pain without lasting damage of any sort. In most cases the animal swapped ends and beat a hasty retreat; in others, the temporary effect of the spray was enough to allow the user to escape.

Using the stuff seems simple. Snap off the plastic safety latch, hold at arm's length, and pull the trigger. Out shoots a yellow-orange plume into the face of the oncoming bear. The effect is twofold. A dab in your eyes (human, anyway, which I can personally vouch for) might as well be boiling acid. Bears are no doubt tougher, but I can't begin to imagine the exquisite pain of a two-second blast full into the eyes of any living thing. But the true power of bear spray manifests itself when it hits lung tissue. Inhaled, it creates an instantaneous, violent, and involuntary bronchial spasm that can literally knock a charging bear off its feet. Its estimated effectiveness under field conditions ranges from ninety-plus percent (Herrero) to the seventy–eighty percent range (Shelton). Why not a hundred? Well, of course, there's a catch or two.

For one thing, it has a maximum effective range of twenty feet; Shelton recommends ten for full effect. Let's say there's a five-hundred-pound bear barreling toward you in all-out-charge mode. It takes more than a little moxie to hold both your ground and your fire until it's almost close enough to touch. Under these conditions (admittedly, a worst-case scenario) you get exactly one chance. As with firearms, a little regular practice seems in order. You don't want to be doing it for the first time. Wind is another issue. A stiff cross-breeze carries your magic airborne goo away, so you need to aim accordingly. And if the bear charges with the wind at its back, you end up spraying yourself—both embarrassing and highly inconvenient under the circumstances.

Other issues: A bear, like ex-President Clinton, doesn't always inhale—at least, not at the right time. And it's the breathing in of the spray that gives that guaranteed knockdown effect. The eyes are small and might be missed, or the force and adrenaline of the charge may carry a bear right through your defense. Also, for reasons not yet understood, bear spray seems to have little effect on some black bears; they may be repelled initially but return within minutes—or hardly slow down at all. And some bears of any species seem to get used to spray quickly; it apparently had little effect, for example, on the brown bear that killed Michio. Shelton recommends a rapid but orderly retreat, if practicable, after any defense using bear spray. He also suggests getting behind a tree, boulder, or similar barrier before you press the trigger, as an added defensive measure. And of course, it needs to be handy, preferably in an elastic and Velcro holster; a can of spray isn't much good in the bottom of your pack.

One last note—bear spray is worse than useless when sprayed on objects (like tents, picnic coolers, or aircraft tires) to keep bears away from them. Seems bears actually have a taste for hot and spicy; the spray residue has been shown to work as a fairly powerful *attractant*, confounding those who don't like to read directions. And if residue is evident in a spot (usually yellowish or orange in color), you might not want to camp just there.

Bear spray, then, isn't perfect, but a solid alternative for those uncomfortable with firearms—or for use in areas (national parks like Katmai, for example) where guns are prohibited. I believe enough in the stuff to have bought several cans and to carry it; but though I've come close, I've never pulled the trigger except for a practice burst or two. (By the way, you want the largest size can possible, and you want it full to the brim. One can for practice, one for the field makes good sense).

I generally carry a nonlethal adjunct to bear spray, copying my friend, filmmaker Joel Bennett: an orange plastic 12-gauge flare gun, of the type carried by boaters. It weighs almost nothing and can be safely carried with a single shot in the chamber, and points and fires about as easily as an imaginary gun made from your index finger and thumb. While bears often ignore gunshots, shouting, and waving, I've yet to see one do anything but skedaddle when faced with a flying ball of fire landing at its feet—and I've used it seven times, even with aggressive bears at close range, and know several people who've also had success. A flare gun has the added advantage over spray of being able to reach out to fifty yards or more, and send a long-distance message to defuse a potential problem. The only real issue is that, in dry conditions, you stand the very real possibility of starting a fire. In a point-blank emergency, I'd go for the pepper spray first; but I don't believe that if (in desperation), I hit a bear with a twelve-hundred-degree flare, he'd continue his charge. Think of that line from Jerry Lee Lewis: *Goodness gracious, great balls of fire.* Yet the gods of bear safety, Herrero and Shelton, are at best noncommittal on the subject of flare pistols. There hasn't been much research done on them, I suppose.

You'd think Tim Treadwell would have worshipped bear spray. It wears off in a few minutes, and no one gets hurt. But he decided, after one successful defense against Cupcake, that the stuff conflicted with his essential philosophy of living in peace among the bears, and wanting them to trust him. Likewise, at one point he had an electric-fence setup like Tom Smith's, but decided not to use it for the same reason. Ultimately, he was willing to risk his own life to that end. One can't argue with his courage or conviction, but you certainly *can* say that not carrying adequate means of protecting himself ultimately put the bears at risk, as the tragedy at Kaflia proved. Camping in that thick brush, right next to a network of trails, was the sort of situation that seemed tailor made for a bear fence. Failing that, the spray.

Bear in camp, uncomfortably close. Timothy leaves his tent, can in hand, just in case, and tries to bluff the bear into leaving— which it's most likely to do. But the bear charges, he hits it square with a blast of spray, it runs, and life goes on for everyone. Or maybe Timothy goes down to a surprise attack and Amie runs out and sprays the bear point-blank (perhaps choking Timothy, a temporary inconvenience) and saves both his and the bear's life.

In the unfailing clarity of hindsight, you might guess Tim Treadwell would have embraced that alternative—no lives lost instead of four. Wouldn't the momentary compromise of peaceful goodwill and high principle have been rewarded by a far greater good? It's another of those curious disconnects that characterized Timothy Treadwell's life and death, a wisp of smoke trailing off into air.

A Selected Bibliography
with Annotations

The following is an abbreviated list of full-length published works I read either as direct or background research. Any comments are purely subjective notations intended to guide the reader. The sheer number of bear books available is staggering; this list is no more than a representative sampling, including some (by no means all) of the best. Publication dates and publishing companies listed in some cases reflect reprint information rather than that of original editions.

Aumiller, Larry, and Walker, Tom, *The Way of the Grizzly* (formerly titled *River of Bears*). Stillwater, Minnesota: Voyageur Press, 1993. A superb combination of accessible, informative text and excellent photography focusing on coastal brown bears. The book is also a detailed history and description of the McNeil River State Game Sanctuary, of which Aumiller is the manager. Crammed with up-to-date bear science and natural history.

Breiter, Matthias, *The Bears of Katmai*. Portland: Graphic Arts Center, 2000. One of those rare photo books where superb images are accompanied by an equally excellent text; both by the author, who is a trained bear biologist. Translated from the original German.

Cheek, Roland, *Learning to Talk Bear (So Bears Can Listen)*. Columbia Falls, Montana: Skyline Publishing, 1997. A thoughtful and thorough exploration of the issue of grizzlies and people coexisting in the lower forty-eight, written by a longtime outdoorsman. Features unique, well-researched information presented in a relaxed, clear voice.

Craighead, Frank, Jr., *Track of the Grizzly*. San Francisco: Sierra Club Books, 1979. An information-packed volume by eminent bear biologist Frank Craighhead Jr. The focus is the bears of Yellowstone, but this research-driven book is a standard bear reference for biologists and laypeople alike.

Dillon, Richard, *The Legend of Grizzly Adams*. Reno, Nevada: University of Nevada Press, 1966. A detailed, carefully researched biography of the famed bear man.

Dominico, Terry, and Newman, Mark, *Bears of the World*. New York: Facts on File, 1988. A solid, well-photographed, and well-written reference volume covering all nine remaining species of bears worldwide.

Herrero, Stephen, *Bear Attacks: Their Causes and Avoidance*. Guilford, Connecticut: The Lyons Press, 1985, updated 2002. A readable yet research-based exploration of bear attacks, by the scientist regarded as a, if not the, top expert.

Kaniut, Larry, *Alaska Bear Tales*. Portland: Alaska Northwest Books, 1983. A solid representative of the "bear chew" book genre. Journalistic treatments of Alaska attacks, many in the words of the victims.

Lynch, Wayne, *Bears: Monarchs of the Northern Wilderness*. Seattle: The Mountaineers, 1993. A must-have reference for anyone fascinated by bears. Focusing on all species of bears across the northern hemisphere, this book combines nine years of exhaustive research and excellent photography.

McCracken, Harold, *The Beast That Walks Like a Man*. Lanham, Maryland: Roberts Rinehart Publishers, 2003 (original edition, Garden City, New York: Hanover House, 1955). As far as pre-1960 bear texts go, this is the best. A far-reaching, scholarly blend of history, science, spiritualism, and adventure filtered through the attitudes of another time; McCracken was himself a bear hunter and notable historian who eventually laid down his rifle. One of the top grizzly books, period. Long out of print and recently reissued.

McMillon, Scott, *Mark of the Grizzly*. Guilford, Connecticut: Falcon, 1998. A well-written book that combines a number of the classic bear-attack cases with other issues concerning grizzlies and humans. Several notches above the typical bear attack book.

Mills, Enos, *The Grizzly: Our Greatest Wild Animal*. Sausalito, California: Comstock Editions, 1947 (original edition 1913). Naturalist Enos Mills's slim classic on grizzly behavior, based on his personal observations of the bears of Colorado and California, now extinct. Though the text is disjointed and uneven, some of Mills's insights are remarkable and far ahead of their day.

Treadwell, Timothy, and Palovak, Jewel, *Among Grizzlies*. New York: Ballantine Books, 1997. Required reading for anyone seeking further insight into Timothy Treadwell. Neither literary nor scientific, but straight from the heart.

Russell, Charlie, and Enns, Maureen, *Grizzly Seasons: Life with the Brown Bears of Kamchatka*. Buffalo, New York: Firefly Books, 2003. A nicely photographed visual chronicle, somewhat short on text, documenting Charlie Russell and Maureen Enns's raising of three brown bear cubs for release in Siberia, and their explorations of the bonds possible between people and bears. If you like cute shots of cubs and people interacting, and a feel-good story, it's one of a kind.

Schneider, Bill, *Where the Grizzly Walks*. Guilford, Connecticut: Falcon, 2004. An up-to-date, solid treatment of bear–human issues by a veteran outdoor writer in a remarkably unconvoluted, reader-friendly form. The focus is on the greater Yellowstone ecosystem area.

Shelton, James, *Bear Encounter Survival Guide*. Hagensborg, British Columbia: Pallister Publishing, 1994. A practical, no-nonsense, and frankly opinionated book written by Canadian bear-defense instructor James G. Shelton, author of two other bear-attack books that favor information over sensationalism. A recommended companion to Herrero's book.

Stringham, Stephen, *Beauty Within the Beast: Kinship with Bears in the Alaska Wilderness*. Santa Ana, California: Seven Locks Press, 2002. A personal narrative of Alaska biologist Steve Stringham's attempts to raise and release three black bear cubs. Sharp observations and insights into bear behavior and learning.

Wright, William, *The Grizzly Bear: The Narrative of a Hunter-Naturalist*. Lincoln: University of Nebraska Press, 1997. (original edition, New York: Charles Scribner's Sons, 1909). A turn-of-the-century perspective based on years of field experience; called by noted grizzly biologist Frank Craighead Jr. "one of the best all-around books ever written on the subject." Combines hunting stories with early black-and-white bear photos.

Index

10